D0298275

SOLDIERS

By the same author

The Duchess of Dino
Addington
The Black Death
King William IV
Melbourne
Diana Cooper
Mountbatten
The Sixth Great Power:
Barings, 1762–1929
King Edward VIII
Harold Wilson
London at War
Osbert Sitwell

ed. The Diaries of Lord
Louis Mountbatten 1920–1922
ed. Personal Diary of Admiral
the Lord Louis Mountbatten
1943–1946
ed. From Shore to Shore:
The Tour Diaries of Earl Mountbatten of
Burma 1953–1979

SOLDIERS

Fighting Men's Lives, 1901–2001

Philip Ziegler

Chatto & Windus
LONDON

20067460

MORAY COUNCIL
LIBRARIES &
INFORMATION SERVICES

355.009

Published by Chatto & Windus 2001

2 4 6 8 10 9 7 5 3 1

Copyright © Philip Ziegler 2001

Philip Ziegler has asserted his right under the Copyright, Designs
and Patents Act 1988 to be identified as the author of this work

This book is sold subject to the condition that it shall not,
by way of trade or otherwise, be lent, resold, hired out, or otherwise
circulated without the publisher's prior consent in any form of binding or
cover other than that in which it is published and without a
similar condition including this condition being imposed
on the subsequent purchaser

First published in Great Britain in 2001 by
Chatto & Windus
Random House, 20 Vauxhall Bridge Road,
London SW1V 2SA

Random House Australia (Pty) Limited
20 Alfred Street, Milsons Point, Sydney,
New South Wales 2061, Australia

Random House New Zealand Limited
18 Poland Road, Glenfield,
Auckland 10, New Zealand

Random House (Pty) Limited
Endulini, 5A Jubilee Road, Parktown 2193, South Africa

The Random House Group Limited Reg. No. 954009
www.randomhouse.co.uk

A CIP catalogue record for this book
is available from the British Library

ISBN 0 7011 6954 0

Papers used by Random House are natural
recyclable products made from wood grown in sustainable forests;
the manufacturing processes conform to the environmental
regulations of the country of origin

Typeset by Deltatype Ltd, Birkenhead, Merseyside
Printed and bound in Great Britain by
Clays Ltd, St Ives plc.

Contents

List of Illustrations	vii
Acknowledgements	xi
Table of Comparative Values	xiii
Prologue	1
Albert Alexandre	7
Archibald Harrington	47
Fernley Small	83
Thomas Parnell	123
Douglas Wright	155
Leonard Pearson	185
Arthur Jeffery	221
James Fergus	259
Alwyn Holmes	289
Epilogue	321
Bibliographic Note	339
Index	343

Illustrations

1 a In-Pensioner Albert Alexandre
  b Bombardier Alexandre, *c* 1929
2 a In-Pensioner Archibald Harrington
  b Sergeant Harrington, 1936
3 a In-Pensioner Fernley Small
  b Company Sergeant-Major Small, 1946
4 a In-Pensioner Thomas Parnell (Sophie Carr)
  b Corporal Parnell, *c* 1938
5 a In-Pensioner Douglas Wright
  b Lance-Sergeant Wright, *c* 1941
6 a In-Pensioner Leonard Pearson (Sophie Carr)
  b Lance-Corporal Pearson, 1940
7 a In-Pensioner Arthur Jeffery
  b Private Jeffery, *c* 1946
8 a In-Pensioner James Fergus
  b Sergeant Fergus, 1943
9 a In-Pensioner Alwyn Holmes (Sophie Carr)
  b Sergeant Holmes with members of his platoon at Celle in
    Germany, *c* 1955

To
The In-Pensioners and Staff
of the
ROYAL HOSPITAL CHELSEA

Acknowledgements

MY FIRST acknowledgement must obviously be to the nine In-Pensioners of the Royal Hospital Chelsea, whose stories comprise this book. Their patience and fortitude under my inquisition was unwavering; I am profoundly grateful to them for their help and for having lived lives which have offered me such rich material.

When I began work on this book General Sir Brian Kenny was Governor of the Royal Hospital; by the time I completed it General Sir Jeremy Mackenzie had taken over: both they and the Lieutenant-Governor, Major General Jonathan Hall – and indeed all the staff of the Hospital – have given me as much support and encouragement as any author could have asked for.

The Adjutant of the Royal Hospital, Brigadier A. G. Ross, and his wife, Cathy, must have a paragraph to themselves. Kim Ross worked miracles for me so far beyond the course of duty that I stand astonished by my effrontery in demanding them. Every In-Pensioner I have met has spoken of him with affection and respect. I can well see why.

My friend General Sir David Ramsbotham was kind enough to read my typescript and to pick up many of my blunders in military lore. I hope not too many remain.

I have been fortunate enough to talk to some of the relations of the In-Pensioners whom I interviewed. In particular I would like to record my gratitude to Frances Bacon, Jean Barlow, Rita Derby, Elizabeth Gill, Vera Hayes, Daphne Isod, David and Alex Jenkins, Sylvannah Mansell, Harold and Nigel Parnell, Andrew Pearson and Christine Penfold.

My old friend Simon Master of Random House championed

this book from its inception; and Carol Brown Janeway of Knopf, whose friendship is rooted even further in my past, was bold enough to feel that it might hold some interest for American readers as well. To them I owe many thanks, as I do to my skilled and constructive editor, Penelope Hoare, to Alison Samuel – both of Chatto and Windus – and to my agent, Michael Shaw of Curtis Brown, who handled negotiations with his usual tact and skill.

My greatest debt, as always, is to my wife, whose perceptive understanding of human nature has contributed so much to all my writing. In this case the debt is even larger than usual, for the idea of the book was hers.

Philip Ziegler,
London
June 2001

Table of Comparative Values

THE POUND STERLING was decimalised in 1969; previously it had been divided into 20 shillings (20s) and 240 pence (240d). A shilling, which comprised 12 pence, was written 1/-; one and a half shillings would have appeared as 1/6d. The main units in the old currency, with their equivalents in new pence, were:

1 farthing ($\frac{1}{4}$d)	– just over 0.1 of a new penny.
1 halfpenny ($\frac{1}{2}$d)	– just over 0.2 of a new penny.
1 penny (1d)	– just over 0.4 of a new penny.
Sixpence (6d)	– $2\frac{1}{2}$ new pence.
1 shilling (1/-)	– 5 new pence.
Half a crown (2/6d)	– $12\frac{1}{2}$ new pence (a crown had been worth five shillings, hence the name).

Comparisons between the purchasing powers of the pound at different periods are notoriously misleading and calculations are further complicated by the fact that the period between the two World Wars was one of deflation, the pound in 1939 buying significantly more than it had in 1918. As a rough-and-ready guide, however, one would not be too grossly misled if one assumed that, between 1918 and 1939, the pound bought approximately 25 times what it would today.

PROLOGUE

Prologue

IT is a minute before eleven on the morning of 8 June 2000. Christopher Wren's great Figure Court, at the heart of the Royal Hospital, Chelsea, is crowded for the prime event of the Hospital's year, the Founder's Day Parade. Its founder was King Charles II, the year of its foundation 1682. Legend claims that Charles II was acting on the prompting of his mistress, Nell Gwyn: there is no evidence whatsoever to validate this thesis, but equally nothing to disprove it. It sounds the sort of thing she might have done. Wherever the original impulse may have come from, the King was inspired largely by the creation of his brother monarch, Louis XIV, the Hôtel des Invalides in Paris. 'Invalides', of course has as much to do with invalids as 'Hospital' has to do with hospital. Both kings wished to provide a hostel where veteran soldiers could find a secure home in their declining years.

The Founder's Day Parade commemorates Charles II's inglorious escape after the Battle of Worcester as well as his restoration to the throne nine years later. One of the more celebrated incidents in his flight from Worcester occurred when he avoided capture by hiding up an oak tree at Boscobel House, some twenty-five miles from the battlefield – hence the designation of his birthday, 29

3

May, as Oak-apple Day and the fact that, before the Parade, every participant is presented with a sprig of oak leaves. Grinling Gibbons' statue of Charles II in the centre of the Figure Court emerges from a carapace of oak-tree branches to survey with mild surprise the scene around him. What the King's statue witnesses could hardly be more colourful.

The plumes of the Governor and Lieutenant-Governor, the Fanfare Trumpeters of the Royal Military School of Music, the band of the Scots Guards, the solitary piper from the 1st Battalion of the Highlanders, the In-Pensioners themselves, splendid in scarlet coats and ceremonial tricorn hats, in their rich pageantry evoke everything that is most memorable about Britain's military and imperial past. Or, to look at it another way, a bunch of superannuated poseurs are poncing around in fancy dress, trying to recapture lost glories that were spurious at the best of times and are entirely irrelevant today. The dichotomy apparent in those points of view is one of the more potent elements in the book that follows.

Eleven o'clock, and the great wooden doors open into the Octagon Porch, a noble space between chapel and Great Hall where trophies captured in battle hang from the walls. As a fanfare sounds from the trumpeters standing on the roof above Wren's colonnade, the Duke of Kent, who is Reviewing Officer for the day, enters the Figure Court. The two hundred or so Pensioners who are fit to take part in the Parade stand as rigidly to attention as their age permits, another hundred sit and watch from the fringes of the court, a handful are too ill or elderly to be present. Attendance at the Founder's Day Parade is the only obligation laid upon Pensioners, otherwise they can come and go as they like; take part in the innumerable activities which the Hospital offers them if they feel the inclination, or abstain if they prefer to. If they are in the Hospital then they must be dressed and out of their panelled cubicle – their berth, as it is called – by half past seven in the morning, but this stipulation is only made because it is the easiest way to ensure that everyone has survived the night. The Royal Hospital is an Army establishment, it is run on military lines, but no attempt is made to impose strict discipline upon the inmates. The good order that prevails reigns at their own wish and by their own doing; the authorities have no sanctions to enforce their rules except the ultimate one of expulsion. It is a sanction that is most rarely and reluctantly invoked.

Ten minutes past eleven, and the Duke of Kent has begun his inspection of the Pensioners. One of the men in front of whom he passes fought at Passchendaele in 1918; almost all of them played a part in the Second World War, one of the youngest was involved in the Falklands – though as a Merchant Navy man. Between them the Pensioners can boast almost ten thousand years of military service. They have served in more than seventy countries, with Northern Ireland thrown in as an extra. The medals that they wear reflect the extraordinary variety of their experience: forty-six Africa Stars, thirty-five Burma Stars, sixteen Pacific Stars, thirteen General Service Medals Borneo, a Polar Medal, a Légion d'honneur, a Polish Cross of Monte Cristo … The Pensioners have been on parade for a long time now. Even among those who are standing to attention rather than sitting to the side the average age is nearly eighty. It is hot in the midday sun, their ordeal is not yet over, but nobody faints, nobody even wavers.

Twenty-five minutes past eleven. The Adjutant calls the Pensioners to attention; the climax of the Parade is near. 'The In-Pensioners Royal Hospital will march past.' As the band plays 'The Boys of the Old Brigade' the first of the four companies of Pensioners responds to the order 'By the left – quick – *march!*' by breaking into what must be the slowest quick march to be witnessed on any parade ground in the British Isles. Some of the Pensioners have pot bellies, few stand as upright as once they did, the drill lacks some of the punch and precision of former years but there is not one of them who does not take pride in the reputation of the Royal Hospital and of the Army in which he once served, and is not resolved to do all he can to reflect credit on them. Behind the marching ranks six Pensioners in electrically powered wheel chairs in their turn pass and salute the Duke of Kent. They suffer from a wide range of afflictions, but in almost every case the ravages of war have played a part in making it impossible for them to march with the others. Their presence is a silent reminder of the many thousands of soldiers who would have been eligible to end their days in the Royal Hospital – but who were deprived of the opportunity by their death in battle.

Twenty-five minutes to twelve. Once more the Pensioners are called to attention. Now the Governor takes over. 'In-Pensioners Royal Hospital – remove Head-dress.' Three cheers are given for 'Our Pious Founder King Charles the Second' – a curious adjective to apply to somebody who possessed many qualities but must have been among the more impious of British monarchs – for the Queen and for the Duke of Kent. The Pensioners wave their hats in the air and cheer with remarkable lustiness, encouraged, perhaps, by the thought that their test is over for another year. The parade is dismissed and with relief the Pensioners shuffle off to relax with friends and families.

Among them are Albert Alexandre of the Guernsey Light Infantry and the Royal Artillery; Archibald Harrington of the Queen's Royal Regiment and the Royal Artillery; Fernley Small of the Northamptonshire Regiment; Thomas Parnell of the Duke of Lancaster's Own Yeomanry and the 10th Royal Hussars; Douglas Wright of the Special Boat Squadron and the Grenadier Guards; Leonard Pearson of the Royal Engineers; Arthur Jeffery of the Devonshire Regiment; James Fergus of the Black Watch and the Royal Electrical and Mechanical Engineers, and Alwyn Holmes of the Royal Army Service Corps.

ALBERT ALEXANDRE

Bombardier Alexandre, *c* 1929

Albert Alexandre

I T would be hard to imagine a less promising upbringing than that of Albert Alexandre. He was born in the Channel Islands, in the little Jersey town of Longueville, on 6 October 1901. The population of Jersey had been almost entirely Norman French until the early nineteenth century, when an influx from the British Isles began. By 1901, though the British element had grown substantially, the majority of the islanders still used a patois incomprehensible to English speakers and likely to cause confusion to the French as well. Albert's Catholic father, however, was an immigrant from France; his mother was born in Jersey but came from English stock. Their children spoke mainly English at home but were fluent in French; they hardly attempted to grapple with the local dialect.

Albert was the youngest of four children but his brother and two sisters were all considerably older and had left home by the time he reached the age of six. His father was a general labourer who spent much of his time in forestry work; money was extremely short but the family was never in need and Albert had enough to eat and was adequately clothed. Then, shortly after his sixth birthday, his mother fell ill and was removed to hospital. Within a few weeks she was dead, Albert thinks of a tumour on the brain. His father followed a few months later, when a tree which he was felling crashed on top of him. Albert knows nothing about the circumstances of the accident: perhaps grief at his wife's death had weakened his father's will to live; perhaps worry or lack of sleep slowed the speed of his reactions. His son found himself an orphan. None of his siblings had a home in which he could take refuge; he had one uncle living in Jersey but he was unable or unwilling to make room for him; Albert was consigned to the orphanage.

The 'Industrial School', as this institution was optimistically entitled, provided shelter for some 120 boys. 'It wasn't really a school at all,' Alexandre remembers. 'I wasn't educated there. I learnt how to read and write a little, that sort of thing, but I never touched arithmetic.' There were only two teachers who were remotely concerned with education in the more liberal sense of the word, otherwise the emphasis was entirely on technical training. There was a tailoring master, a shoemaker master: any boy leaving the orphanage, it was hoped, would have acquired at least the rudiments of a trade. But though the surroundings were dour and the ethos utilitarian, the boys were not Oliver Twists oppressed by some latter-day Mr Bumble. 'It was a really good place,' Alexandre insists. 'They were very kind to you.' The food was adequate if sparse; it was neither the time nor the place for displays of affection but the exiguous staff were concerned about the boys' welfare and did their best to ensure that they were happy as well as healthy.

He stayed at the orphanage until he was nearly twelve, during which time he scarcely saw any members of his family or ventured far beyond the grounds of the institution. Then the elder of his two sisters, who had married a farmer's son and lived in St Peter Port in Guernsey, volunteered to take in her little brother. She could not afford to provide any further education for him, but at least he would have a home and be living with relations.

Albert left the orphanage without regret but without bitterness –

bitterness seems, indeed, to have been unknown to him at any time; the singular sweetness of his disposition defied every brickbat that fate might fling at him. He at once looked for work and found it in the local brewery, washing bottles and occasionally filling them with beer. He had no wish to drink the stuff himself, but his sister deplored the temptation that was being put in his way and felt that a brewery was no place for a twelve-year-old boy. Instead, she found him a job in a market garden, where he washed pots and performed other menial tasks in the winter and picked flowers for export in the summer. It was hard and uninspiring work, ill-rewarded too, but Albert always did his best to perform whatever duty was imposed on him and it would never have occurred to him that he might be qualified for something more exacting and better paid.

Then, in 1913, his brother-in-law joined the Army and was posted for his training to the neighbouring island of Alderney. Albert's sister soon joined him there and Albert followed in their wake. He lodged in St Anne's with an elderly lady, who loved him like a son and whom he came to consider almost as his mother. His first job was on a farm, in fact little more than a smallholding, but though he enjoyed the work the owner could afford to pay him only a pittance. For himself he would have been satisfied – throughout his life, what he was doing seemed far more important to him than the money he earned by it – but he knew that his landlady was making very little money out of him, was perhaps even losing, and he wanted to pay her more. The principal source of employment in Alderney was the quarries run by the Channel Island Granite Company and soon Albert was employed by them as a driller. With the outbreak of the First World War many of the Company's workers joined up and left the island. Albert was still only thirteen, but he was tall and strong and looked considerably older. Strictly speaking he should not have been allowed to handle explosives until he was eighteen but in wartime nobody was too fussy about the regulations and within a few months he was carrying out blasting work as if he was a man.

At first the war did not impinge on his life but by the time he was fifteen he looked so mature that people began to ask him why he was not fighting for his country. One night a soldier stationed in Alderney accused him of shirking his duty. 'And what are you doing out of the Front on a cushy island like this?' Albert retorted, but later the same evening he asked himself whether perhaps he should enlist. Restlessness, a wish to see the world, a craving for adventure, were as strong as patriotism among his motives but his brother and several of his friends were already in the Army and a feeling that he should do his bit by joining them was an element in his thinking.

At the age of fifteen and eleven months, Albert Alexandre took himself to the recruiting centre in Alderney and volunteered to join the Army. Though lying did not come easily to him he had prepared himself to claim to be much older than he was. He need not have worried; the question of his age was never mentioned. In the summer of 1917 the war had reached its most desperate stage. The United States had entered the war but any substantial help from the other side of the Atlantic still seemed a distant prospect. On the Eastern Front the Russians had been routed. The Allied High Command concluded that an all-out assault must be mounted if an overwhelming German offensive were to be pre-empted. Recruits were urgently needed for the Western Front, and provided a volunteer was not obviously a child he would be welcomed with alacrity. Alexandre was despatched to Guernsey to become a soldier.

He had wanted to follow his brother into the Royal Artillery but the recruiting sergeant told him that the Guernsey Light Infantry was in dire need of recruits and urged him to join his local regiment. Obligingly he agreed. The Guernsey Militia, as it had originally been styled, was a highly respectable and antique body whose oldest existing ordinance dated from 1546 and provided that *haquebutes* must be kept in good order and *les boulvers* (earthworks) properly maintained. Alexandre found that the new intake consisted largely of Irishmen who had been resident in the Channel Islands or of recruits to the North Staffordshire Regiment who had been drafted in to make up numbers; he preferred to consort with these foreigners rather than the native Guernseymen, whose patois he could hardly understand. He found that the sergeants knew their jobs and were firm but fair. The senior officers were equally acceptable – 'mostly gentlemen, ex-militia and that sort of thing'. It never occurred to men like Alexandre to question the higher strategy. Siegfried Sassoon pictured an affable general greeting the troops as they went up to the Front:

> 'He's a cheery old card,' grunted Harry to Jack
> As they slogged up to Arras with rifle and pack.
> But he did for them both with his plan of attack.

Alexandre was Harry and Jack, and though some of his regimental officers may have joined Sassoon in cursing the General's staff 'for incompetent swine', he had no such feelings himself. His only reservations were about the younger officers who were frightened by their new responsibilities and tried to ensure that nothing would go wrong by fussing endlessly over trifles and bullying those under them: 'They didn't really know how to handle men.'

Seven weeks' basic training in Guernsey were followed by a move to Rouen at the end of October 1917, where training continued six or seven days a week from 7 a.m. to 9 p.m. and sometimes overnight as well. Reinforcements were desperately needed to confront the big German push that it was feared was coming, and hardly a moment could be spared for rest or recreation. For all Alexandre knew or cared he might have been in Timbuctoo; he had neither time, energy nor inclination to get to know the country and its inhabitants: 'When I was in France I did what I was told I had to do and that was that. Where I was didn't interest me whatsoever.' Nor was he told, or even concerned, about the progress of the war. While still a civilian he had been influenced by official propaganda presenting the Germans as brutal barbarians but once he was enlisted this was spared him; he just got on with his work day by day and waited with some apprehension for the action that could not lie too far ahead. The actual training caused him few problems. He was among the fittest of the recruits and proved adept with rifle and bayonet. Because he was used to working with explosives and had a good throwing arm he was selected to specialise in grenades; soon he found that he was particularly skilled at manoeuvring himself into the right position to launch his missile without drawing attention to himself. But though a success, he was at this stage entirely without ambition; it never occurred to him that he might be promoted, nor would he have welcomed promotion if it had come his way.

Even if the schedule had left him free time or he had felt inclined to indulge himself, he would have had little money to spend on his pleasures. His basic pay was 7 shillings a week and of this half was paid directly to his former landlady and 'foster mother' in Alderney. The payment was voluntary; the Army made a point of ensuring that its soldiers contributed to the livelihood of their dependants at home but in a case like Alexandre's, where there was no blood relationship, would have seen no moral, let alone legal obligation. The result of Alexandre's generosity was that – after various extra deductions made from his pay by the authorities – he had barely enough left for a mug of tea and a very occasional pint of beer. Even if he had hankered after wine or women – concepts, in fact, far beyond his imagining – he would have been unable to do much about it.

While Alexandre was finishing his training the Guernsey Light Infantry had been taking part in one of the bloodiest and most futile offensives of the war. The advance at Cambrai in November 1917, cost the regiment six or seven hundred casualties in ten days;

the shattered remnants were pulled back and sent to rest and absorb their reinforcements forty miles or so behind the lines at Houvin. It was there that Alexandre joined them at the beginning of November. Any remaining illusions about the sort of fighting that awaited him were quickly dispelled when he spoke to the survivors of the battle; even though they had been the lucky ones who escaped serious injuries these men were scarred by the horrors that they had seen and the massacre of so many of their friends. But the mood was one of resignation and a bloody-minded determination to carry on; when on Christmas Eve they began the march to the front morale was high, astonishingly high when one considers what so many of them had been through and what they all suspected might lie ahead. Nor was this spirit unusual. There were, of course, moments of apathy or despair, but the resilience of the British infantryman in intolerably hideous conditions was one of the miracles of the First World War.

Christmas Day was spent at Verchocq, reached after an exhausting route march of more than twenty miles. It was marked by a febrile gaiety as any money the soldiers chanced to have left was squandered on drink and the commissariat did miracles in eking out the rations with a few extra titbits. The festivities, recorded the regimental history grimly, gave rise to 'an unbounded vein of hilarious humour and uproarious chorus in celebration of a Christmas that many knew would be their last'. The hilarity quickly faded when the march to the front was resumed next day; by the New Year problems of supply meant that rations were cut and bread almost disappeared from the daily diet. Then came the news that in two weeks or so the regiment was to be consigned to the most dreaded of all destinations, the Passchendaele–Ypres sector. When the announcement was made, from the ranks of the veterans came 'continuous outbursts of growling'; the new arrivals were less immediately downcast but had learnt enough over the previous few weeks to share their seniors' apprehension.

In mid-January 1918, the Guernsey Light Infantry relieved a

battalion of the Worcesters near the main road running between Poperinghe and Ypres. They paused to absorb the latest horror stories of flooded trenches, constant shelling, gas, days without food when the ration parties were unable to get through, then resumed their trudge along a duck-boarded track through the sterile and pockmarked desolation that had once been prosperous farmland. A final halt was made for the men to wash their feet in warm water and to grease and powder them, and for two days' rations to be added to the full pack, rifle, Mills bombs, Lewis gun ammunition, spade and sheet of corrugated iron which comprised the average private soldier's burden. On 18 January 1918, Albert Alexandre arrived in Passchendaele. He was exactly sixteen years and three months old.

'Do you believe in hell?' Alice Keach asked Mr Birkin in J. L. Carr's novel *A Month in the Country*. 'Hell? Passchendaele had been hell. Bodies split, heads blown off, grovelling fear, shrieking fear, unspeakable fear! The world made mad!' Alexandre was more phlegmatic than most and had the resilience of youth, but the memory of that battlefield would never be expunged. The so-called 'front' consisted of little more than a series of shell-holes, most of them waterlogged, connected by inadequate trenches which crumbled regularly into muddy ruin. Gas shells were sent over day and night, hampering the ration parties and stretcher teams and forcing the men to spend hours at a time in hot and claustrophobic respirators. Alexandre caught whiffs of gas but not enough to do him any serious harm; the smell reminded him of musty hay and left him feeling that he was suffering from an attack of influenza. The danger of death or mutilation by shell or mortar fire, hand grenade or sniper's bullet, was omnipresent, by day and night. 'I expected it to be bad,' says Alexandre, 'because of the casualties we'd heard of, but it was a lot worse than I had expected. Mud, snow, ice, everything...'

In February the regiment was pulled out of the front line for a period of rest at Poperinghe, though the 'rest' was hardly recreational; working parties were sent out every day to repair roads and fill up shell-holes. A major German offensive was believed to be imminent and in March it came. The regiment was hurriedly thrown back into the line and spent a few days digging trenches in the spongy soil outside the village of Passchendaele.

They were never to be used, the front was crumbling, collapsing almost. The Germans had advanced ten miles at Saint-Quentin, Passchendaele was outflanked, and the regiment began to withdraw, then was thrown into a gap in the line at Doulieu. A powerful German attack was almost immediately upon them, they were ordered to retreat under murderous machine-gun fire, made a stand, then again fell back when a battalion on their right was overrun. For several days the retreat went on, the Germans attacking with overwhelming numerical superiority, the battlefield a scene of carnage, made more hideous by the helpless and hopeless refugees clogging whatever roads existed, half-starved pigs, cows moaning in agony for want of anybody to milk them. Finally the line stabilised; the German offensive ran out of steam; the war, though nobody would have dared predict it at the time, was won.

Alexandre had endured several months of bombardment and brutal fighting without a scratch. Not many of the thousand or so soldiers who went into battle with him could say as much; more than a third of them were dead. To survive unscathed required a great deal of luck but also physical strength, quick reactions, cunning and an ability to strike first and quickly. It is not a period on which Alexandre cares to reflect. 'I wouldn't like to say if I killed a German – that's something that I never said to anyone. I don't like to think about it. All I can say is that it was hand-to-hand fighting and you had to defend yourself.'

But though the enemy had not hurt him he did not escape untroubled. Before the regiment was again involved in any major action, he had been struck down by what was described, with some imprecision, as 'trench fever' and taken to hospital. From there he was moved to a convalescent home near Trouville, only discovering after he had left that the brother whom he had not seen for nearly five years was within a few hundred yards of him. At the convalescent home he was asked if he would like to volunteer for some sort of work. He said he would and was hailed as a godsend when it was realised that he had some experience of working on the land and was also fluent in French. For six weeks he lived with a French farmer, helping out in various ways and in particular liaising over the provision of horses for the British Army. After the horrors of the front line the work seemed infinitely to his taste. For the first time since he had joined the Army he began to look ahead to a world in which he would be free to lead whatever life he wanted.

First, however, there was a job to be finished. As soon as he was passed as being fully fit he was sent to Rouen and then to rejoin his comrades at Bertincourt. On 11 November the regiment was marching towards the front line, knowing that German resistance was collapsing but foreseeing much hard fighting before the war was won. A despatch rider on a motorcycle hurtled past the column and stopped where the Colonel was standing. Within minutes word was passed down the line that an armistice would be signed at 11 a.m. 'We were all very excited,' remembers Alexandre. 'We jumped for joy but some of us couldn't believe it.' They marched on to take up their place in the front line to find there a scene of unnatural inactivity – nothing was moving except for a few German troops packing up their belongings in a mood of mingled mortification and relief. Alexandre looked at them with loathing: 'Propaganda is a terrible thing, it lives with you for a long time. We were taught to despise them as the enemy, to hate them. It was either you or them all the time.'

Demobilisation could not come too soon for Alexandre but its date was calculated after considering a man's length of service and the importance of his future role in civilian life. On neither ground could he hope to be granted any priority. Several months had passed and twenty batches of demob-happy soldiers had preceded him before he marched into Boulogne on the way home. It was cold and wet, their hobnailed boots slithered on the slippery cobbles, the euphoria of victory had long faded, tempers frayed. It was 'a horrible march with much sliding and falling, resulting in cursing and even fist fights'. At last they boarded a boat and were taken to Southampton. Alexandre and a few friends rushed to a nearby pub. 'Now then, you lot,' the landlord greeted them, 'before you take one more step, SHOW US YER MONEY!' Thus the land fit for heroes welcomed back its champions.

Disillusionment was not dispelled over the next few weeks. He returned to Alderney and had a rapturous reunion with his honorary foster mother, but there it ended. Even if he had wanted to go back to the quarry, every place had been taken by ex-soldiers who had been demobilised before him. There was no job on the land that offered any prospect of permanency. He had no other skills or strings to pull. What was more, rather to his surprise, he found that he missed the camaraderie and structured pattern of military life. For the first time he began to consider the possibility that he might re-enlist. The more he thought of it the more the idea appealed to him; partly for want of any more promising alternative, still more because he felt that peacetime soldiering would suit him well.

The next question was what sort of a soldier he wished to be. The Guernsey Light Infantry would have taken him back without problems, but he felt no particular loyalty towards them. 'We Channel Islanders are all the same,' he remarks. 'We fight each other – they called me a *crapaud*.' He felt that he would do better to make a fresh start, and so reverted to what had been his first idea, the Royal Artillery. At the depot of the Royal Garrison Artillery at Plymouth he explained that he had always wanted to be a gunner and enlisted for eight years in the Colours and a subsequent four in the Reserve. He was still well short of his eighteenth birthday but if he had been old enough to fight at Passchendaele, the recruiting officer not unreasonably considered, he was old enough to carry out his basic training for the Royal Artillery.

Strictly speaking he should have spent twelve months or so training as a foot soldier before starting work in the Artillery but since he obviously knew all about it already he was quickly despatched to a riding course at Winchester. By the time he had finished that he was qualified as a driver. He was then posted to Lydd where he joined a brigade group of 60-pounders and 6-inch howitzers and learnt the crafts of loading and firing guns as well as dragging them from one point to another. Life in the Royal Artillery was to be an endless process of mastering new techniques but the basic foundations had been put in place. The real work was now to begin. In August 1919, he was sent on embarkation leave. He went to say goodbye to his foster mother in Alderney but found no one else there whom he particularly wished to see. Nor were any of his relatives immediately accessible. It was not so much a case of a soldier going on leave to visit his family as of a soldier returning from leave to rejoin his family. For Alexandre, though he hardly yet realised the fact, the Army had become and was to remain his family.

His posting was to India, with the 9th Heavy Battery of a new Artillery Brigade. After 1918, planning for the armed services was carried out on the assumption that there would be no major war for at least ten years; there would therefore be no serious involvement on the continent of Europe and the Army could revert to its traditional and proper role, that of policing and defending the British Empire. Before 1914 – indeed, until the transfer of power in Ireland in 1922 – India and Ireland had figured in the life of almost every soldier except those belonging to a few units which, for one reason or another, were doomed to stay at home. Ireland was now fading from the scene but India retained its role until after the Second World War. Its importance to the British Army cannot be overstated, either in terms of the forces it provided for use in other parts of the world or of its own vulnerability. Whether the threat was deemed to be from Russia and dissident tribesmen in the north or from subversion within, there was nowhere in the Empire where defence and policing were more evidently called for.

During the First World War the demands of Europe and the Middle East had meant that the British military presence in India was much reduced, but with peace restored and a potentially dangerous Communist Russia posing new threats from beyond the Himalayas, there was a need to rebuild the Army in the sub-continent. By the end of 1919 there were about 50,000 troops in British units in India, predominantly near the North-West Frontier, as well as 180,000 Indian and 20,000 Gurkha troops whose officers and sometimes senior NCOs were for the most part also British. Some of the soldiers were scattered in small cantonments around the country where, willy-nilly, they were forced into a measure of contact with the local Indians, but more were concentrated in large barracks in the potential trouble areas: Lahore, Peshawar, Rawalpindi.

For officers with a sporting bent India was close to paradise: hunting, shooting, polo, all at a quarter the price of the same delights at home. For the men there were fewer such advantages. There were compensations for their exile: the nastier chores in barracks were looked after by Indian cleaners, most of the time the schedules for work were undemanding and there were plentiful opportunities for games. But that was the end of it. Except for the temperature and the weight of uniform they might just as well have been in Britain; even the food was substantially unchanged. For most other ranks – indeed, for most officers unless they had unusual tastes – there was no contact with Indian society nor involvement with Indian culture. Alexandre learnt to refer to the 'syce' rather than the groom, the 'dhobi' rather than the laundry, but in most important respects his life in barracks differed little from what it would have been at home. As for his life *outside* barracks – it could hardly be said to exist at all.

His first stay in the sub-continent lasted little more than a year, at first with coastal artillery, then with a heavy battery in Central India. He had assumed he would stay for longer but was unflustered when told that he was to be posted to Malta: the ways of the military authorities were unfathomable and it was not for him to question their mysteries. He did feel that he was being hard done by, however, when, on arrival at Malta, he was despatched to learn how to be a signaller. This meant that he would forfeit his proficiency pay as a driver, worse still he felt himself incompetent to undertake the new work. 'I'll drop dead!' he told the Regimental Sergeant-Major. He would need at least a Third Class Certificate of Education before he could qualify as a signaller, and that seemed as far beyond him as a First in Greats. The RSM was unsympathetic: orders were orders, Alexandre was on the list, and he must be at the signalling school the following afternoon.

It proved to be even worse than he had feared. On the first afternoon the class assembled for arithmetic; the subject was the Lowest Common Denominator. The men were told to write down the answers to certain problems on the blackboard. Alexandre stared aghast at the virgin sheet in front of him. 'Come on, have a go, it's easy!' urged his neighbour. 'It's easy if you know how to do it,' retorted Alexandre. '*What* don't you know?' asked a voice from behind him. A captain had come into the room and was standing a few feet away. 'I don't know any arithmetic at all, sir,' protested Alexandre. 'But you must have been to school?' Alexandre explained about the orphanage and how he could barely read and write. The Captain called him out of the classroom and told him that he must continue to follow the course but that he should come back every evening after sport for half an hour's private tuition. It was the schooling that he had never had and Alexandre relished it. He 'really got stuck into the work he gave me', and amazed both himself and his teacher by his progress. It was not just arithmetic; he was taught grammar, encouraged to read and write, made to learn words and then to search in a dictionary until he had found other words related to them. The Captain held him back until he was confident that his pupil could pass the examinations, then let him loose on the Third and, after that, the Second Grade. Alexandre passed both without difficulty. 'I felt quite good about it,' he remembers, with what must have been classic understatement.

That year in Malta transformed Alexandre from an ill-informed and unthinking cog in a vast machine to a reflective and questioning human being. The process still had some way to go, however, when his battery was ordered urgently to Turkey. After less than two years of peace, renewed war seemed imminent. The Greeks had been encouraged by the Allies to occupy Smyrna and 'colonise' part of defeated Turkey. Rising from the ashes of the Ottoman Empire, a resurgent Turkish army swept away the feeble Greek resistance and marched towards the Sea of Marmara. The British found that those on whose help they had been counting, notably the French but also the Australians and Canadians, were singularly unenthusiastic about any proposal that they should join in checking this advance. Soon a tiny British force, strung out along the coast around Chanak, was confronting a vastly superior Turkish army, well armed and itching to repeat the injuries they had inflicted on the Allied forces in the World War. Theoretically, the guns of the Royal Navy were at hand to come to the rescue of the British troops, but the flat trajectories of the naval guns made their usefulness limited in the undulating and broken ground in which the Turks were massed. The only land-based British artillery unit was the 92nd Field Battery of 4.5 howitzers in which Alexandre was serving. Bellicose messages from Whitehall instructed the British Commander-in-Chief to defy the Turks and to order them to withdraw their forces from the Chanak area. Otherwise 'all the forces at our disposal – naval, military and aerial' would open fire. Mercifully General Harington, who knew all too well just how inadequate 'all the forces at our disposal' would prove to be if put to the test, ignored his orders and did a deal with the Turkish commander whereby the Turkish forces fell back from Chanak. In the end, as was inevitable, the Turks secured most of what they wanted; Harington's action ensured that this happened without pointless loss of life.

Alexandre knew nothing of all this, nor of the reasons for his presence on the Anatolian coast. He could hardly escape noticing, however, that the Turks were massed in overwhelming strength in the hills only half a mile away, that the British position was indefensible, and that evacuation by sea in the face of a Turkish attack would have been a difficult and probably bloody undertaking. Some of the British troops, notably those who had just joined the Army, were eager to stand their ground and 'have a go at the Turks'. Alexandre and most of the other veterans had no such aspirations. When it was announced that a ceasefire had been agreed he felt nothing but profound relief: 'I'd already had enough of the war.'

The next five years were spent in Malta. Alexandre was naturally disposed to enjoy life and Malta offered every chance to do so. The work was light, the climate pleasant, the barracks, by the standards of anything he had known before, comfortable, even luxurious. There was plenty of time for games, bars to visit, entertainments to attend: he was richer than he had ever been. But though the Maltese were on the whole well disposed towards the British, he made no friends among them. Many British soldiers found themselves Maltese girlfriends, some ended up by marrying them. Alexandre might wistfully have envied them but he experienced little urge to do the same. He had scarcely met any girls of his own age, was ill at ease with them and felt himself still more debarred by the barriers of race and language. It was an age in which men married late – particularly in the Army, where early matrimony was deplored if not actually forbidden – and pre-marital sex was unusual. Brothels existed in Malta but they were mainly patronised by the older, married men who, for one reason or another, were deprived of their wives. Nobody thought Alexandre was eccentric, still less were his sexual proclivities put in question, because he sublimated his urges in violent exercise and remained firmly celibate.

But his monastic dedication did not long survive his return to Britain. Militarily, his career had begun to take off. The years of conscientious hard work and patient self-education reaped their reward: he was sent on an instructors' course, certified a first-class signaller, given his first stripe, sent on another course as a signaller, and then promoted bombardier and posted to Shoeburyness, the Royal Artillery barracks just outside Southend in Essex. By now his pay was 33 shillings a week and he felt close to affluence. Though the Army had done much to educate him, he had still not acquired the art of easy letter-writing and had lost touch with his foster mother and remaining family in the Channel Islands. Many of his colleagues were in the same boat but he was none the less aware, sometimes painfully aware, of his solitary position. He was thirty-three, well past the barrier of twenty-six after which a soldier was free to marry without being required to present himself to his Commanding Officer, explain his intentions and no doubt be heartily discouraged from any such premature adventure. Almost without realising it he was looking around for a wife.

He found her in Dorothy Axcell, the twenty-two-year-old daughter of a family which was originally of Dutch-Jewish stock but had long been wholly anglicised. He met her at a garrison dance, was immediately attracted by her, took her roller-skating in Southend, after a few months proposed and was accepted and, being a man with a great capacity for love and loyalty, never looked at another woman so long as she lived. But she had to compete with his prior loyalties. Shortly after they became engaged he was told that he was to be sent back to India. His Sergeant-Major made it clear that he had done very well as an instructor and that they would be happy to retain him at Shoeburyness if he applied for the posting to be cancelled. The curiously stubborn determination to carry out orders, however irrational or undesirable, which so often marks the regular soldier, now possessed Alexandre: 'I don't think they wanted me to go . . . but once they'd put me down for it, I wouldn't back out of it.' Regretfully he told his fiancée what the future held: 'You'd better find some other young man; I'll be out there at least six years.'

Her response was what he had hoped for. 'That *would* happen!' she said resignedly; rather than give him up or wait six years she would marry him immediately and either accompany him to India or follow as soon as it proved possible. He explained that she might find herself in some remote jungle station – she accepted the possibility with equanimity. She might not have been quite as amenable if she had known that Alexandre could have got out of the posting, but he remained discreetly quiet about his Sergeant-Major's offer. In fact Dorothy quite liked the idea of a stint in India; it was his future mother-in-law who was most put out and who would have been indignant if she had known that her beloved daughter could have had her man and yet stayed at home.

Dorothy's mother got a year's grace. Only ten per cent of any given gunner unit could take their wives with them, with fares paid and accommodation provided at the other end, and Alexandre had to wait twelve months before there was such an opportunity. By this time he had put signalling behind him and had been promoted to lance-sergeant. His first posting in India was to the 5th Medium Battery at Ambala – 'not a bad station at all' – and it was there that Dorothy joined him. She liked the relatively ladylike existence, the cleaner and the cook, the tennis, the society of the other sergeants' wives, but she found the ever-present sense of hierarchy oppressive and never became wholly reconciled to the fact that her husband had two families and that she must always share him with the Army. She became still less enthusiastic when the battery was transferred to Ferozepur. This was much more of a frontier camp and appropriately well fortified; barracks and married quarters were confined within ramparts, a huge arsenal divided the two, in summer a searingly hot wind lashed across the plains and made life almost intolerable. At the worst time of year wives and children could escape to the hills, but though the authorities did their best to let husbands join their families, the unit was on active service and could not be denuded of too many of its officers and NCOs. Alexandre was in Ferozepur in 1937 for King George VI's coronation, an occasion that was celebrated with as much pomp as heat and sandstorms would allow.

From Ferozepur the battery moved back to Ambala and then to the so-called 'jungle station' of Motra, between Delhi and Agra. In each post there was a routine of training, gun drills, exercises; the British Army in India had to remain in a state of suspended animation, knowing that theoretically it might find itself in action at any moment yet knowing, also, that the chances of it being involved in any fighting were few and far between. The nearest Alexandre got to real warfare came when his battery was posted to Peshawar early in 1939. The region between Peshawar and the Afghan frontier was perpetually in disorder; the mountain tribes-men resented any form of external authority and, anyway, found their principal source of entertainment in attacking each other or, better still, foreign troops. It was only eighteen months since a force more than 30,000 strong had had to be assembled to suppress the Fakir of Ipi in Waziristan. By the time Alexandre's unit got to the area things had become comparatively calm but it was still felt necessary to mount periodic forays so as to show strength and deter potential troublemakers. Twice Alexandre found himself in the Khyber Pass; not a shot was fired but the history of the Pass was such that every rock seemed likely to conceal a sniper and an ambush was expected at every corner.

The Alexandres had two children while they were in India, both born in the hills at Simla. The first, christened Muriel but always

known as Alex, enjoyed her life in India. She remembers a
Christmas party for the Army children with her father dressed as
Father Christmas and mounted on an elephant; she was given a
doll's tea set which she kept for many years. Her younger brother
was less fortunate. He was just a year old and seemed to be thriving
– 'a bonny child' his father remembers sadly – when he inexplicably
contracted pneumonia. It was coming up for the hottest time of
year but he was deemed unfit to travel to the hills. Within a few
weeks he was dead. Alex cannot help blaming herself. Her brother
was in a pram on the veranda and she took sand from the bucket
nearby and trickled it through the mosquito net on to his face. He
chuckled and enjoyed the game but she panicked at what she had
done, ran into the house, and summoned the grown-ups to scrape
the sand out of his nose and mouth. It seems unlikely that this can
have been a factor in his later illness but Alex could never
altogether rid herself of the conviction that she had contributed to
his death. For his parents the loss of their child blighted their life
in India: 'It was really terrible,' Alexandre remembers; so much
love, so much hope, extinguished so brutally. His baby son's
sufferings became, with the horrors of Passchendaele, a memory
that he wished to suppress but which could never be altogether
exorcised.

By 1940 Alexandre would have served twenty-two years with the
Colours. The way would have been open for him to retire with full
pension rights or for the Army, if it so wished, to dispense with his
services. Probably they would have been happy for him to carry on
for a few more years; probably, too, he would not have availed
himself of the opportunity. In conversation with his wife no
conclusion had been reached, but their first feelings were that, if a
new life had to be made, it would be better to start on it while
Alexandre was still the right side of forty than to hang on in the
Army and face the same problems a few years later. Such debate
proved academic, however; by 1939 it was obvious to everyone that

war was coming and that the possibility of retirement would have to be indefinitely postponed. The process began of running down the British Army in India so as to have more seasoned troops available in Europe. In the early summer of 1939 Alexandre boarded a ship on his journey home. He had no idea how soon room would be found for his wife and daughter to follow him but before he had even finished his period of leave he heard that they were on the way. They arrived in Britain the day war was declared, Alexandre met them at the docks and carried his daughter in triumph down the gangway.

As a veteran, Alexandre was considered unsuitable to go to France. Instead he was posted to Arborfield, a garrison town between Reading and Camberley, to train the deluge of new recruits. There was a sense of urgency and the work was hard but he knew it all already and felt no particular stress. He had barely time to settle in, however, before he was transferred to Devizes, to help take over an infantry training camp which was being adapted, section by section, for work with radar and searchlight equipment. Shortly after he arrived 250 young women joined him, the majority of them clerks or cooks but including some officers. When he left, by which time he had been promoted to battery quartermaster-sergeant, the women numbered more than two thousand. His wife was not entirely happy to see him installed as pasha of this gigantic harem but there was little she could do about it. In theory it might have been possible for her to follow him to Wiltshire but accommodation there would have been extremely difficult to find and such a move would have meant giving up the house that they had secured at Wokingham, near Arborfield. Anyway, even if she had overcome these difficulties, there was no reason to believe that Alexandre's stay in Wiltshire would be any longer than it had been in Berkshire. Dorothy consoled herself with the reflection that things could have been a great deal worse. Devizes and Arborfield were only sixty miles or so apart and weekend leave was not too hard to come by, so they were better off than many families in their position.

Their second son was born in August 1940. A year or so later there was a polio epidemic. The child died at the age of sixteen months. At that time they had no telephone; a neighbour took messages from the hospital and came round with the news that all was over. 'Young as I was, I knew there was something very wrong,' says the baby's sister, Alex. 'I remember my father coming out in tears, picking me up and giving me an extra cuddle. They were so distressed.' To have lost one son in infancy was a cruel misfortune, to lose two must have seemed unbearable. It was a wound which had hardly begun to heal when their second daughter, Daphne, was born in 1942.

By that time Alexandre knew that he was likely soon to be posted abroad. With the Japanese armies overrunning Malaya and Burma and poised on the frontier of India there was an urgent need to rehabilitate the shattered Army and build up resources. His colonel sent for him and told him that his name was on the list for a posting to the East. He knew the family circumstances and sympathetically asked whether Alexandre had any good excuse for not going back to India. This seemed to Alexandre a rather odd question to put in the circumstances of 1942; he answered diffidently that he had been abroad a long time already and that perhaps enough was enough. This was the furthest he felt it proper to go by way of protest. But that was the problem, the Colonel replied; it was just because Alexandre knew India well and was used to handling native troops that the authorities wanted him back there again. Alexandre in fact had never worked with Indian troops, but he felt he had already said as much as was permissible and accepted his destiny without further demur. In July 1942 he sailed for India, leaving his wife and daughters in the house near Wokingham.

The journey proved protracted, not for the first time in his military career Alexandre found himself wondering why, if his

presence somewhere was so urgently required, it should take quite
so long to get him there. His ship sailed in convoy from the north
of England and took five weeks to reach Durban. Then occurred
one of those inexplicable but not uncommon hiatuses in which the
Army seemed to have forgotten what it had intended to do in the
first place. After seven weeks at Clarewood Camp in the Durban
area, Alexandre was shipped up-country for some ill-specified
liaison job with the South African Army. The South Africans
made it clear that they had no idea why he was there and wished
he was somewhere else; Alexandre shared their view – 'I was just
floating about there,' he said. Eventually he brought himself to
request a transfer back to England. Before he had even registered
his protest, however, momentum was suddenly regained; he was
rushed urgently back to Durban, embarked, and after another three
weeks decanted at Bombay.

His work kept him far behind the fighting area. The British and
Indian Armies were massed on the border of Burma, preparing to
attack the Japanese yet uneasily conscious that they themselves
were vulnerable to a counter-strike. Alexandre was in a transit
camp in Bihar, responsible for reclothing and rehabilitating
survivors of the fighting. At one point the authorities meditated a
surprise attack on the Japanese at a time of year when the weather
was supposed to make such a move impossible. If it had come off
Alexandre would probably have been involved. He would have
accepted such an assignment without complaint, but when the
project was abandoned he was heartily relieved to escape what
would have been a dangerous and extremely disagreeable campaign. At the age of forty-one, with a wife and two daughters
dependent on him, he felt no urge to indulge in heroics. He would
do whatever was required of him but no more.

Not that Kunta, the barracks where he was stationed, was either
congenial or salubrious. It was classified as a 'jungle post' and the
only town within ten miles was infected by leprosy. His unit did
not technically form part of the Fourteenth Army – he was not to

be deemed eligible for the Burma Star – but he looked on General Slim as his Commander-in-Chief. Lady Slim lived near the camp, visited it, and was shocked by its desolate isolation. She bussed in a contingent of girls from the Auxiliary Territorial Service for a dance; this brief brush with something approaching normal life may have caused more frustration than it gave pleasure but the gesture was well intentioned and much appreciated. She was 'a lovely old lady', thought Alexandre. He stayed at Kunta less than a year, then moved to the real jungle at Chinwara, where he took detachments into the great ravines that were scored across the landscape, to teach the men how to handle their guns in rough conditions.

It was a comfort to him to believe that his family, however far away, were at least safe in the English countryside. His wife never disillusioned him, but in fact they were nearer the action than he was; a bomb fell about four hundred yards away from their house and rattled the windows menacingly. By this time Alex was at a conveniently situated Catholic school. Alexandre's wife had been born a Protestant but had turned Catholic out of solidarity with her husband. He was pleased and touched, but more because he knew it was done for his sake than because he valued the gesture in itself: 'It wouldn't have made any difference to me if she had refused to let the children be Catholics. I'm not a very good Catholic. I say my prayers, that sort of thing, I go to church, but I can stay away from it just as soon as go to it.' In the children's experience, staying away was the general rule. Their mother used to insist on their going to church on Sundays, and to start with, the parents went as well, but first one thing would occur to make it inconvenient, then another. In the end only the reddest of red letter days would see the senior Alexandres in church; 'I don't need to go to church to be a Christian,' Alexandre would declare defiantly.

By the beginning of 1945 it was clear that the war was won but there was still the prospect of much hard fighting before the

Japanese were driven back to their homeland and finally subdued. In anticipation of an enduring need for tired troops to recuperate, the Army decided to open a rest camp near Poona – a holiday camp in effect – 'and a wonderful camp it was too,' remembered Alexandre. By now he had been promoted to regimental quarter-master-sergeant and, under the command of a peppery retired colonel who happened to live in Poona, he was put in charge of the development and administration of the camp. It was an imaginative concept, laid out like a map of England with a block of huts called Kendal in the north and other towns or cities – Plymouth, Portsmouth – giving a name to appropriately sited sections of the camp. No doubt it would have proved most popular but the first troops on leave were only just beginning to trickle in when the Americans dropped the atom bomb on Hiroshima. The news was not a total surprise – there had long been rumours of a devastating weapon that would somehow harness the power of the split atom – but nobody had known when it would be ready or, indeed, whether the bomb existed at all. 'That's bound to end the war,' Alexandre thought. He felt immense relief that the killing would soon be over, but he also sensed that something terrible had happened. If at any time in the future he could have disinvented nuclear weapons, or at least ensured that no further development took place and all stocks were destroyed, he would instantly have done so.

The immediate result, however, was that the war was over. By then Alexandre had been moved to an air transit camp, also in Poona, where he worked with the Royal Air Force, receiving troops as they came in from Britain or from the front line and despatching them in the appropriate direction. He was only there for a few weeks; on grounds both of age and of length of service abroad he was among the first to be sent home. He hoped that his liaison work with the RAF might win him a return by air but he had no such good fortune. He returned by ship, though at least taking the short cut through the Suez Canal rather than via the

Cape. At Gibraltar the Captain obligingly announced: 'Now I'll put on speed so as to get you old gentlemen home earlier.' He had barely spoken before he was ordered to divert to the Azores to pick up another group of veterans. It was the end of September 1945, when Alexandre disembarked in Scotland.

Immediately he found decisions thrust upon him. Before he even had a chance to rejoin his family he was sent to the documentation centre at Carlisle and told that his term of service had technically ended in 1940, at which date he had elected to take his pension so as to ensure that his wife and children had enough to live on. If he wanted to he could sign on for another two years; otherwise, after whatever leave was due to him, his military career would be at an end. He had originally signed on in the Channel Islands and so, unless he specified otherwise, it was there that he would be sent to be discharged. His reception was not callous or unfriendly but he was not given much in the way of advice or encouraged to take time for reflection. The staff at Carlisle had many such cases to deal with and were grossly overworked. The sooner Alexandre made up his mind and got out of their hair, the happier they would be.

'I was muddled up. I didn't know what to do. I was in a bit of a flummox, actually.' It would have been kinder to have given him a few weeks to sort himself out in peace. Perhaps he could have secured such a breathing space if he had been more assertive, but the final result would probably not have been different. He quickly decided that he did not want to renew for a further period. 'I can't afford to take them, sir,' he said, when offered two more years in the Army; if it had been ten years, or even five, he would probably have succumbed but he was already old to be looking for a job; in two years' time millions of others would have left the services and flooded into civilian life, better to take the plunge now while there were still openings and he was young enough to take advantage of them. His links with the Channel Islands had all been severed, jobs there were hard to come by, his future lay in mainland Britain and it was there that he would take his discharge. On 29 September 1945, after twenty-eight years with the Colours, he entered civilian life. He was within a fortnight of his forty-fourth birthday. He would have been startled and probably dismayed if he had been told it, but well over half his life lay ahead of him.

His homecoming was hardly propitious. His second daughter, Daphne, had been too young to remember him when he left England; now she was three and a half years old. Her sister, some six years older, was at school, and Daphne was used to having her mother's exclusive attention for much of the time. When a strange man arrived at the front door she was suspicious, when he greeted her with affection she was disconcerted, when he took up residence she was outraged. What initially was something of a joke became more serious when Daphne continued to reject her father. 'Don't go into your room with that man!' she would instruct her mother, and throw ferocious tantrums when her orders were ignored. Things became so bad that the Alexandres even contemplated separation, for a period at least. Then time blunted the edge of Daphne's rancour, she began to take her father for granted, within a few months both parents were equally acceptable.

This problem solved, the most urgent need was to find a job. Because he had taken his pension in 1940 it was tied to his rank at that time; this might just have sufficed for food and lodgings but not for the education of two daughters to the standard their parents found desirable. Throughout his life, Alexandre had been told where to go and what to do. Now he was on his own. He had become used to the structured existence as well as the comradeship of the Army – 'I missed it. I missed it very much indeed.' He felt like some subterranean animal blinking in the sudden light of day, disorientated, ill at ease. He had been doing important and responsible work, with many people under his command. Could he hope to find anything of similar status in civilian life? Could he find any job at all? The future seemed uncertain and uncompromisingly bleak.

He was, in fact, eminently employable. In the course of his Army life he had acquired a range of skills which were relevant to a career in industry. Even more important than this, he was a hard worker of total reliability and conscientiousness, a man who would accept responsibility but not repine when it was denied him, who was easy to get on with and would never throw his weight around or try to come the sergeant-major in a civilian setting. Within a few days of starting his quest for work he had met Frederick Miles, who had established a light-aircraft factory on a disused airfield a few miles from what was still the Alexandres' family home near Wokingham. 'Can you read drawings?' asked Miles. Alexandre proved that he could. At once he was taken on probation as a progress-chaser, responsible for ensuring that the innumerable operations involved in the making of an aircraft were synchronised and ran smoothly. Six months later he was offered a permanent job and a rise in pay.

He liked both Miles and the work and would have stayed where he was indefinitely, but the job died under him; in the winter of 1946–7 the firm ran into financial storms and was taken over by Handley Page. The new owners kept Alexandre on but moved him to a factory just outside the perimeter of the airfield where they manufactured Biro pens. His job was simple but required unrelenting attention; the tube inside the pen casing had to bend back upon itself, Alexandre was called on to immerse it in hot water and then mould it to the required shape. Biro pens were a cherished novelty and the firm could sell as many as it could produce; as Alexandre was paid by results, for a time he made extremely good money. Then Handley Page devised a machine which moulded the tubes without human intervention. Alexandre was out of a job. They offered him instead the task of filling the tubes with ink, but he was not interested. He had not found it too hard to perform a relatively humble role in a civilian firm – 'I was sort of disciplined to jobs,' he says – but the tedium of the assembly line was too much for him. 'It was very, very boring indeed ... eight hours a day, working to a kind of rhythm, never talking to one another, it went on and on and on.' He did not resent the hard work, merely the monotony. To be bossed around by people younger than himself was occasionally irritating, but this too he could stomach provided they knew their jobs. Sometimes they did not, however, and sometimes their man-management skills were limited. 'They treated me as a dummy, sort of thing, as if I didn't know anything. You see, I've never been very good at talking but my mind has always been very keen. Some of these people didn't know how to govern you; in the Army you were taught how to treat people.' He had had enough, and by now he was sufficiently confident of his value to potential employers to take a risk, leave Handley Page, and set out in search of something more fulfilling.

For a few years he wondered whether he had made a mistake. He threw up his job two weeks before Christmas 1949. For the short term he got a stop-gap job in the Post Office, helping with Christmas mail. When this ended, he was told of a nearby chicken farmer who was looking for people to clean out the incubators. He gave it a try, but found that he could not stand the foul air in which he was required to work and gave notice after a few weeks. 'You'll have to go on the dole,' a friend told him. Alexandre was determined to do nothing of the sort; partly because the dole would not have been enough to keep his family in modest comfort, still more because his pride and spirit of independence revolted at a course that would have involved reliance on the state. For a time he loaded vans with groceries in Reading, then moved back into engineering, working for a firm that had taken over part of Miles's factory and was manufacturing brakes for motor cars. The worst was over. Soon he met C. F. Taylor, who had worked with him in the early days at Miles's and had subsequently built up his own business with a factory only a mile from the Alexandres' home. Taylor was working, under sub-contract from Handley Page, on the Herald aircraft; he needed reliable and experienced hands and he knew Alexandre's capabilities. When the contract was completed he asked Alexandre to stay on to work on galleys for aircraft, a rapidly expanding business. This led to employment as a progress-chaser, then as a pre-selector, getting together all the necessary assemblies and sub-assemblies. Alexandre remained with Taylor until his eventual retirement in 1969. He enjoyed almost every day that he was there.

It was just as well that he had got a steady and well-paid job. Encouraged by his high earnings while manufacturing Biro pens, and with the help of a 100 per cent mortgage from the Wokingham District Council, he had bought the house where they had been living since the early years of the war. The mortgage was supposed to be paid off over twelve years; Alexandre managed it in seven. The house had four bedrooms, which was ample for their needs, and a big garden, 260 feet deep and 47 feet wide. The garden had been a wilderness when he returned after the war and every spare minute was devoted to taming it. He kept hens, so as to provide eggs for his family, and developed a passion for growing vegetables. Soon he had more than enough of these for his own needs and began to supply them to a number of former prisoners-of-war of the Japanese who lived in the neighbourhood: 'They couldn't get them anywhere else, you see.'

Shortly after the death of his second son, Alexandre had discovered his daughter – by now a mature six-year-old – being kissed by a grubby little boy outside her school. Possibly the recent tragedy had made him over-protective; at all events Alex spent the greater part of her school years immured in a convent. In spite of her infantile escapade her father had nothing to worry about – she proved to be enough of a *jeune fille rangée* to satisfy the most censorious parent. It was a fee-paying school and the Army contributed nothing, but the local priest helped find the money and probably picked up some of the cost himself. She finished school at seventeen, leaving nothing but glory behind her, and trained as a nurse. Her younger sister, Daphne, started on the same course but proved as rebellious as Alex had been amenable to discipline. After only a year the headmistress asked her parents to remove her: she was charged with no particularly heinous crime, she had just proved a disruptive influence and the nuns felt unable to cope with her. Daphne finished her education at the local comprehensive.

Albert Alexandre was disappointed but neither shocked nor angry. Anger, indeed, was an emotion in which he rarely indulged. He had high standards himself and hoped for great things from his children, but if the great things were not forthcoming, he was understanding and tolerant. At home he expected and obtained a measure of good manners, punctuality and cleanliness, but though he was ready to assert himself – 'If he said jump, we jumped' – he was never a martinet, still less a bully. On leaving school Daphne announced that she wanted to be a model. Few occupations could have been more remote from Alexandre's conception of what was worthwhile but he accepted the proposal with equanimity – comforted by the thought that it was highly improbable his daughter's ambitions would be realised. His scepticism was justified; Daphne tried to save up the money to go on a modelling course but instead spent it all on clothes; her mother took her to Lucy Clayton's modelling agency but the encouragement that she got there was not sufficiently ardent to inspire her to greater efforts. She followed her sister into nursing, decided the discipline was unacceptable, and left for the United States to continue her training there. Though she sometimes found her father's absorbed interest in her education irritating or oppressive, she never resented it: his own upbringing had been so bereft of opportunities that it seemed to her quite reasonable that he should hope for better things where his daughters were concerned.

It would, indeed, have been hard to quarrel with him. His capacity to see both sides of a question was formidable; a handicap, perhaps, from the point of view of material success in life, but endearing to all who loved him. He did not vote in the 1945 election because he felt too uncertain about the merits of either party: 'I wasn't very interested in who got in at that time. There was so much else to think about.' He approved the installation of the Welfare State, thought that Attlee's government had done a reasonably good job and was disappointed when Labour was bundled from office in 1951, but never did he qualify as a partisan supporter of any party. One of the very few issues on which he felt passionately was the Suez operation of 1956. He was moderately affronted by Nasser's seizure of the Canal, but believed that the Anglo-French invasion was immoral and, even more important, that it was 'a silly war. I don't think we needed it. I can't forgive Anthony Eden for that.' There were few other people whom he would ever have condemned so unequivocally.

When he retired at the age of sixty-seven money was not a problem. His employer gave him a generous pension on top of that which he received from the Army and the state; he owned his house; the children were independent. The first question was where he and Dorothy would live. The house at Wokingham was too large for their needs, they had no particular ties with the area and they wanted to settle where the children and grandchildren would like to come to visit them. The choice seemed to be between the Channel Islands and Brixham, in Devon, where they had spent enjoyable holidays. Alexandre had affectionate memories of the Channel Islands but had lost touch altogether. Without much difficulty they decided on Devonshire. They sold their house in Wokingham for £6,000 and bought a bungalow in Brixham for £3,800 – it all seemed most satisfactory. Then, a few months later, the route of the M4 motorway was announced and property prices in the Wokingham area soared extravagantly. A house identical to the one they had just left was sold for £90,000. Alexandre felt mild chagrin but did not let the lost opportunity distress him. 'Actually, I've never been sort of a greedy man,' he says. 'I was happy as long as I could live comfortably and have *most* of the things I wanted – because you always want *something*, even if you're rich, something beyond your reach. I've had sufficient practically all my life.'

At first Alexandre found that his time in retirement hung heavy on his hands. Then a neighbour, who had been a painter and decorator and was also now retired, suggested that they join forces and do some work in the neighbourhood. It was hardly a money-making enterprise – they worked mornings only, and usually for elderly widows who could not afford to pay much more than the cost of the materials – but it filled his time and left him feeling that he was putting something back into the community. In the afternoons he would work in his garden which soon became one of the showpieces of the area. He rarely watched television but he read a lot – 'detective stories, travel, and all that sort of thing', never romance, which he found cloying and unsatisfying. There was a good public library at Brixham and he used it regularly. Sometimes in the summer they would drive out into the surrounding countryside for a picnic – but they rarely went further afield and were content to stay at home: 'We decided to stick together as much as we could because we'd had some very long partings during the war.'

Alexandre would happily have stayed at Brixham but after twenty years his wife began to hanker for a home closer to their daughters. He pointed out that there was no guarantee that their daughters would go on living where they were at present and that they might find themselves in a few years packing up again to follow the children to some other part of the world. He had to admit, though, that at eighty-seven, he was finding the garden a bit much for him and that it might make sense to look for a home where the responsibilities were lighter and help more readily to hand. Reluctantly he agreed to move east, to Bexhill on the coast of Sussex, where they bought a flat in sheltered accommodation.

Their new house was not a success. Alexandre missed his garden and resented the lack of privacy: 'It wasn't like living in one's own place.' Some of the fellow residents were pleasant enough but others proved less companionable and there was an atmosphere of the 'twilight home' which he felt premature and depressing. His recollections of Bexhill may have been coloured by subsequent events. They had been living there for four years or so when Dorothy began to feel ill. Until then she had seemed perpetually young, always smartly dressed as if ready for an outing. Suddenly she was old. Cancer was diagnosed and she was taken to hospital. It soon became obvious that she was dangerously ill, there was little hope except for a peaceful end. Alexandre was prepared for the worst but it did not make it any easier to bear. Her death when it came shocked him into a desolate inertia which seemed to rob him of the capacity to survive. 'I thought he would go as well because they were very close,' remembers his daughter Alex. Then one day he asked her: '*You* want me to live, don't you?' 'Of course,' she replied. 'Then I'll do something about it.' And he did.

For the next two years he made a pretty good job of looking after himself. He enjoyed his visits to the supermarket, cleaned and cooked, taught himself how to make cakes and casseroles. He could have carried on for several years more. But he was ninety-two years old. He knew that a time would come when he would be unable to look after himself. It was surely better to act now than to wait until the need was cruelly thrust upon him.

Long before his wife died his daughters had insisted that they would look after him if he were left a widower. 'I wouldn't if I were you,' his wife had warned him. She knew that the children would have been as good as their word but she knew too how much her husband would hate being dependent on them, feeling himself a burden even if he was not one. Fortunately, there was an alternative. His wife had urged him, if he were left alone, to apply for a place at the Royal Hospital Chelsea. He had said that he would 'if necessary'. No absolute need yet existed, but the prospect was beginning to seem more attractive by the day. Had he left it too late, though; would the Hospital be ready to take on somebody whom they must anticipate becoming a burden in the near future? While he was still hesitating a card arrived from the Hospital saying, in effect, 'Don't leave it too late!' Immediately he wrote back to say that, if there was a vacancy, he would like to be considered for it.

In March 1994, he went to Chelsea for a three-day trial visit. He had long talks with the Adjutant, who wanted to 'make sure that I was the right sort of person', and was shown every aspect of Hospital life, so that he could be sure that it was the right sort of place for him. He was entirely satisfied by all he saw: 'I thought to myself, you haven't got to worry about much if you're here.' The three days were barely over before he telephoned his daughters to announce in triumph: 'It's lovely here. I've made up my mind.' Remembering his dislike of the sheltered accommodation in Bexhill, Alex was uncertain how well he would support the hugger-mugger existence. Her doubts increased when she saw the size of his cubicle or 'berth' – a mere nine feet by nine feet. But she knew that she could not possibly have matched the facilities of the Hospital or offered her father the same opportunities to get about and lead an active life. In her home, she recognised, 'he'd have died of boredom'.

In fact he never regretted his loss of independence – indeed, there *was* no real loss; provided he caused no annoyance to his fellow Pensioners he was free to do or not do whatever he might choose. The close proximity to his neighbours, which had seemed so irksome at Bexhill, became acceptable, even desirable, when those neighbours were fellow soldiers. Alexandre was sociable by nature; only when he got to Chelsea did he realise how much he had been missing the company of friends from the world which had for so long been his life.

He remained astonishingly fit, walking every day in Battersea Park or the gardens of the Hospital, doing press-ups until he was ninety-seven, regularly first on the exercise bicycle at ninety-nine.

His days were as full as he wanted them to be. As one of the dwindling band of those who had fought in the First World War he was in regular demand by historians and journalists. He was constantly invited to unveil memorials, attend regimental reunions, be photographed with one celebrity or another. Once he went with a small group of veterans to the battlefields at Ypres. He met the Queen but otherwise found the occasion rather disappointing: 'It was very wet, everything was sodden. No trenches or anything, mostly just the cemetery.' Sometimes his schedule, in the view of his children at least, verged on the hyper-active. Aged ninety-six, he was invited to Colchester to join in the festivities of a Scottish regiment of the Royal Artillery. He loved and still loves dancing and the first night stayed up till 3.30 a.m. at the regimental ball. Next night he complained he felt a little tired and only stayed up till 1.30 a.m. – 'They kept him topped up with whisky,' says his daughter, with mingled admiration and dismay. He touched base for one night in Chelsea and then was on his way to celebrations in Guernsey. This time the ball was given by the Governor and Alexandre stayed up till two. By the time he got back to the Hospital his legs were so painfully swollen that he could not use the seat offered to him at the Cup Final and had to spend a day or two in the infirmary. But he did not regret a moment of his outings and would have done just the same again.

Gradually time caught up with him. He used to read the papers every day, and many books as well, then his eyesight deteriorated. For a time he tried to struggle with large-print books with the aid of a magnifying glass, but after a few words his vision would blur and he would not be able to find the place again. After a cataract was removed there was a slight improvement, but not enough to make a substantial difference. 'The backs of the eyes are done for, they can't do anything for me,' he says regretfully but without self-pity. Nor could they do much for his hearing, even with the most powerful aid he finds it increasingly difficult to conduct a conversation. He spends longer periods in the infirmary and, though he still walks around and marches in the Founder's Day Parade, he has had to curtail his longer excursions.

'I've got really nothing to grumble about whatsoever. Except illness sometimes – I don't like that at all. On the whole I'm pretty fit.' Blind and deaf, orphaned at six, survivor of one of the bloodiest battles in the First World War, father of two sons who died in infancy, survivor of a beloved wife, Albert Alexandre is a man of radiant contentment. Always his refrain is how happy his life has been, how kind everyone is to him, how lucky he is to be in so beautiful and secure a place. Mortality is everywhere around him and he is always aware of it. He has made no intimate friends during his years at the Royal Hospital: 'I don't want to get too close – they die.' He views his own future with wry resignation; very occasionally when he is feeling ill he will say, 'I think it's time I curled up,' but then he will remember how much there is still going on in which he takes an interest: football matches and elections, the doings of his children and grandchildren, gossip from the Hospital. One day it will be time for him to curl up, but until that moment comes he will live his life to the full so far as it is within his powers to do so, with the same generosity and the same selflessness as have marked his almost hundred years.

ARCHIBALD HARRINGTON

Sergeant Harrington, 1936

Archibald Harrington

To be born into a family of fourteen was unusual even in the first decade of the twentieth century, but it was by no means freakish. To have three out of the eldest seven children die in infancy was similarly out of the ordinary but not that far out. The Harringtons were more numerous and poorer than the majority of their neighbours, but most families in the Hampshire countryside were both large and poor and they never felt themselves in any way exceptional.

They lived in the little town of Alton. Archie Harrington's father, Henry, had served in the Army for six or seven years and was now working as a timber carter. Archie was officially recorded as having been born on 11 April 1906, though his mother later admitted that she had not got round to registering his birth until a fortnight after the event and that he must be at least a week older than the state considered him to be. He was the seventh child but before he was five years old he was the fourth, only two elder brothers and a sister having survived their infancy. They lived in Turk Street, the road leading to the Alton Brewery, and one of Archie's earliest memories is the sound of the brew-hands' clogs on the cobbles in the early morning as they clattered their way to work. The house had two bedrooms and an outside lavatory; it was taken for granted that the children would sleep two or three to a bed. The death of his siblings relieved the congestion, but by the time Archie was five it seemed more than time for a move. His father looked around and found work in the gasworks at Haslemere, fifteen miles or so to the east of Alton. Their new house had three bedrooms, hardly palatial for a family which now included six children but a great deal better than anything they had known before.

The rent, however, was also larger: 7/6d a week. Harry Harrington was earning 30 shillings a week in his new job and was a hard worker, but he was also a heavy smoker and drinker. He was a tall, good-looking man who had complicated his life by having too many children too soon, found his existence at home verging on the intolerable and took refuge in the pub. His children welcomed his absence; when he was at home he was a menacing presence, taking little interest in their achievements but quick to complain if they made too much noise. He was 'better on correction than guidance', says Archie, who remembers him as 'uncouth' and 'oafish'. He was not brutal – although he had a leather belt and threatened to use it on the children, he never did so – but he contributed nothing to their pleasures and spared no time to help with their education. Not that he could have done much in the latter respect: neither of Archie's parents was more than semi-literate, able to read and write up to a point but with little grasp of grammar or spelling.

Harry's drinking also meant that he contributed less to his family's upkeep. Fortunately his wife, Annie, daughter of a wheelwright's smith, was a good manager and resolutely cheerful in the face of what must have been almost overwhelming problems. She was constantly pregnant yet her daily work was never done; at the time her children took her role for granted but today Archie realises that she was little better than a slave, confined to the house and perpetually occupied in feeding and dressing her ever-growing brood. A cauldron of stew was almost always on the hob; a half sheep's head provided its meagre element of meat; swedes, turnips and other root vegetables were added as they became available. Potatoes were expensive and rarely to be seen but Harry Harrington had an allotment and produced green vegetables at certain times of the year. There was always bread and margarine or dripping; honey-sugar, the molasses left over from the production of treacle, was the most common sweetener. Exotic fruit was a rarity – perhaps an orange at Christmas – but the children would forage for themselves on the way back from school, picking blackberries, hazel cobs, and with luck an apple from an ill-guarded orchard.

But it was a happy enough home. The children had hoops, tops and other homemade toys; marbles were the only playthings that came from a shop. Their mother seemed never to repine, all day she would spend at the wash-tub or the oven, 'singing away like stinko,' usually the old music-hall songs. Treats were rare, but all the more appreciated for that; Archie remembers particularly a Sunday School outing on a haywain. King George V's coronation in 1911 took place just before the family left Alton; there was no bonfire but there were sports and each child was given a mug, an orange and a penny. The family was strongly royalist, as everybody else seemed to be in Alton and Haslemere, but this was only part of a more general deference to those in authority. The gentry, the vicar, the schoolmaster, the policeman composed an unchallenged and, so far as could be seen, immutable establishment. 'Subservient but not obsequious', is how Archie defines the children's attitude to those whom they had been taught to consider their betters.

No one at school ever contemplated mocking, still less disobeying, the teacher. Archie spent a few months in the infant school at Alton but when the family moved to Haslemere he was allowed to skip a year and join the Church of England elementary school, so as not to be separated from his older siblings. It was a well-ordered if uninspiring establishment comprising seven classes – each of thirty to thirty-five children – with a teacher for each class and the headmaster in charge of the final year. Religion was prominent if taken for granted; there were prayers and a hymn every morning, but since there were no hymnbooks and none of the children knew the words, the cacophony was sometimes fearful. The vicar would come in once a week to preach a sermon. Patriotism was almost as much a part of life as Christianity; on Empire Day a flag was hoisted and 'Land of Hope and Glory' sung with due fervour – unlike the hymns, the words were learnt in advance. Archie proved to be a convinced joiner of institutions and pillar of the establishment: he was in the choir and the Boy Scouts and ended up as Head of the School. He was one of the brightest pupils, as well as the most hard-working, and could easily have got a scholarship to the grammar school in Guildford. The possibility hardly occurred to him. The tuition would have been virtually free, but someone would still have had to pay for his fare, his clothes, his books: 'I had to be earning money, not spending it. It just wasn't on.' At the time he, anyway, had no particular wish to stay at school; even in retrospect, he feels no bitterness at the fact that the stationmaster's son, though far less clever and industrious, went on to grammar school just because his father had a little money: 'It was how life was in those days.'

The First World War made little difference to Archie's life. His father rejoined the Army but his absence hardly affected his family; he did not go abroad and was anyway invalided out in 1916 with double pneumonia. None of the children was old enough to fight and, though the battles and fearsome casualty lists were much talked of, they were more a source of excitement than distress. The family did not take a newspaper and when Harry Harrington was away they relied for information about the war on what the children picked up at school. News came rather more rapidly after Archie began to supplement the family income by doing a paper round for W. H. Smith's and sneaked a quick look at the headlines as he went. It was hard work – he would get up at 5.30 a.m., boil the kettle, have a slice of bread and margarine and a cup of tea, then go to the station to collect the papers and deliver them in the course of a four-mile walk on the way to school. He enjoyed it thoroughly, though, and became something of a favourite in the houses he visited, being encouraged along the way with sweets and pieces of cake. He was paid 2/6d a week, of which 2 shillings went to his mother.

In one way the war proved positively beneficial. The 'ladies of the aristocracy', as Archie thought of them, did their bit for the country by preparing dinners for the children at the elementary school. No one paid more than a penny or two for these meals; the Harringtons, being so numerous, got them free. Archie was introduced to hitherto unknown delights such as tinned salmon. It never occurred to him to resent these Lady Bountifuls who emerged from their large and comfortable homes to bestow charity on the underprivileged; on the contrary he was very pleased to be given a square meal. In the same way, he was happy to accept the hospitality of the local Co-operative who organised evenings of talks, singing or dancing for the youth of the neighbourhood. Once they imported a mesmerist and thought-reader. Archie was impressed but not entirely convinced. An open-minded but healthily sceptical attitude towards the paranormal has remained with him all his life.

In 1920, shortly after Archie had left school, his father made a bold decision about the future. The Surrey County Council was encouraging smallholdings by setting up would-be farmers on plots of thirty or so acres. The rent was nominal and stock, including six cows, was included with the land. The Harringtons were offered a farm near the village of Leigh and migrated from Haslemere – Annie Harrington, the children and all their possessions in a cart drawn by a single horse, their father riding ahead on a bicycle. For six months, Harry Harrington ran the farm with the help of Archie but it soon became obvious that it was far too small to support so large a family. Reluctantly he went back to work at the gasworks and, at the age of fifteen, Archie found himself effectively in charge. He relished the responsibility and believed that under his management the farm was doing well. There were plenty of siblings to help out with odd jobs; by now there were eleven living children – the youngest born in 1919 – and though one of his elder brothers had joined the Army and three of the girls were in domestic service, there were still seven of them at home. The house was remote and had running water but no gas or electricity. If a doctor were needed he had to be fetched from six or seven miles away, and a reluctance to bother so remote a dignitary meant that most ailments were, in effect, left to heal themselves. Two of Archie's brothers would probably have survived if their parents had plucked up the courage to summon a doctor, or had easily been able to pay his fees.

Social life was limited, though Archie would occasionally indulge in a whist drive in the village hall or a silent movie in Redhill or Reigate. On red-letter days he would buy a tin of condensed milk before the film began and slurp it rapturously during the action. He loved village cricket but his duties on the farm made it hard for him to play with any regularity. Girls were at first anathema; at the age of fourteen he was pursued by a girl a year younger than he was and repelled her in dismay: 'Go away, you silly bitch!' he would exclaim. Within two years all had changed and he was chasing girls as assiduously as previously he had fled them. The chase was conducted within strict bounds, however, with all the propriety and reticence that the mores of rural society demanded in the early 1920s.

By then his father had returned and displaced him in charge of the farm. Archie went to work as a carter and ploughman on a neighbour's farm, being paid £2 a week, of which he kept 10 shillings and gave the rest to his mother. He was not unhappy, but it was obvious that the family smallholding would never provide a worthwhile living and that his present job was leading nowhere. His elder brother, who had joined the Royal Artillery, had taken part in the expedition to support the White Russians at Archangel and had returned, resplendent in his spurs, puttees and bandolier and with stirring tales of 'hair-breadth scapes i' the imminent deadly breach'. Archie was not wholly satisfied that he himself was cut out for such a destiny but he was sufficiently interested to join the Territorial Army as soon as he was old enough. The Queen's Royal Regiment had a county Territorial Battalion scattered all over Surrey. 'A' Company had a Drill Hall at Reigate and at this Archie presented himself. The battalion took itself seriously, being unusual in that it expected its members to wear uniform for its evening drills. There were twice-weekly drill nights, several weekend or Sunday exercises in the summer and a grand rally in an annual camp at Arundel. Archie enjoyed the parades and found that he took easily to drill; marching behind the band in the park at Arundel in 1924 was an intoxicatingly exciting experience. The Army as a career seemed ever more attractive. He asked his father what chance there was that he might one day take over the farm. 'Nix' was the response; Harry Harrington had no intention of making way for anyone and even if he had, Archie had a superfluity of brothers with as good a claim. Harry raised no objection, indeed was positively encouraging, when his son said that, in that case, he thought he would like to become a soldier.

On 1 April 1924, Archie Harrington joined the British Army. He should, in fact, have waited another ten days to his sixteenth birthday but the recruiting officer was perfectly happy to mark him down for the earlier date, thus adding a third birthday to the two which he enjoyed already. He loved working with horses and would probably have put in for the cavalry if it had not seemed a more prudent course to follow his brother into the Royal Artillery. The Gunners at that time were anyway entirely dependent on horses for the transport of their guns, so there was no question of cutting himself off from his favourite animal. Nothing in the Army ever happened quite as quickly as might have been expected – at least where the workings of bureaucracy were involved – but in this case all went relatively smoothly and it was only a few weeks before he found himself at the Artillery depot at Woolwich.

The shock was considerable. On arrival at the depot new soldiers were given a brutal haircut and had their civilian clothes packed up and sent home. For the next sixteen weeks they were harried from dawn to dusk with an endless series of parades, drills and sessions of basic weapon training. The food was execrable, comfort minimal. But nearly all the new recruits had joined the Army because they came from intolerably crowded homes and were either unemployed or finding it difficult to make a decent living in civilian life. They grumbled about conditions at Woolwich, but were not seriously discomposed. Of the thirty-two recruits in Harrington's squad, only two dropped out: one could not stand the pressure and deserted, the other was a previous deserter who had hoped to sneak back unobserved under another name but was detected and arrested. There were not even many complaints about the bombardier in charge of the squad, who was deemed to be strict but fair. Discipline was tough but there was no bullying; indeed, Harrington claims to have witnessed no bullying in his whole military career; a judgement which perhaps says as much about his own character and expectations as about conditions in the Army. He emerged from his preliminary training with credit: 'A very good recruit,' read his report. 'Keen. Clean and smart. He is very much all there.'

Since he was used to horses and obviously of a calibre superior to most of the new recruits, there was a move to post Harrington to what was generally felt to be the elite wing of the Gunners, the Royal Horse Artillery. He was appreciative of the honour but dubious about it. There was a flavour of snobbishness and of the archaic about the Horse Artillery. Archie had not yet contemplated a world in which the Artillery would operate without horses but he was clear that their role was that of draught animals. In the cavalry, he suspected, horses were as much designed for amusement or for showing-off as for the business of war. Amusement and showing-off were to be deplored. Gunners' horses should be 'unsuitable for fun and games'; there was an element of fun and games about the Royal Horse Artillery. Fortunately there was a rule that a gunner could ask to be allowed to serve with an elder brother; Harrington's brother was a sergeant in the Field Artillery and it was to the Field Artillery that he was duly assigned.

He was posted to Brighton, to the 19th Field Regiment, where he learnt how to work with guns. The food had been bad at Woolwich – at Brighton it was 'absolutely blinking ghastly'. For breakfast there was thin porridge and never a hint of an egg, supper was a 'grisly chicken soup' with what seemed to be a dog biscuit. He could, of course, supplement his rations in the canteen, but money was far from plentiful. He was paid 19/3d a week. Of this 7/6d was allotted to his family and another 2 shillings deducted for 'barrack room damages', whether or not any such damages existed. That left 10 shillings or so for everything else; not an insignificant amount at a time when five Woodbine cigarettes cost only 2d and a pint of beer $2\frac{1}{2}$d, but certainly not giving scope for lavish spending. Though organised games featured prominently in the curriculum there were no recreation rooms in the barracks; in the evenings there was nothing the young soldiers could do except mooch around the town, for the most part unable to afford what was on offer, even if it was to their taste.

Harrington's solution was to work. The Army offered the chance of securing three Certificates of Education. To pass out from Woolwich the recruit had to get at least a Third Class Certificate; this Harrington did with ease, and then passed the Second Class as well. Now at Brighton his sergeant urged him to tackle the First Class. This was considerably more difficult and he was by no means sure that he could manage it. It was the gateway to promotion, however, and he was determined to get on in his career. It took six months of intensive work every evening, but in the end he succeeded; not with great distinction, for his mind was businesslike rather than brilliant, but by a comfortable margin. It was his first important breakthrough – after winning a First Class Certificate 'you were something,' he remembers. 'You began to get a bit of respect.' His determination to get ahead and very reasonable pride in his own achievements did not leave him with much sympathy for those whom he felt had had as good or better opportunities but had failed to make use of them. He despised failure and had no time for grumblers. The General Strike of May 1926 took place while he was at Brighton. For nine days every union member in Britain refused to work. Secluded in their barracks, he and his companions felt remote from such goings-on, 'it was in a different world'. But Harrington could not understand the point of view of those who would refuse to work in the hope of securing better pay. 'I never had sympathy with strikers and I never will have. If a man doesn't like his job he's always free to leave it and go on to better himself.'

Promoted to lance-bombardier, only the first step up a vertiginously steep and far-extended ladder but a vastly important one for all that, he was posted to Greenlands Farm on Salisbury Plain. Here he worked with a battery doing range duties, an administrative job more like the work of the police than that of a conventional artilleryman. It was not particularly stimulating but the period was nevertheless of great significance in his life, for in it he performed the one impetuous, indeed foolhardy action of his life. Frances, the daughter of an officer in the Edinburgh Fire Brigade, was spending a few weeks' holiday with her soldier uncle at nearby Larkhill. She met Harrington, they fell in love, within a month they were engaged. Harrington's explanation of this *coup de foudre* is characteristically unrhapsodical: 'Dare I say it, but in the first instance she was the only woman available.' This cannot be the whole story. Both of them were under twenty-one, the age before which couples at that time could not legitimately marry without their parents' consent. The Army not only deprecated early marriages, it did everything it could to prevent them. Until a soldier was twenty-six he would not be eligible for marriage allowance or married accommodation; implicitly it was understood that his promotion prospects, even his continued employment in the Army, would be put at risk by what was felt to be a premature entanglement. For an intensely ambitious and committed young soldier like Archie Harrington, such defiance of the authorities was extraordinary. He himself admits that he can barely understand it. 'The heart knows no reason,' he suggests. They were very much in love, 'and she was every bit as keen as I was'. Strong physical attraction, combined with a conviction that it would be wrong to gratify it without first going through the marriage ceremony, was probably at the root of it. At all events, they procured a special licence and were married at the Register Office in Salisbury on 17 December 1926. Because he was under the age of twenty-one Harrington wrote a false date in the register, thus adding a fourth and final birthday to the bewildering miscellany which he already boasted.

Frances was certain that her parents would disapprove and decided to go ahead without their consent. Harrington knew only too well what his father's response would be: 'Do what you bloody well like but don't expect any help from me!' The fact that his mother might be hurt if she was left in ignorance of his intentions seems not to have occurred to him. Not even his Royal Artillery brother was told of the marriage. It was a month before the news leaked out, during which time the marriage remained unconsummated. When they at last heard the news Frances' parents were indignant, but they soon decided that their new son-in-law was responsible and loving and that they had better make the best of it. The Sergeant-Major at Greenlands was equally put out, since he had felt Harrington to be his particular protégé, but though he grumbled he too accepted the *fait accompli* and did not refuse the culprit a sleeping-out pass. The couple moved into a small and primitive thatched cottage, for which they paid 2/6d a week. Their first child, a son, was born after sixteen months, in 1928. Frances went back to her parents' home for the birth; by now they had completely come round to the marriage and were beginning to believe that they had been in favour of it from the start.

Frances proved an ideal wife for an ambitious young non-commissioned officer. She was economical, even frugal, but proved capable of adapting her style of life as her husband rose further up the military hierarchy. She was sociable, and enjoyed the society of the wives of the bombardiers and sergeants; she was deferential to superiors without being obsequious and affable to inferiors without being patronising. But though Harrington realised how much he owed her, there was never any doubt in his mind as to which of them was the leading spirit. 'She went along with me in my ways,' he says. 'She was subservient, happy to be the lesser one in the partnership.' The word 'subservient' is one which occurs several times in his conversation. Harrington was autocratic and some-times inconsiderate, he genuinely believed that women – not just his wife – were the weaker sex and less able to cope with life, but he protected and cherished Frances and they had a lot of fun together.

Soon they had to give up their cottage – cold, damp but in its way idyllic – and move to Newcastle, where their accommodation was quite as cold and damp but less idyllic. They lived in a one-room flat and were desperately poor. Perhaps once a month, probably less often, they would walk a mile or so to the nearest cinema. The treat cost them 1/9d: two cinema tickets for 1 shilling; fish-and-chip supper at 2d each for fish and 1d each for chips; 3d for the babysitter. Dinner at the Ritz followed by dancing at the Café de Paris could not have given them greater pleasure.

But it was a bleak period. The order of the day for the armed forces was retrenchment, morale was low, the officers in the field battery to which Harrington was attached took little interest in the work or the men who did it. The battery commander, so far as Harrington could tell, was scarcely even aware of his existence.

One day, however, he happened to notice and be impressed by some work which Harrington had done on a horse which had the reputation of being particularly difficult. By this time Harrington was a lance-sergeant; his Major asked him what he would like to do next and offered to help if he could. Harrington at once asked if he could have a transfer to the Territorial Army; not an appointment that would normally have appealed to a young man hungry for further promotion but with the signal advantage that it would entitle him to married accommodation. The Major duly did his stuff and Harrington was soon posted to 85 East Anglian Brigade of the RA Territorials on the fringes of London at Grays in Essex.

There followed several comfortable if professionally unexciting years. The Harringtons had spacious quarters within the grounds of the Drill Hall, he was paid an extra £1 a week as caretaker of the Hall, most of the time he wore civilian clothes, they could ask friends or relatives to stay. They still only had the one child, a state which Harrington, remembering his own crowded childhood, was content to leave unchanged for a while yet. The work was light, though he characteristically made use of every opportunity to go on courses – one on signalling, for instance – which might prove valuable in his future career. His only regret was that part of his duties was to recruit for the Regular Army; a thankless task, for the area around Grays was grossly underprivileged, unemployment was high, Communism flourished, and the Army – or, indeed, any other manifestation of traditional authority – was heartily detested. Harrington saw the Drill Hall as an oasis of good order and established values in this unpromising desert; he cherished it and his efforts were evidently appreciated by his employers, for his original period of duty was prolonged by a year and would have been extended still further if the Territorial Army had had its way.

Sooner or later, however, in the 1920s and 1930s, almost every gunner was bound to do a stint in India and Harrington knew that his turn could not be long delayed. Most people dreaded the posting, because it involved several years far from home, often separated from wives and children. To bring out one's family with one it was necessary first to be established on the 'married quarters roll'; only about 10 per cent of sergeants and 5 per cent of private soldiers were so privileged. When he had joined the Territorial Army, however, Harrington had jumped the queue; he was now firmly established on the roll ahead of men far his senior. He knew that when he went to India his wife and son would accompany him or at least follow quickly. He looked forward to the adventure with pleasure and excitement.

In 1934 he was posted to Shorncliffe, to get back into the ways of the Regular Army before his India posting. He found himself working with horses again, the only battery of greys in the British Army; he professed enthusiasm for his charges but was privately sceptical; he suspected that already horses were an anachronism and that within a few years they would have disappeared from active service. Nostalgically he regretted it, but nostalgia must not be allowed to stand in the way of efficiency and progress; vehicles would be much less trouble and time-consuming: 'There's all the difference in the world. Sentiment doesn't come into it, I'm afraid.' He was clearly on top of his job; when the Battery Sergeant-Major was posted he was chosen to act in his place. The appointment was improper, or at least most unusual, because it meant that he would order around sergeants considerably senior to him, but the Major insisted and Harrington did not demur.

In December 1934, the Harringtons set sail for India. Families were segregated, his wife and son were confined to the worst part of the ship, the forward end, and he was allowed to visit them only for an hour each evening. Nobody travelled in luxury: as a sergeant Harrington found himself uncomfortable enough; for the men conditions were atrocious, sleeping in hammocks on the lower deck, cramped in the foetid heat of the Red Sea and the Indian Ocean. There was hardly any contact between the various groups; 'Nowhere in the Army is the social difference between ranks so apparent.' But there were few complaints and no formal protests: 'We were soldiers, we were volunteers, we accepted anything like that.' Besides, for Harrington at least, the novelty of seeing a new world far outweighed the tedium and discomfort. He was glad to arrive in India but he would not have shortened the journey by a day.

At Bombay he had his first surprise when on the quayside he was offered a meal of corned beef, boiled potatoes and peas. He had vaguely supposed that, when in India, the British would have had at least a gingerly stab at doing as the Indians did. He was quickly disabused of this naive idea. In Rawalpindi, the nearest military base to his eventual destination, he was amazed by the gracious style of living of the Sergeant-Major who entertained him, the spacious rooms, the cook, the bearer waiting at table. But the lunch consisted of roast beef and stodgy pudding. Solar topees were still worn but at least the practice of covering every inch of skin under heavy flannel had now been discontinued. No one suffered from sunstroke, or even bad sunburn, in Harrington's experience; prickly heat was the worst affliction. But when the temperature went up to 126°F in the shade in the weeks before the monsoon, no one could pretend that life was enjoyable. Women and children migrated to the hills, officers and senior non-commissioned officers took their local leave there and, if they had families, joined them at weekends. The men, if they were lucky, might do some training in the hills but for the most part sweated it out in the plains below. It was a single battery station, based halfway between Rawalpindi and Peshawar on the North-West Frontier, and facilities were sparse. There was no proper doctor but an 'assistant surgeon', a matron and a two-bed hospital. The assistant surgeon was an Anglo-Indian who was not allowed into the Officers' or even the Sergeants' Mess and was despised by Briton and Indian alike. If a man fell seriously ill he had to go to Rawalpindi eighty miles away.

As a married sergeant Harrington thoroughly enjoyed his time in India, but he realised how dire conditions must be for the men. They were starved of female company; and even in the larger towns brothels were out of bounds to the soldiers, who were anyway afraid of contracting venereal diseases. Yet Harrington knew of no cases of homosexuality and believes that if they had existed he would have heard of them, if only because it was virtually impossible to find a place where men could make love to each other in privacy. One gunner married an Indian teacher, but he was mocked so unmercifully by his fellow soldiers that he soon wondered whether he had been wise.

On the whole, relations between British and Indian troops were amicable if not intimate. The relatively small number of Indians holding the King's commission were treated in all respects as if they were British. In Harrington's experience this only once posed a problem – when a Sikh officer was posted to his battery and found himself having to check a white soldier for being improperly shaved. Given the amount of hair on his own face, this must have seemed a little ridiculous. Fortunately the Sikh officer was well liked by the men and, though there was some joking afterwards, there was no discontent. As for the Indian sergeants, Harrington liked them and knew them well. He and his wife were invited to weddings or sometimes to a meal in their houses. 'We never, ever invited them back, though. It was not customary and you abided by the custom. It would have caused embarrassment, particularly to the sergeant's wife.'

Since 1937 he had been a sergeant-major, promoted unusually though not phenomenally young. 'It was not necessarily merit,' he says, 'though it *was* merit, of course. I joined at a fortunate time.' The old Army had been disbanded, the cutbacks were over, rearmament was the order of the day. There were many vacancies for young and thrusting NCOs. But his new responsibilities did not involve him in active service. There were spasmodic outbursts of violence on the North-West Frontier and twice expeditions were mounted to quell the unrest, but the guns used by his battery were deemed too big and the trajectory of the shells they fired too flat to be suitable for mountain warfare. Some men from his unit were posted to the war zone to operate howitzers, but Harrington was unlucky. He was disappointed though unprotesting: 'I would have been honoured to go, it's what you're aspiring for, it's what you want.'

By the time the Second World War began, the changeover from horses to motor vehicles was complete. Harrington was in Kashmir on 3 September 1939. It was unusual for anyone except an officer to venture so far afield on holiday and even officers were usually content with the facilities of some salubrious hill station; Harrington and his wife, however, were inveterate travellers and would never have missed a chance to see the distant prospect of Mount Godwin-Austen or the gardens of Shalimar. They had rented a houseboat in Srinagar but had only been there two days when the recall came. Harrington explained the situation to the houseboat's owner, who insisted on refunding the rent in full. ' "Sahib, you are going for the Empire," he said. Wonderful, wasn't it?' In fact it turned out that it was unnecessary for him to have hurried back. The sergeant who was in charge in his absence was managing perfectly well and Harrington was anyway to remain in India till November 1940. He accepted the delay philosophically: 'I let matters take their course. You go where you're told, you know; you haven't much blinking influence in the Army.'

Meanwhile Harrington had been commissioned. Though the infantry and cavalry were slower to embrace the principle of promotion from the ranks, the Royal Artillery and Royal Engineers quickly accepted that if vacancies existed it was often better to appoint experienced warrant officers on the spot than to draft in newly commissioned officers who would have to learn the job. There was a regimental sergeant-major who should have got promotion before Harrington but the Commanding Officer deemed him a drunkard and unsuitable. Harrington's response when the news was given him was peppery: ' "If you think I'm fit to hold a commission in wartime, you should have thought about it a long time ago," I said. I really laid it on with him. I wasn't annoyed, I was honoured, but . . . ' His Commanding Officer took these strictures calmly and Harrington was commissioned as a full lieutenant.

Usually, a ranker who became an officer was transferred to another unit but Harrington stayed where he was. The move from Sergeants' Mess to Officers' Mess could have caused embarrassment but in this case was free from problems; the pomp and circumstance of peacetime soldiering had been much reduced and Harrington found no difficulty in adapting his habits to fit his new circumstances. It was harder for his wife, who found that her husband's promotion inevitably severed her from her former friends while not necessarily making it easy for her to come to terms with the wives of the officers. Worse still, she now had to find accommodation for herself and her husband. She was 'somewhat inept', Harrington comments tartly, but 'she got along'.

After four months as an officer on the North-West Frontier Harrington was transferred to the newly formed 5th Indian Division. About a third of the men were British, the rest Indian. The equipment was depressingly out of date, mainly First World War guns, and signalling apparatus which might have been used even earlier. He was appointed adjutant of a divisional ammunition unit: 'A very low-grade job,' he considered it, 'not at the sharp end.' 'The sharp end' was where the fighting took place and where he wanted to be; not because he felt himself particularly heroic or because he was spoiling for battle, but because that was what soldiers were for: 'I felt I ought to fight if I was going to get on.'

The division went overseas in November 1940. It was hard to leave his wife and children behind (a second child, a daughter called Vera, had been born in 1936), but he knew that they would be safe and well looked after in India, and the thought of action after so many years of peacetime soldiering gave him great satisfaction. Not that he had any idea where the action was likely to take place. The fact that the troops were dressed in tropical gear was a clue, but not a very precise one. When they asked where they were going they were told that it was essential that security be maintained. They accepted the force of the argument but would have been more impressed by it if in the past they had not constantly been left in the dark about what was going on. Rarely if ever were even officers given any information about how the war was progressing, still less about what part in it they might be expected to play. The radio was their only source of information; it was 1941 before the more fortunate officers began to receive a periodical pamphlet called 'Current Affairs', the gist of which they were supposed to pass on to their men.

Only when they disembarked at Port Sudan and piled on to a train for Khartoum did they guess that they were on their way to fight the 300,000 or so Italian troops in Abyssinia, Eritrea and Somaliland. The 5th Indian Division formed part of General Platt's army which advanced into Eritrea from the Sudan; meanwhile another force under General Cunningham was pushing north from Kenya. Platt's two Indian divisions bore the brunt of the fighting. They went into action in January 1941 and Harrington almost immediately had the discouraging experience of seeing the local British 'airforce', consisting of a dozen or so Wellesley bombers, destroyed on the ground by Italian fighters. The Italians retained control of the air for most of the campaign. Harrington was once reconnoitring in a jeep when he saw an Italian fighter cruising overhead. He pulled over under cover and shouted to another jeep immediately behind him to do the same. 'We must push on!' replied the then Brigadier Slim. Five minutes later the Brigadier's jeep was in the ditch and Slim on the way to hospital with a bullet in his backside.

The first part of the campaign was an advance of ninety miles across mountainous terrain to the fortress town of Keren. Held with resolution, Harrington believes, Keren could have been impregnable; even as it was, it took two months to capture, hill after hill being taken under heavy fire. Casualties were high and he was close enough to the sharp end to satisfy all his aspirations. Often he was frightened, but fear, he believes, is a healthy reaction, certainly nothing of which to feel ashamed. Cowardice was different, an inescapable part of a man's nature, perhaps, but never to be condoned. In 1942 in the Western Desert, his driver lost his nerve after persistent attacks from the air and sneaked away one night. He was posted as a deserter and eventually arrested. After the war his case was reviewed. Harrington was asked whether he wished to stick by the evidence which had led to the man's conviction. 'I wrote back an emphatic "Yes". He let us down badly. He was scared, poor lad.'

Cowardice, Harrington felt, was common among the Italians; indeed, their whole approach to war disgusted him. In the advance after the fall of Keren they overran a 'comfort company' of native women, 'their tents filled with condoms, cosmetics, scents and powders'. That, he believes, showed up the Italian Army in its true colours: 'They really came down in our estimation very much.'

After the fall of Keren the Italians put up little effective resistance. The main British force drove on towards Asmara but Harrington took part in a headlong rush to the Red Sea port of Massawa. That for him was the end of the campaign; now with the 4th Indian Division he was switched to the Western Desert to join Wavell's army, which had been weakened by the need to detach forces for the defence of Greece and Crete. For a few months, now with the acting rank of captain, he found himself commanding an independent anti-tank battery of 2-pounder guns. It was a disillusioning experience, the guns were accurate and easy to use but the shells bounced off the heavy armour of the German tanks and caused the occupants no more than discomfort. Meanwhile the German anti-tank guns shattered the more lightly armoured British tanks. Having been altogether too much for the

Italians, Harrington now found that his unit was out-fought and out-gunned by the new opposition.

Personally, however, he continued to prosper. When his anti-tank battery was recognised to be useless and pulled out of action, Brigadier Mansergh, his Commander Royal Artillery, picked Harrington to be staff captain in his Headquarters. 'I'd much rather have been in a unit, but your career is the thing that matters,' he reflects. During a lull in the fighting he was sent to Cyprus, where it was feared a German attack might be imminent, and told to make himself as conspicuous as possible so as to give the impression that a large force was on the point of arriving. In fact the whole division shortly followed him for a period of rest and training.

After Eritrea and the desert, Cyprus was a delight: a roof over one's head; wine and brandy which, if hardly refined, was at least cheap; Greek girls who were 'very free with their favours – and in wartime, when one never knew whether one would be alive the next day, one took one's pleasures as they came.' Once he felt so unfit after his excesses that he took himself for a run along the beach at 6 a.m. There he met the General, who later that day sent for him and told him to take the officers on the staff out for physical training first thing every morning. It won him few friends, but 'you did it all light-heartedly,' he remembers hopefully. 'You had a laugh with them.' He enjoyed Cyprus so much that he seriously contemplated settling there after the war – a decision which now he is profoundly grateful he reconsidered before it was too late.

Another of his miscellaneous duties as a staff captain was to censor the men's letters. He was struck by the number who worried about the possible infidelity of their wife or girlfriend. 'Dear John' letters were a source of endless jokes: 'Dear John, I have seen a lot of your father, as you asked me to, and have tried to cheer him up after your mother's death. We have got close to each other and I have become very fond of him. So now I sign myself, with love,

Mother.' But though the jokes were bawdy, the pain was real; soldiers were lonely, anxious and quick to feel betrayed; too often they *were* betrayed. Harrington himself remained closely in touch with his family throughout the war and congratulated himself that he had nothing to worry about on that score; as for the girls of Cyprus, they signified nothing and, anyway, Frances would never know.

Briefly he was sent to Kirkuk in Iraq to help defend the oilfields against possible German attack through the Caucasus. He took the chance to visit the Holy Land, 'magic, absolute magic, the Bible came to life'. The experience possibly helped him make up his mind to be confirmed in Baghdad Cathedral, though he himself denies that there was any strong religious conviction behind his decision. He had been baptised as a baby but, like many working-class children, had missed out on the next step because of the expense and loss of time involved. It seemed sensible to repair the omission now; he got on well with the chief padre and, anyway, felt that to be a confirmed member of the Church of England was appropriate for somebody in his position – it was 'merely conforming to the general pattern of life'.

From Kirkuk it was back to the Western Desert again. Early in 1942, after the failure of a premature British offensive, the Germans under Rommel had counter-attacked, captured Benghazi, and driven the Eighth Army back to the lines at El Alamein which Harrington had helped prepare the previous year. He arrived in time to take part in what was close to being a rout. In terms of the cataclysmic conflict which was simultaneously being waged in Russia, this campaign was no more than small beer, but to Harrington and his fellow-officers it seemed all-important.

The British defeat was not due to any failure in generalship, he insists, but the price paid for inferior equipment. Most historians would agree with him, but this did not save the then Commander-in-Chief, General Auchinleck, from dismissal. Harrington mourned his departure and was outraged when General Bernard

Montgomery took his place. Monty had let it be known that he had little use for Indian troops, something not likely to endear him to a man who had served so long in India, but quite apart from this, the flamboyance and would-be Churchillian rhetoric of the new arrival was wholly alien to Harrington's dour and down-to-earth style. 'I have today delivered orders that there will be no further withdrawal,' proclaimed Monty. 'Utter balls!' comments Harrington. 'There was nowhere else we *could* go.' Mere captains do not often have dealings with Commanders-in-Chief, but Monty made himself familiar to every man in the Eighth Army. Among the other ranks, in particular, he often inspired confidence and affection, but sometimes he proved entirely antipathetic. To Harrington he was 'a horrible man', and it was something of a relief when his unit was pulled out of the front line and sent to Iraq to re-equip and take in reinforcements.

His commanding officer in Iraq was an Indian, Lieutenant-Colonel Chaudhri, a very able and polished soldier, educated at Cambridge and Sandhurst and speaking perfect English. He was to end up as the Commander-in-Chief of the Indian Army. Harrington admired and liked him, though with reservations: he was 'cunning as a wagonload of monkeys, as are all these Eastern people. They haven't the same principles as you and I.' It didn't seem that there was much to be done in Iraq and Chaudhri suggested an escapade: an eight-day trip to India by way of Isfahan, Kwm and Afghanistan – allegedly to bring up to date the existing road maps – followed by a couple of weeks' holiday before they returned to their unit. Harrington himself would not have conceived anything so frisky, but was delighted at the thought of the adventure and, even more, of a reunion with his wife. The two men set off in the highest spirits and thoroughly enjoyed their excursion.

Frances had by this time joined the Women's Army Corps and was a sergeant living in an hostel near the North-West Frontier. Finding the discipline intolerable and the work tedious, she kicked

over the traces and flatly refused to wear the regulation solar topee
and army boots. Harrington was ready to condone a revolt against
any authority except his own – 'not a disgrace at all,' he considers
it. 'It was damned funny!' By this time both the children were away
from home. Their son, who was hyperactive and missing a father's
authority about the house, had been 'becoming a damned
nuisance'. He was packed off to the Boys' Depot of the Royal
Corps of Signals at Mayo, where he quickly became a resounding
success: sergeant of his company, captain of football, hockey . . .
'What a lad! It was the place for him.' Their daughter was at a
convent school in the Muree Hills, where she had been sent when
only six years old. She is barely aware of having met her father
before the family was reunited after the war.

Soon after Harrington and Chaudhri got back to Iraq they were
told that the Division was destined for Burma, where the Japanese
had been building up their strength for a final thrust into India.
Harrington was responsible for the movement of the troops and
equipment, a job which in any circumstances would have posed
difficult administrative problems and in India was further complicated by questions of caste and diet. He was the last man in the
Division to leave Baghdad, rejoining it in Central India for
training in jungle warfare. They were now part of the Fourteenth
Army, commanded by General Slim, under whom Harrington had
already served in Eritrea. 'We didn't admire Slim, we revered him,'
Harrington remembers. For the first time in his service in the
British Army he found that the High Command wanted the rank-
and-file to know what was going on and to feel part of the
campaign. Slim explained frankly that the Fourteenth Army was
starved of resources and for the moment could do little more than
conduct a holding operation. But the tide was turning; it would
not be many months before the initiative would switch to the
Allied forces. When the Japanese launched their offensive around
Kohima, their last desperate attempt to break through into Assam
and reach the Brahmaputra and Ganges valleys, Slim addressed the

senior officers and explained that the enemy could not possibly maintain the momentum for long and that they were beaten men. 'We went out sceptically, shaking our heads and saying "Silly bugger!"' Harrington recalls, but in fact they had absolute confidence in Slim's judgement – there was a 'wonderful spirit in the Army, smiles not scowls'.

As Deputy Assistant Adjutant-General, with the rank of major, Harrington had a multiplicity of duties relating primarily to people (as opposed to a deputy assistant quartermaster-general who was responsible for things). One of his less significant but more amusing functions was to look after entertainers who were flown out by ENSA. One of these was Noël Coward, who annoyed the troops by bringing his piano with him in the plane. The men thought the space could have been better used. George Formby, the ukulele-playing comedian whose most celebrated song dealt with the adventures of a libidinous window-cleaner, so offended Harrington that he walked out in the middle of the performance – 'he was too lewd'. The DAAG's work normally kept him some way behind the front line but Harrington was often near the fighting. Once he was responsible for clearing a large supply dump which was at risk of falling into Japanese hands. His Lieutenant-Colonel came along to lend a hand but, in spite of Harrington's remonstrances, refused to wear a tin helmet. They were in full view of the Japanese and soon came under fire. A shell fell a little way beyond them, a second a little short. 'Dive for the ditch, boy; the next one's going to hit us,' cried the Colonel. It did: he was killed by a fragment of shrapnel piercing his brain. With a helmet he might have survived; Harrington, as on other equally dangerous occasions, was unscathed. He might no longer be 'at the sharp end', but he was quite near enough to it to satisfy himself that he was 'doing what soldiers were supposed to do'.

He was soon to have more reason to question his role. Slim's prophecy was proved correct: the Japanese offensive was broken, the tide turned, a motorised division was formed to drive south

towards Rangoon. Harrington found himself further and further
behind the spearhead of the advance, first two miles, then ten,
finally two hundred. At this point he was appointed lieutenant-
colonel and posted as Assistant Adjutant-General to General
Headquarters at Jhansi in Central India. 'I could have refused,' he
reflects. 'I would like to have refused. I was happy with the division
. . . but I couldn't refuse it, I was a career soldier.' The work he was
doing was connected with records and he was entirely at home
with it. Meticulous, hard-working, conscientious, he was ideally
suited to such a task: 'I made quite a name for myself there. I really
got down to it.'

After the end of the war, his work was to involve collating much
information about the Japanese prisoner-of-war camps; it did not
need this, however, for him to conclude that he hated the enemy.
When the atom bomb fell on Hiroshima he felt nothing except
exultation: 'I wanted to exterminate the Japanese race.' And, he
adds darkly, 'the leopard doesn't change its spots very easily'.

In 1946, with India about to become independent, the Headquarters was moved to Singapore. Harrington, who was in charge of
the train carrying the staff and its impedimenta, found the orders
for the journey 'damned stupid' and disputed them vigorously. 'I
was getting a bit uppish at that time, feeling a bit important,' he
admits. Nothing about the style of his life in Singapore was
calculated to bring him down to earth. The Harringtons – for they
had now been reunited – lived in a palatial sixteen-room bungalow,
deferential Japanese prisoners who had been recruited as domestic
servants bowed to him whenever he left the house, a staff car was
permanently at his disposal to take him to the swimming pool and
the club as well as to the office. There were about ten assistant
adjutant-generals at Headquarters, but though Harrington was
among the most junior he was by far the most effective and it was
he whose work was honoured by the award of the Order of the
British Empire.

Their son was now with the Royal Corps of Signals and off their hands, but Vera had rejoined them. The education on offer in Singapore struck them as inadequate and they decided to take a few months' home leave, in lieu of the permanent repatriation for which Harrington was now overdue, and try to settle their daughter at a school in England. They found one that was suitable in Hertfordshire: 'We couldn't afford it but we put her there nevertheless.' Harrington's younger twin brothers had now built up the original smallholding at Leigh into a prosperous farm and cattle-trading business and old Mrs Harrington was still going strong, relishing her sons' success but finding it impossible to adjust her way of life to take account of this belated affluence. Her home would provide a base for Vera during the school holidays. To Harrington this seemed an ideal solution, to him his mother was still the same generous, uncomplaining spirit who had nurtured him as a child and 'sung away like stinko' over the wash-tub. Vera was less happy, however. She found her grandmother gruff and unwelcoming, taking no pains to help a thirteen-year-old girl who was finding it hard to settle into an alien environment.

Before he went on leave Harrington had been sent on a three-day course, after which he was given a permanent commission. At that point he was a temporary lieutenant-colonel with the war substantive rank of major. When he returned to Singapore he began seriously to consider his future. He was nothing if not a realist, and though he was self-confident and justifiably proud of his achievements, he suspected that he had got as far in his career as he was likely to. When the Brigadier selected him for a senior officers' course near Devizes he was sceptical about his prospects but accepted, on the grounds that he had nothing to lose and, anyway, would be glad to be posted back to the United Kingdom. The course was not a disaster but certainly far from an unqualified success. He was 'completely out of his depth', the equipment and tactics to which he was used were out of date, he had no idea how rockets worked or what they did, he had no parent unit in the country to help out with text books and manuals, he was elderly for his rank and found it harder to assimilate information than he had when he was younger. To add to his problems, he had to find accommodation for himself and his wife and provide all the furniture and cold-weather clothing that they were lacking. It was a difficult period, and though in the end he passed the course, the going was tough and its conclusion undistinguished: 'I didn't sparkle by any manner of means. I was on the way down. I can see now there was no place for me in this modern army.' For the first time since he had become a soldier he began to contemplate a civilian life.

In the meantime he was despatched to the Isle of Anglesey, as a major, to act as administrative officer to an artillery unit that was doing experimental work on guided missiles. The nearest village was three miles away, rented accommodation was expensive; his daughter was still at boarding school; the pay was 'abysmal, absolutely shocking'. Luckily, at the end of 1949 the officers' mess was still run on frugal, wartime lines; otherwise he might have been seriously out of pocket. He had managed to save up a certain amount of money while he was in India but this was a nest-egg he was determined not to touch until he left the Army. That this should be sooner rather than later was becoming more and more clear to him. He still enjoyed the life, the comradeship, the swimming, the sport, but by 1952, when the posting to Anglesey was likely to end, he would be forty-six years old. With luck he might be able to spin out his military life until he was fifty-five but every year that passed would make it more difficult to find a decent job in civilian life. He applied for discharge and was allowed to go with disconcerting alacrity; the Army was in a period of overall decline. The outbreak of the Korean War in mid-1950 had to some extent checked this process, but, though British forces were soon heavily committed, Harrington's skills were not those that were needed most. When it came to the point, his passage into civilian life was eased by the fact that, in a moment of absentmindedness, the authorities gave him six months paid leave instead of the two to which he was entitled. Harrington saw no need to call attention to their blunder.

But what to do? He had no claims to the family farm and even if he had, would not have wished to impose himself upon his brothers. 'I'm a pretty useless fellow,' he reflected. 'I don't know much, do I?' He decided that what he needed was a small business which required no special skills and not too large an amount of capital, and which with common sense and hard work could be built up into something more substantial. A shop seemed the obvious answer and he began to study the trade journals to see what was on offer. Soon he found a fruit shop in a side street in Hayes, Middlesex. It was badly run down, and so he could afford it without taking out a mortgage; it was small enough to be run, at least initially, by him and his wife alone; it had accommodation above the premises so there would be no need to look for a separate house. As a job it was something of a come-down from the sixteen-room house and chauffeured car of Singapore; but Harrington never supposed the world owed him a living and he was confident he could built up the business into something better.

He did so too. His predecessor had bought his stock through bulk retailers, Harrington cut out the middleman and went himself to the market. It meant getting up at 5 a.m., but that was a small price to pay. He made some mistakes at first but nothing serious; the first year was tough but after that all prospered; within a few years he had built up the business to a level where it brought in an income sufficient for all his needs. But there was a limit to expansion unless he moved to larger premises and the work, involving much humping around of heavy sacks of vegetables, was bound to become more onerous as he and his wife got older. The social life too became arduous. In retirement he had become the anonymous Mr Harrington of the fruit shop. Then the British

Legion discovered that he was in fact Lieutenant-Colonel Harrington, and he became patron of the local branch while his wife took charge of the women's section. The Legion flourished in Hayes and Harlington; social functions were not that numerous but there were too many of them to be compatible with his gruelling work load. Escape to another area seemed the only hope. As soon as the shop had reached a point at which he could sell it profitably, he began to look elsewhere.

It was back to the trade journals. This time he found a small antiques business for sale in Watford. There was no living accommodation but a house with a large garden was available about half a mile away. From the sale of the fruit shop and their savings they could just about afford to buy both properties and enough stock to open with. The ins-and-outs of the antique trade were harder to pick up than fruit and vegetables but Harrington was shrewd, hardworking and ready to start at the bottom end of the market. He decided that, at first at least, it was more sensible to buy cheaply and sell quickly for a small profit than to go for the more expensive articles and risk having them on his hands for months or years. Every morning, Sundays included, he would go down early to the East End markets to buy bargains from the totters; his mark-ups were modest, he knew his customers, the business flourished. He was working a seventy-hour week but found it endlessly fascinating. His natural caution served him well; what he didn't understand or couldn't afford he didn't buy. Gradually as his knowledge and his ambitions expanded, he rose above the level of tawdry bric-à-brac to handle pieces that were respectable in quality. His wife worked alongside him in the shop, her particular interest being porcelain, Staffordshire above all the rest. Her turnover built up, until eventually it became common sense to rent another shop further along the road for her to run. 'One of the biggest satisfactions for me was that we were at last real partners,' says Harrington.

By 1970, when Harrington was sixty-four, he found the routine of early-morning visits to the dealers and constant night work was beginning to become oppressive. He would shortly be on full pension, the business was well established and would be easy to dispose of; without being rich he knew he would never want for money. He still felt that he was not ready to retire but he took a resolution to give up in 1976, when he would be seventy. He rarely changed his mind and did not do so in this case. The shops were sold for a satisfactory profit, a few of the choicer items were put in the attic for eventual sale at auction, others were kept at home or given to the children. The big garden now came into its own. Gardening became his passion; he found it both good exercise and 'a marvellous hobby for relaxing'. Relaxation had never been his forte, and without the garden he would have found time dragged and would have fretted uneasily. He took on his daughter's garden too, and those of two of his neighbours, and turned his lawn into a playground with slide and sandpit where his grandchildren and other children from round about would come to play. It gave him pleasure to feel that he was being of service to society: 'It's the feeling of satisfaction in helping people. You don't want them to bow down, you don't want them to recompense you, you just want to help. If they appreciate it, so much the better.'

Retirement seemed idyllic and his health remained remarkably good as he advanced into the eighties. But then his wife fell ill, with bad arthritis in the hip. Soon she could no longer get upstairs and slept uneasily in her chair. Her husband acted as a full-time nurse. Always she resisted calling in a doctor, saying that the pain and inconvenience were tolerable; anyway, there was nothing to be done. Finally she gave way and was almost at once carried off to hospital. An operation on her hip seemed to have been a success but she was eighty-two years old and her kidneys and her heart began to fail. In 1985 she died.

'I didn't grieve a great deal,' Harrington remembers, with that devastating honesty that is one of his most notable characteristics. 'More than anything else, I think, it was a relief. Grief is self-pity.

Why grieve for someone who's in another world? There's no point in grieving.' Even in the blackest hours he continued to get pleasure from tending the various gardens, soon he was finding satisfaction in ensuring that all ran smoothly in the house as well. His daughter felt that her mother's death ought to provide an opportunity for breaking down the barrier which existed between her father and herself. For six months she came to see him at least once a week, then he said: 'It's all right. I'm OK. There's no need to come so often.' He seemed reluctant, even unable, to express his emotions: 'He gets "wordy" if he has to say something sympathetic.' His self-sufficiency seemed to his daughter to cut him off from other people and to lead him to reject overtures from those who wanted to establish any sort of intimacy. She tried to give him 'love and affection, but this curtain comes down all the time'. She wonders whether it had always been so, even in his childhood, or whether his carapace had grown thicker with the years. 'I sometimes say to myself, it's the Army that's done this. I think the Army is responsible for a great many fragmented families.'

The high spots of Harrington's civilian life have always been those that recalled the glories and pleasures of the Army. In mid-1966 the Emperor Haile Selassie held a reception in the Tower of London and invited many of those who had been involved in the campaign to liberate his country. Harrington put on his bowler hat, took up his carefully rolled umbrella, and walked between lines of sergeants from the Guards into the commemorative service that preceded the party. 'I was back in the Army again. I had a wonderful time there.' He felt 'a glow of recognition, of satisfaction'. In the same year the Royal Artillery celebrated three hundred years of its history with an enormous reception at the Festival Hall. The Master Gunner, General Mansergh, spotted his former staff captain, strode across the room, put his hand on Harrington's shoulder and announced: 'Archie is my best friend.' 'It was absolutely wonderful,' Harrington recalls today. 'I've never forgotten.'

With such nostalgic urges it is not surprising that he should have played with the idea of ending his days back in the military womb at the Royal Hospital Chelsea. He vaguely assumed, however, that by becoming an officer he had rendered himself ineligible. It was his son who pointed out that this was not so; having served more than ten years in the ranks Harrington had earned his passage, his subsequent career was neither here nor there. He duly applied, paid the obligatory three-day visit, decided he liked it and within a few weeks was installed. In 1997, his first year in residence, he was one of the twelve pensioners who represented the Hospital at the Albert Hall Remembrance Day Festival. When they marched in, the audience rose to its feet and applauded. In military life, Harrington recalls, 'let me tell you, one is somebody. For many years I'd been Mr Harrington, an anonymous man, a nobody.' In the uniform of the Hospital 'one was recognised as a man who'd given something.'

He had feared that, as a former officer, he might encounter some resentment from other Pensioners who would feel he had no business to be there. His policy was to lie low, to keep quiet about his record during conversations in the dining hall, to present himself as a former sergeant-major. It was not until the Remembrance Day Festival, when the broadcaster revealed his background, that his new colleagues realised they had got a lieutenant-colonel in their midst. 'Then I got respect for not having thrown my weight around. I'd been one of the boys.' He found no difficulty in fitting in: 'Remember, my bearing and my speech are from the lower deck.' And, after all, though he might have shuffled off his commissioned status, he was still a former warrant officer, 'at least I'm something different to the ordinary rank-and-file'. He is richer than most of the other Pensioners but equally, because like everybody else he forfeited his military pension when he joined the Hospital, his financial sacrifice has been greater. The thought does not bother him: 'I've never had one moment of regret, never unhappy, perturbed or disturbed.'

His daughter once asked him how he was getting on. He replied that he wished he'd come in ten years earlier. She was put out: 'That's not a nice thing to say. If you hadn't been here, you'd have been with your family, wouldn't you?' But she was also immensely relieved. She was surprised at the ease with which he adapted to the world in which he was no longer boss: 'I'd always viewed him as a solitary figure and I couldn't honestly see how he was going to fit in. He likes his privacy and to make his own running.' The peculiar strength of the Royal Hospital is that it is possible to live there in a community that seems almost claustrophobically congested and yet retain one's privacy and one's individuality. His daughter underestimated the potent appeal of the military machine; the attractions to a veteran – be he never so independent, cantankerous or proud – of fitting back into a world where he is respected and where he has no need to assert or to humble himself, a world in which he belongs. In the Royal Hospital Harrington happily accepts restrictions on his individual liberty which he would find hard to tolerate in any other circumstances. By giving up the independence of civilian life, the satisfaction of being master of his own house, he has come home.

FERNLEY SMALL

Company Sergeant-Major Small, 1946

Fernley Small

ERNLEY Millbrook Ernest Small was known as 'Fern' when he was a child, but for almost all his life was referred to as 'Sam'. His father, Henry, had worked on the railways during the First World War, a reserved occupation which meant that he did not have to fight. One of Henry's brothers was a sergeant-major in the Devonshire Regiment, however; another had served more than twenty years in the Royal Navy: military values and discipline were taken for granted in the Small household. After the war Henry Small had become a bricklayer, a hard job that often involved him in a six-mile walk before he even began to work. He was not a cruel man and was sincerely concerned about the welfare of his family, but he found it hard to connect with them as individuals. Sam cannot remember anything approaching a conversation with his father nor any warmth or affection in the relationship. Henry Small had rigid beliefs and translated them into an equally rigid code of rules governing his children's behaviour. They suffered if they did not observe them. Many times Sam 'felt his belt across my backside' for some offence such as stealing apples from a neighbour's tree. He was distressed at the time but he bore no malice – 'to be fair, I'd done wrong'.

85

His mother, born Ada Biddle, would never have dared oppose or criticise her husband, but her disposition was very different. As a girl she had been in service at the local great house, Powderham Castle, and had there imbibed a code of propriety and good order which she sought to apply in her own home. She was anxious to bring her children up virtuous and Godfearing and when Sam was given his bath in the tub in front of the fire she would sing a hymn or tell him what he had to do to be a good boy. But 'it wasn't a question of making me a sop,' Sam insists; she was as warm as her husband was chilly, and her admonitions were based on deep love and a determination that her children should do well in life.

Sam was by far the youngest of the five children and the most precious to his mother for that reason. He was born on 5 August 1916, an afterthought, or more probably a mistake; his three sisters had left home before he was conscious of their existence and his brother was seven years the elder. His mother was forty-one when he was born and what to her was a God-given dispensation, to her husband must have seemed an infernal inconvenience. Sam got the impression that his father did not like him and ignored him whenever possible; he clung the more closely to his mother to whom he was 'deeply devoted'.

The family lived in East Budleigh, a Devonshire village a few miles north-east of Exmouth, and it was there that Sam went to school. Drake's Charity School – which still exists under that name, although shorn of its somewhat demeaning adjective – had been called after Francis Drake's brother, who founded a number of schools in Devon. There were about 150 pupils, divided into classes of thirty or so, with the usual emphasis placed on history – particularly imperial – and the basics of literacy and mathematics. It was a Church of England school and in the Small household church attendance on Sunday was taken for granted. Sam sang in the village choir for seven years. He enjoyed school and thought that he owed it a great deal, particularly admiring the headmaster, whom he describes as 'a wonderful man'. The headmaster took the senior boys, from whom were selected those who were to go to grammar school. Sam passed the necessary examinations but his father felt that he could not afford the money for books and other expenses and, anyway, considered that, at the age of fourteen, his son should be earning. 'I wasn't disappointed,' says Sam. 'I didn't realise the importance of it then. One just got on with the job. It was a question of living and existing.'

Possibly his mother, who believed fervently in the value of education, might for once have made a stand against her husband and pleaded Sam's cause. When he was within a few weeks of leaving school, however, she was diagnosed as having breast cancer. In the early 1930s this was little better than a sentence of death. The only redeeming feature about her illness was that it was all over quickly. She was in dreadful pain: 'I can hear her screams now,' her son relates. 'It upsets me to think of it. It virtually broke my heart.' It took him many years to get over it; sometimes he wonders whether he ever did. He was not allowed to attend the funeral but he sat for hours beside the coffin and 'cried his eyes out'. His father, too, was devastated: 'I must give him that. He was a hard sort of man but I heard him talking to himself many, many times, as if he was talking to my mother.' But the fact that both of them suffered did nothing to bring them together; his father found himself unable to talk about his loss, for weeks after Ada's death the household was frozen into a silent desolation.

Sam was now put to work with a newsagent in Budleigh Salterton. He would get up at 5.30 a.m. in a silent house, with his father sleeping upstairs, bicycle two miles to the railway station, do a small newspaper round near the station, then go on to the shop to pick up more stock and embark on a longer round. If it rained the papers got wet and he would find himself the target of angry complaints: 'Nobody ever asked how wet I was.' He worked until 12.30 p.m. and was paid 7/6d a week, out of which he kept 6d as pocket money. But the customers – who included a fair sprinkling of retired admirals and captains – must have been more appreciative than he had supposed; when the time came he was amazed to be given Christmas boxes adding up to more than £25. It was a fortune; it kept him and his father in clothes for the next twelve months.

His father often did not get back from work before 7 in the evening and when Sam returned to the empty house he had to prepare the vegetables for supper. There was enough to eat – they had an allotment and his father taught him how to snare rabbits and even the occasional pheasant – but there was little or no variety and he used his pocket money to buy cakes or sweets. He had friends from school with whom he would sometimes go on long walks or birds'-nesting expeditions but at home there was a melancholy, even a hostile, silence. Almost the only words his father addressed to him were orders; twice a week, for instance, he would have to take the ashes from the fire in a wheelbarrow and spread them on the allotment, a journey taking half an hour each way. Sam missed his mother desperately and felt lonely and unloved: 'It was terrible. I don't quite know how I dealt with it.'

The summit of his ambitions was to escape from home. To become a soldier offered a possible solution. He took on an extra paper round on Sunday and used the 8d he was paid to go into Exmouth to visit the recruiting office. Since his uncle George was a sergeant-major in the Devonshire Regiment he first applied to them but they looked at him scornfully and told him that he was under age, under the regulation height, underweight, under everything. It was the same story with the Royal Marines. The recruiting sergeant of the Devons later told him that if he had only declared himself as George Small's nephew he would have been at once admitted, but he had not realised at that stage that in the Army a judiciously pulled string was worth as much as a cornucopia of martial talents. By the time he was seventeen he was in despair.

It was one of his elder sisters who rescued him. She had been working abroad as a nanny in the household of a Captain Barthorp, who was Adjutant of the Northamptonshire Regiment which had recently returned from the Middle East. She was horrified at the life her little brother was leading and told her father roundly that he was not providing his son with a proper home. Sam explained that he had tried to get into the Army but had been rebuffed, whereupon she appealed to her employer. The ploy worked, Sam was given a travel warrant and told to apply to the recruiting officer in Exeter. Once there he was asked how old he was. 'Seventeen,' he replied, honestly but injudiciously. '*What* did you say? I didn't catch that. Go out and come in again.' Sam duly obliged. 'Now, how old are you?' 'Eighteen.' He was signed up without further debate. His father, who had got into the habit of making expensive visits to the pub in the evening, was sorry to lose his son's 7 shillings a week but showed no other signs of regret: 'If you've got to go, you've got to go,' he said resignedly. On 30 October 1933, Fernley Millbrook Ernest Small enlisted in the Northamptonshire Regiment.

He did his basic training at Northampton – a twenty-week course, which would have been hard going for anyone but for Small was particularly arduous. He was not merely small for his age and underweight but he had taken little exercise outside his newspaper round and his muscles had not developed as had those of most of his contemporaries. He was resolved to put this right. Every spare moment he spent in the gym, following a special course worked out for him by a sympathetic gym sergeant-major. It was tough but immensely rewarding; he grew dramatically both in strength and in self-confidence; in height too – when he joined the Army he was 5 feet 8 inches tall, within two years he had grown two inches. He was an exemplary recruit; always the best turned-out man on guard; designated as 'stick orderly' and responsible for turning the pages of the regimental roll of honour in St Sepulchre's Church, Northampton; punctual, meticulous and obviously determined to do well. 'It was a new life, it was something totally different.' He savoured every minute of it.

The past caught up with him at Christmas 1933. Even before he had escaped to join the Army, the atmosphere at home had become intolerable. He had no sort of relationship with his father, who at best ignored him, and now a ferocious feud had broken out between his siblings. His sisters – justifiably as it in the end turned out – accused their sister-in-law of having an affair with a local gamekeeper. She hotly denied the charge, and her husband took her side. Sam Small was bombarded with letters demanding his support. For someone of his sensitivity, it seemed inconceivable that he should venture back into this morass of hostile passions, so when the new recruits were asked where they intended to go for Christmas he found he had no answer. 'I just went into the toilets, shut myself in and sobbed my heart out. I must have seemed an awful wimp.' His squad sergeant, who had sensed both Small's potential as a soldier and his vulnerability, followed him into the toilets and told him to come out. 'He put his arm round me, it was just like a big brother, he was wonderful.' When he realised Small had nowhere to go for Christmas he invented a vacancy in the kitchen of the Sergeants' Mess; there was some work involved but not much – 'really they gave me a wonderful time'.

When Small moved on from Northampton to join the 2nd Battalion at Aldershot, the spate of letters from home continued unabated. He was determined not to be drawn into the battle but found it increasingly difficult to stand aloof: 'Being so young I didn't know what to make of it.' Someone noticed that whenever he got a letter he would sit on his bed reading it and then retreat into gloomy silence. The Sergeant-Major was warned that all was not well with one of his flock. One day Small got a letter, read it and threw it dejectedly on his bed. The Sergeant-Major asked to see it. 'I don't think it'll interest you,' said Small, but the Sergeant-Major persisted. Once he had found out what the problem was he took Small to the Company Commander, who at once wrote stern letters to Small's sisters, telling them that this persecution must now stop. In future any communication should be made through him; he, for his part, would let the family know how Small was getting on. Until that moment Small had felt totally cut off from the world, 'as if I didn't belong to anyone'. Now he felt secure. 'That was typical of the Army at that time. If you were somebody who tried to be a good soldier you could be sure that it wasn't a waste of time. I was lucky.' The Army, Small several times repeated, became his family. He never went home on leave until after his marriage in 1940. Every Christmas till 1937 he volunteered for duty so that a married man could be with his family. In 1938 the Regimental Sergeant-Major asked him why he never went home. When Small confessed why he preferred to stay away he was sent to Sandes House, an Irish equivalent of the YMCA, which prided itself on catering for soldiers with no family.

At the end of 1935 the 2nd Battalion was posted to Ballykinter in Northern Ireland. Small was put into the signals section, communicating by helio lamps over distances of two miles or more. Unfortunately this assignment coincided with one of the hardest winters Ulster had known for many years; the glare of the lamps reflected on the snow damaged Small's eyes and for three weeks he could barely see. He was sent to hospital and then employed, while convalescing, as a waiter in the Sergeants' Mess. One of his duties was to see that outstanding bills were settled and it so happened that the Regimental Sergeant-Major had a penny owing on his account. Small harried him politely but relentlessly for weeks, at which point the RSM paid his bill and told his persecutor that he was being taken into the regimental police as a lance-corporal: 'That's how I got my first stripe. I've often laughed a bit when I think of it.' His contemporaries were not best pleased by Small's promotion above their heads, especially when it was in a branch as generally disliked as the police, but 'we had our job to do and that was that'. As a private he had been paid 15 shillings a week, of which he actually received 10 shillings; as a lance-corporal these sums increased to £1 and 15 shillings respectively.

In Northern Ireland, 'I became a much harder person. I grew up,' Small remembers. Partly this was because of his new responsibilities and increasing self-confidence, but, he believes, the episode which toughened him most markedly occurred in the summer of 1937 when the battalion was mechanised and motor vehicles replaced horses. Homes were found for most of the displaced animals but some of them were deemed to be too old at sixteen and were shot. Small had never ridden himself, but the police office was at the back of the stables and he had got into the habit of stroking and petting them. 'They had a better life than I had when *I* was sixteen,' he recalls. 'I sort of tied myself in with them.' Their execution caused him much distress: 'It was the only time I felt I wanted to rebel against the Army.' He resisted the urge, sensibly concluding that rebellion would have done nothing to help the horses. Instead he went on a course at the School of Chemical Warfare at Shrivenham and found that he had a phenomenally well developed sense of smell. He became a self-appointed bloodhound for his colleagues and would walk in front of them, warning if any trace of gas was in the offing.

In October 1938, he was posted to the regimental depot at Northampton to take charge of the dining hall. It was the first time he found out that all was not invariably high-principled and honourable within the military family. The young civilian who had previously been in charge had got into the habit of handing out rations to married families who were not entitled to them. Worse still, items from the stores were being sold in pubs across the road. Small was told that he must put a stop to this petty theft and he installed a strict system of control by which he alone held the key to the stores. A sergeant who had been doing nicely out of the racket tried to bully Small into giving him access to the provisions. Small referred him to the Quartermaster, a proposal which the Sergeant unsurprisingly did not follow up. Instead he decided to engineer Small's downfall, and put him on a charge for using dirty tea buckets in the dining hall. Fortunately for Small, he had already complained to the Quartermaster that the tin of the tea buckets had deteriorated beyond repair, and had been promised that they would be replaced. He tried to defend himself when he came up before the Company Commander, but the Sergeant's story was accepted and Small was reprimanded, 'the first entry on my sheet since joining'. Incensed by this injustice, he availed himself of his right to appeal to the Commanding Officer, a risky tactic since, if the reprimand had been upheld, his future in the regiment could have been permanently blighted. The Quartermaster, however, came to the rescue, and promised to make sure that the true facts were known. He did so to such effect that, when Small was marched in, the Commanding Officer smiled and said: 'You have a clean sheet.' The Sergeant was marched in next and, to judge by his appearance when he reappeared, was given a rough time. Justice had been done, but Small was still dismayed and disillusioned. He told the Regimental Sergeant-Major that he wished to revert to the ranks and return to the battalion. 'Revert be buggered!' said the RSM. 'You're next on the list for promotion.'

Small was sent on a promotion course and bullied ruthlessly. The RSM seemed to take a malign delight in picking him out for special tasks and finding fault with every detail of his drill and appearance. Small's reaction was one of defiance; he resolved that whatever the RSM might demand of him he would do, and do better than expected: 'I put my heart and soul into it and got very high marks.' On 1 July 1937, he was promoted corporal. 'Now I suppose you think you're finished?' said the RSM fiercely. Small replied that he very much hoped so. 'Well, you're not, now you're on the promotion list for sergeant.' Again he passed with very high marks. He had to wait until February 1940 before he could put up his third stripe but it was clear that, in the eyes of the RSM at least, he was destined to play a major part in the regimental machine.

He was in the Corporals' Mess when Chamberlain announced that Britain was at war. The reaction was one of startled silence; everyone had known that it was almost inevitable yet, until it actually happened, no one had believed that it could be true. There was no elation but equally no dismay; they just accepted it as professionals – it was their job, 'that was it'.

A few months later, now a sergeant, Small was put in charge of training the young militiamen who were by then arriving in droves. He moved out of the depot into billets behind the Northampton branch of Woolworth's, a change of address which was to prove unexpectedly significant. Though by this time he was twenty-three, he had hitherto had no girlfriends nor felt the need of them. Then he met and got to know a girl who worked at Woolworth's. 'I was so attracted to her, it was as if I'd been hit by a boxing glove.' He took her out two or three times, all seemed to be going swimmingly, then suddenly she grew cold and would have nothing to do with him. He was hurt and greatly saddened: 'She was an extremely nice, bubbly person and I'd lost my heart to her.' He was too inexperienced and unsure of himself to do anything except put up with the rebuff; then a few months later they met again and the truth came out. Someone had told her that he was already married; she had felt betrayed and angry, not for a long time did it occur to her that her informant might have been mistaken or even just malicious.

The reunion was rapturous and they got married in December 1940 in the regimental church of St Sepulchre's. Blanche Rodhouse was the daughter of a farm labourer. Her father had liked Small from the start and was wholeheartedly in favour of the match; her mother did not like the idea of her daughter marrying a soldier but realised that in wartime Britain she could hardly sustain her opposition. It was very much a wartime wedding; they married on a Saturday with a minimum of formality, took their honeymoon on Sunday, and on Monday Small was back in barracks as orderly sergeant. There were no married quarters available so they started their life together in the home of Blanche's parents. Small had to be back in barracks by six each morning but this hardly damped their pleasure; their first child, a daughter, was born at the end of 1941. Both mother and child nearly died; for this reason the child was peculiarly precious to her father. He was to have four others: 'I love 'em all, but she's the apple of my eye.'

Now the real war began for Small. In February 1942 he was posted with the 5th Battalion of the Northants to Callander in Scotland where they were to train as assault troops. What was in store for them was made all too clear on the first Monday after their arrival when they were sent on a 46-mile route march. Only the determination to justify the stripes on his arm kept Small going; when he went to Scotland he had thought himself reasonably fit, within a few days he realised that he hardly knew what fitness was. By that autumn the battalion had been trained endlessly in the techniques of amphibious warfare and were ready to storm the world's fiercest cliffs if that was required of them. In October they were unexpectedly given leave – 'to even up the roster,' they were told. The Smalls guessed that in fact this was embarkation leave, though they had no idea where the battalion might be headed. They devised a code. They had a dog called Rap. If Small included in a letter the phrase 'I am sorry Rap's poorly', she would know that he was on his way and that she could not expect to hear from him for several weeks at least.

Within a few days Rap duly fell ill. Small was transported to an unidentified port, boarded an unidentified troopship and sailed for an unidentified destination. Various other unidentified vessels were sailing with them so an operation of some size was clearly intended, but where it might be was still a mystery. When they hung around for several days off the Azores the men speculated that Dakar was their objective, but then another convoy joined them from the United States and the combined armada headed for the Mediterranean. They knew that they were part of the 78th Division and that their companions on the troopship were the 6th

Battalion of the West Kents; beyond that they were in the dark and had merely to wait and see what the future and the War Office had in store for them.

On 1 November all was revealed. The Commanding Officer assembled the battalion and told them that they were bound for Algiers. This was 'Operation Torch' – no more than a substitute, perhaps, for the Second Front in Europe, which the Chiefs of Staff were convinced would be dangerously premature, but still an undertaking of immense scale and complexity. The plan was to secure French Morocco and Algeria and then advance into Tunisia, crushing the German forces in North Africa between their advance and the onslaught of the Eighth Army sweeping westwards across Libya. It sounded all too easy; Small suspected that in practice the Germans might prove not to be the helpless victims portrayed by the Allied strategists.

He was relieved when the landing was unopposed. Small was told that the landing craft was safely aground and 'being a keen young sergeant, shouted "Jump!"' He followed his own instruction and promptly vanished below the surface of the sea, eventually struggling ashore having swallowed an inordinate amount of salt water. He blames his mishap on the crew of the landing craft who had drunk too freely of the rum ration assigned to the invaders and hopelessly misjudged the distance from the shore. The only casualty was a luckless lieutenant who slipped and fell when climbing down the landing nets on the side of the ship and was dragged by his heavy equipment into the propeller. 'The sea was red with blood,' remembers Small, a grim if unconscious echo of Macbeth's fear that his bloody hand would 'the multitudinous seas incarnadine, making the green one red'.

When the 78th Division went ashore there was hardly a German within miles of the landing place but the enemy rallied with startling speed. It was soon all too evident that much bloody fighting lay ahead before the 560 miles to Tunis could be covered.

Shortly after the landings Small was appointed Company Quarter-master-Sergeant to a small mobile column under the command of Major Hart. 'Hartforce', as it was christened, was ordered to push ahead to support the commandos and paratroops who had landed at Bône, halfway between Algiers and Tunis. The hectic rush towards Tunis was continued but it was slowed at Medjez, where Hartforce was severely mauled, and checked at Djedaida, where Hart himself was killed.

Small found himself in charge of a motley group of cooks, stretcher-bearers and other non-combatants, under constant attack from the air – since the advancing British had far outstripped their air cover – and with German tanks advancing towards them. A shell from one of the tanks landed only a few feet from them but failed to explode. Small set fire to the cooks' truck, grabbed the wireless, and led his band back along the coast to Brigade Headquarters at Tabark. There, to his fury, he was accused of cowardice. 'If you think that, sir,' he said, 'I'm off.' 'Where to?' 'To join the Royal West Kents.' Fortunately an officer from the Northants was also present, who knew enough about Small to recognise the absurdity of the charge. He insisted that Small should go back to his own battalion, and it was with them that he saw some of the fiercest fighting of the war as Rommel threw in all his reserves in an attempt to destroy the Allied forces in Tunisia before the Eighth Army was ready to storm the Mareth Line to the west.

A coward was one thing Small would never be. He did not consider himself a hero, nor even particularly brave; but under fire, he says, he was 'as cold and callous as could be'. His main feeling was one of rage against his enemies and a determination to kill them before they killed him. He had no time to be afraid: 'I was one of those lucky people who seem to have no nerves.' To a degree he believed that he was immune from death or serious injury. Three times he was pulled out of action when his unit was in a particularly dangerous position; twice his replacement was killed almost at once, the third time he was severely injured: 'I'm not a religious man, but I'm compelled to believe there is something.' At twenty-four he was too old to apply to join the Special Air Service, otherwise he would have found the glamour and the promise of adventure irresistible. As it was, he belonged to one of the elite fighting formations of the British Army. The 78th Division was rightly held to be matched by few others when it came to morale and discipline. To Small it was an extension of the regimental family, something to which he belonged and could pledge total loyalty. 'Such a feeling I've never known elsewhere in all my career. It didn't matter what your cap badge was, it was that little yellow battleaxe on the side that mattered.'

Yet once removed from the fighting and the need to kill or be killed Small was the least belligerent of men. He took no particular pride in his prowess and in tranquillity preferred to put all thought of battle out of his mind. At the Royal Hospital the Governor once asked him why he never went up to the Field of Remembrance. 'Sir, I've a Field of Remembrance in my head,' Small replied. But though the memories could never be wholly exorcised, he did not court them. If he had been asked what aspect of his conduct in battle he viewed with the greatest pride he would not have spoken of his gallantry or his coolness under fire but of his determination to give the men who fought under him the greatest possible chance of surviving compatible with doing their duty. He believed in the importance of training and discipline, but only because of the results that they produced, not because training and discipline in themselves were meritorious. 'If somebody told you to jump, you jumped; if somebody told you to dive, you dived, for you never knew what was coming next.' Once Small was with a new arrival in the front line when he saw a puff of smoke. 'Duck!' he shouted, but his companion was slow to respond and died with a bullet through the neck. A German sniper was responsible. 'We got the sod in the end. He didn't kill any more.' Small's comment may sound bloodthirsty, but to him it was the fact that no more of his men were killed that was important, not that the German sniper had been eliminated.

As a company quartermaster-sergeant Small was unusual, almost unique, in that he took out patrols. At several points in the operations all the officers or other warrant officers had been killed or wounded. He found himself in effect acting as platoon commander. The men were happy when they knew he was in charge because they trusted his judgement and were confident that under his command they would never be sacrificed unnecessarily. By the time the final advance on Tunis resumed in April 1943 he had been appointed Sergeant-Major of C Company. His company commander was Major Cook, an ex-ranker who made few concessions to the politer usages of the Officers' Mess. Sometimes the relationship between a senior non-commissioned officer and a commissioned officer who had risen from the ranks could be an awkward one; in this case there was no trace of a problem, the two men respected, trusted and liked each other. 'He was brilliant,' says Small. 'We got on like a house on fire.'

The last few weeks of the battle for Tunis tested Cook to the uttermost. In a joint operation with the Lancashire Fusiliers the battalion suffered eighty casualties, more than a quarter of which were fatal, and the final offensive, at the end of April, brought further heavy losses. But though battered, the battalion survived as a viable fighting unit. On 8 May the 78th Division led the way in triumph into Tunis, the 5th Battalion of the Northamptonshire Regiment led the Division, and C Company led the Battalion. Small was the first sergeant-major to enter the city: 'I can smell it today. A great big Frenchman put his arms round me and kissed me. He stank of vino. I just shoved him off.'

The reaction of the men of the 78th Division when they finally linked up with the Eighth Army was something less than rapturous. Small was shocked by what he felt to be the slackness and indiscipline: officers wearing silk scarves, camouflage casually applied, a logistic back-up of what seemed extravagant dimensions. British soldiers in North Africa were usually admirers either of Alexander or of Montgomery. There was no doubt who commanded Small's loyalties. He met Alexander by chance when crossing a pontoon bridge. To his amazement the Commander-in-Chief came over to him, shook him by the hand, questioned him about the condition of his company and gave him some packets of cigarettes to distribute among the men: 'He was a gentleman, truly a gentleman.' When Montgomery handed out cigarettes he would throw them out of the window of his car and appeared to enjoy the sight of the soldiers scrabbling in the mud to pick them up. 'I stopped my men doing it, to my mind it was lowering to their dignity,' says Small. 'I got a very black look but nothing was said.' When Montgomery was made a field marshal there was so much hostile comment in the regiment that the Commanding Officer came into the Sergeants' Mess and said that all talk about senior appointments in the British Army was to cease forthwith. 'The next man I find discussing it, I don't mind what his rank is, will be before the Divisional Commander.' Protest might have continued even after this stern warning if Montgomery had supplanted Alexander but fortunately – in the eyes of Small and his fellow sergeants at least – Alexander too was promoted and retained his seniority.

As a result of the unskilful use of forceps at his birth and the deformation of his jaw Small had all his life endured trouble with his teeth. In the course of his Army career he saw no less than thirty-eight dentists, none of whom could do more than offer a temporary palliative. Towards the end of the North African campaign he was in almost constant pain, so much so that he could eat nothing except the softest of foodstuffs. He refused to do anything about it while the fighting was on, then collapsed and was taken off to hospital. At one point the doctors threatened to downgrade him medically, a step that would effectively have ruled him out for future combat. Small exploded indignantly; having come through some of the fiercest fighting of the Second World War, he did not intend to be driven from the front line by toothache. The doctors nevertheless keep him in hospital for several weeks and he was unable to rejoin his regiment until after the landings in Sicily. He could well have lost his post as Company Sergeant-Major but Major Cook stuck by him and insisted that there should be no permanent replacement. By the time he was able to rejoin his unit they were stationed below Mount Etna training for the next phase, the invasion of Italy.

Mussolini had fallen and an armistice had been signed with the Italians by the time the 78th Division landed at Taranto at the end of September 1943. At first opposition was light, but once again the Germans rallied. The division found itself on the right wing of the Eighth Army, battling its way up the east coast, 'slogging up Italy' as Alexander described it. It was one of the harshest winters of the war, food and other supplies had often to be dropped by parachute to the front-line troops, progress along the narrow coastal strip became progressively more difficult. The division was switched in an exhausting cross-country trek across Italy to Capua. The plan was that it should advance on Rome but instead it became involved in the battle for Monte Cassino.

Small survived it all, then, when the worst of the fighting seemed to be over and the road to Rome open, ate a handful of unwashed grapes and succumbed to amoebic dysentery. Delirious and with a high fever he was evacuated by ambulance. He was barely conscious of his surroundings; fortunately, perhaps, since the driver behaved with criminal irresponsibility. He paid no attention to his charges and was carousing in a canteen when the Military Police heard groans from inside the ambulance, forced open the doors and found it stinking like a sewer and with three out of its five occupants dead. The driver got ten years in prison, the episode almost cost Small his life. He had been a slightly overweight fourteen stone eight pounds when he fell ill; by the time he reached hospital he was a mere eight stone.

While Small was away the division had been involved in further fierce fighting around Lake Trasimene. He rejoined shortly before it was pulled out of the line for a badly needed rest period. For this they were despatched to Egypt, first to a camp about twenty miles from Ismailia, then to the outskirts of Cairo, within sight of the Pyramids. The British women in the city had been warned that the men of the 78th Division would be sex-starved and rapacious. Some of the girls from the Auxiliary Territorial Service were supposed to have told the new arrivals that they would not be prepared to dance with them unless first they removed their divisional insignia from their shoulders. 'That was a damned insult to us,' Small recalls indignantly. Everything conspired to inflame the resentful troops. The Military Police seemed to take a malign pleasure in harassing them over petty details of dress and discipline, what the regimental history describes as the 'insolent profiteering and open contempt of the tradesmen' broke down whatever restraint was left. Who actually began the trouble was never established but for a few hours the division ran amok. A piano was thrown from the upper windows of a five-storey building, a taxi with the driver still on board was pushed from a bridge into the Nile, £3,000 worth of damage was done to the Cairene shops. Small did not join in the mayhem but made no effort to check it: 'You couldn't do nothing about it. If we'd tried to stop it we'd have been done ourselves.' Eventually passions subsided and the police regained control. Next morning more than a hundred British soldiers were nursing their hangovers in gaols and guardrooms around the city. The 78th Division left Cairo a few weeks earlier than had been envisaged.

Small disapproved of but understood such excesses. His own tastes when it came to celebration were more restrained. Shortly after the division returned to Italy he and two or three other warrant officers were given a few days' leave in Rome. They went intending 'to let their hair down' but were so enraptured by the buildings and the paintings that they had no time for carousing and returned without having had a single drink: 'Not a drop! When we got back to the battalion they couldn't believe it.'

In fact their stay in Egypt would probably have been cut short in any case. Many of the British troops in Italy had been recalled to take part in the war in France and reinforcements were badly needed to overcome the stiffer-than-expected German resistance on the Gothic Line. By the end of September the division was back in the Appennines, some twenty-five miles south of Florence. Major Cook had been killed by a sniper some months before and though his successor in command of C Company had come with a high reputation he and Small never enjoyed the same mutual affection and trust. The division fought its way through the mountains to the last ridge before the Po valley and the Northants were told to storm the strongpoint that was the key to the situation. C Company was on the right. They reached the summit and one platoon continued down the other side in the wake of the retreating Germans. The flame throwers opened fire on the troops remaining on the ridge. Small, with the headquarters' staff, returned the fire and put three of the flame throwers out of action before their ammunition was exhausted.

By now a German counter-attack had begun and the leading platoon was pinned down and in danger of being overrun. 'I'm wounded,' announced the Company Commander. 'I can't go on, Sergeant-Major. We must withdraw.' Small could see no signs of a wound but offered to put on a field dressing. His Major refused, there was no time to waste, he insisted, they must withdraw immediately. Small protested that the forward platoon could not just be abandoned and must be told of their withdrawal. He went forward himself to try to establish contact, stumbled into a German position and found himself looking down the barrel of a machine-gun.

His captor put him on the back of a motorcycle and headed

towards a nearby farm, while another German in the sidecar covered him with his pistol. An officer of impeccable courtesy interrogated him; he knew everything about Small's background, he said, there were just a few points of detail which he wanted to clear up for the record. Small quoted the Geneva Convention and refused to give more than his name, rank and number. He was then locked up while the Germans entertained themselves by firing a machine-gun through a window into the wall above the spot where he was lying. Covered with plaster and 'shaking like a leaf' he was then put in with the other men from the Northants whom he had been trying to rescue when taken prisoner. Together they were bundled into a lorry and driven to Imola, where they were joined by a Sikh who spoke perfect English and took a keen interest in their doings. Small knew that there were collaborators at work and suspected that this man was one of them. 'Don't speak to him,' he ordered. 'And you, get out! You're a traitor!' Whether or not Small's suspicions were justified, the Sikh was removed shortly afterwards and never seen again.

Meanwhile his Company Commander had walked two miles back to the battalion headquarters and had reported that Small and many others were dead or missing. Something of a scandal followed. Small was later told that he had been recommended for the Distinguished Conduct Medal but that the proposal had been dropped because the award of such an honour would have highlighted the conduct of the Company Commander and possibly led to his court martial. The Commanding Officer of the 5th Battalion wrote to Blanche Small to tell her that her husband's body had not been found on the battlefield so there was every reason to hope he was a prisoner. 'He and one officer and eighteen other ranks were the only personnel to reach their objective after a night attack. They held on for two hours against three counter-attacks. Dawn was breaking when it was decided to withdraw as they had no ammunition left. They split up into two bodies, but only three of the Sergeant-Major's party got back . . . He was just about to get promotion, so his loss is doubly felt.' It was a sanitised version of the truth, but the Army was never keen on stirring up dirt if it could be avoided. The Company Commander left the Regiment and Small heard of him no more.

Gradually the number of prisoners at Imola built up and after a few days they were taken to a railhead, loaded into trucks and despatched to Germany by way of the Brenner Pass. Conditions were decidedly unpleasant, the only sanitation was provided by a tea-chest in the corner and there was barely room to sit on the floor, let alone stretch out. As the senior warrant officer in the party, Small was in a painfully difficult position. He knew that it was his duty to organise an escape if any opportunity arose; equally he felt that he must do all he could to avoid unnecessary loss of life. 'The responsibility rested heavily on me. I didn't want to land them in the cart.' It was something of a relief to him that the Germans proved efficient gaolers. Small was never put to the test. The party arrived at Moosburg, north-east of Munich, without a vestige of a chance of escaping having been offered them.

There were 17,000 prisoners in Stalag 7a at Moosburg, divided into laagers according to the nationality of the prisoners. Small no longer had to carry the burden of being the senior warrant officer but the dozen or so sergeant-majors were something of an elite group and were excused the working parties in which all the other prisoners had to take part. In no other way was he better off, however; he shared the same meagre rations: boiled potatoes, a slice of bread with margarine which they believed was made from coal oil, a triangular piece of horsemeat about the size of a segment of Swiss processed cheese. The tea was herbal and horrible – Michaelmas daisies were said to be the main ingredient. Inadequate though it was, the food was shared with scrupulous fairness, lots were drawn as to who would have which piece of bread. Though Small's rank protected him from disagreeable duties it could sometimes prove a disadvantage. Once the prisoners from the British laager were assembled to hear a harangue in English about the Führer. One of the men blew a raspberry in derision. Small was suspected of being the culprit or at least held responsible as the nearest warrant officer. He was marched off, pushed down a slope into a dark cell and kept in solitary confinement for fourteen days. He had already been feeling ill because of the after-effects of his dysentery and the problems in eating caused by his defective teeth; the semi-starvation and the cramped conditions which he now endured added to his discomfort. By the time he was released he was near to collapse. Fortunately there was an English medical officer in the camp who managed to patch him up with the help of the extremely limited resources available.

Defiance of the gaolers was a part of life in Stalag 7a, but normally took a more muted form than obscene noises on parade. The prisoners had an illicit radio hidden up a chimney and thus kept themselves in touch with the progress of the war. The Germans suspected such devices existed and conducted periodic searches. One humorist put a wire through the floorboards, concealed but not so carefully concealed that it would escape examination. At the base he put a lump of excrement. A German guard spotted the wire, triumphantly thrust in his hand to capture the radio, and took it out fouled and evil-smelling. He got his revenge by slapping the faces of everyone in the hut with his dirty hand. Another way of scoring off the Germans was to remove the contents of a tin of cocoa received in a Red Cross parcel, fill it almost to the brim with the dust from crushed bricks, put back a little cocoa at the top and then offer the resealed tin to the German sentries in exchange for loaves of bread. Since the trade was anyway contrary to the rules, the cheated Germans had no redress, and in a few weeks, when fresh sentries were on duty, the trick could be played again.

On the whole the relationship between guards and prisoners was correct without ever being cordial. The English laager was fortunate in that its commander came from the Regular army rather than the SS. He had himself been a prisoner-of-war in England during the First World War, had been treated decently, and was resolved to do as much himself. He was strict over such matters as saluting or being properly shaved on parade, but he was also fair; if a prisoner pleaded that he was unable to shave because he had no razor blade the Commander would procure him one from German sources. Things were different in other parts of Stalag 7a, in particular in the adjoining Russian sector, where the rations were far worse and the treatment of prisoners brutal. When the moment of liberation came the officer in charge of the whole camp was shot for war crimes but the Commander of the British laager was handed over to the relieving forces with a recommendation that he be well treated.

Even if they had not known from their radio that victory was near, the prisoners-of-war would have guessed as much from the sudden influx of refugees from other camps being marched back by their gaolers to escape the Russian advance. The immediate result was still greater overcrowding and still more meagre rations but this hardly dulled the euphoria at knowing the ordeal was almost over. It was the Americans who arrived first. General Patton swaggered into the camp with his pearl-handled revolver in his belt: 'You had to see it to believe it,' remembers Small. 'Talk about Tom Mix!' The released prisoners made their way to Munich. Small still recalls his distress when he saw a group of Jewish refugees, probably some of those who had been fortunate enough to emerge alive from Dachau: 'There was nothing more than skin and bones. I had never seen anything like it in my life. You'd see those gaunt faces and those eyes staring at you. It made you appreciate how lucky you were.'

They moved on to an airport, where thousands of British troops were milling around, all wishing they were somewhere else and pulling every string at their disposal to get there. Small found himself sitting beside a man who seemed vaguely familiar, looked more carefully and recognised the son of the chemist from the Devonshire town next to the village where he had spent his childhood. The two had often played football together as boys. 'I was never more surprised in my life, nor was he. We took each other's hand and held on as if we were never going to let go.' They got on the same plane bound for England. A sobering note was struck when they were almost home. The plane was abruptly diverted to another airfield. The plane ahead of them, with a full load of long-term ex-prisoners-of-war had crashed on landing. Everyone had been killed.

A cup of tea and a bar of chocolate were offered on arrival. Small drank the first with relish and refused the second; his digestion was still alarmingly frail and the last thing he wanted as he set off on the final stages of his journey home was a bout of debilitating diarrhoea. After a night's sleep all their clothes were taken away and they were shepherded to the bathrooms. It was one of the most sublime experiences of his life. 'You never saw anything like it. Have you ever seen kids that don't want to come out of the sea after they've been paddling? It was just the same. All this damned stuff coming off your body. It was heaven. In the end they chased us out.' New clothes were issued, the receipts which the Germans had meticulously furnished when their money was confiscated on capture were honoured and reimbursed, £50 was given to each man as an advance on the pay that had accumulated.

And so Small found himself on the train to Northampton. As he approached his front door, he suddenly realised he had no idea what he was going to say, he knew only that he felt intense excitement. He knocked and waited. 'There was the sweetest little girl came out. It was my daughter and she said: "Mummy, there's a soldier at the door." Blanche came out and I embraced her and I couldn't let her go.'

He had four months' leave. For the first two months or so he found it hard to sleep and had nightmares when he did, reliving former actions. Gradually they died away. 'If I hadn't had this wonderful wife I don't know what I'd have done. She nursed me back. She encouraged me to go out. We talked, it seemed to quiet me down and get me back to normal.' But the memories of what he had been through never wholly faded. Even now, when the fireworks explode on 5 November, 'I can smell death. It's awful, a terrible thing.' His daughter, Rita, remembers how difficult he found it to go out into crowds, even to stand in a bus queue was at first too much for him.

When Small rejoined the regiment he took over the training of recruits. The work was congenial and he liked the idea of spending some time in Northampton, but all was not well at home. During his absence his mother-in-law had grown very close to his daughter. Rita now wanted always to be with her father and looked to him as the source of all wisdom. Her grandmother knew that this was natural and proper but could not help herself resenting it; her chagrin took the form of a barely concealed dislike of Small. It became more and more difficult for him to share her home, yet no married quarters were available and other accommodation in Northampton was expensive and anyway difficult to find. It never occurred to him that he might leave the Army and find a new job elsewhere; apart from the fact that this was his life and he knew no other, he would have forfeited a large part of his pension by premature retirement. Instead he volunteered to join the 1st Battalion of the Northants in Malaya; it would mean leaving his wife and daughter behind, probably for a few months, but they would then be able to follow him.

The Emergency was still in its early stages when he arrived and techniques for combating the Malayan People's Liberation Army (which, in spite of its name, was almost entirely Chinese in its membership) were still in their infancy. Small went on one patrol, raiding a site where the presence of Chinese terrorists was suspected, but if they had ever been there they had certainly departed by the time the British infantry arrived. His first outing proved uneventful. It was also his last. The Colonel called for him and told him that the Battalion had unexpectedly been called back to the United Kingdom. Having only just arrived, Small would not be accompanying them. General Headquarters was in need of a senior warrant officer with police experience to take over a prison in Singapore. It was not a conventional military glasshouse but a holding prison for war criminals who were either awaiting trial or serving sentences. It was, Small gathered, in something of a mess, and it would be up to him to put it right. It was not work which he would have chosen for himself, especially since it would mean his temporary secondment from his beloved regiment to the Military Police, but he did not feel that it was for him to question orders; at least a comfortable house went with the job, so his wife and daughter would be able to join him sooner than expected.

He got off to a difficult start when he found that much of the furniture and equipment was missing from the prison. His predecessor, who was on the point of being transferred to a civilian gaol, tried to persuade him to sign the inventory as it stood. Small refused, and insisted that the barracks inventory clerk be called in. 'Oh, we don't want that,' said the former incumbent. 'I don't care what *you* want,' retorted Small. 'I'm a regular soldier with a pension to look forward to and I'm not losing that for you or anyone else.' He appealed to the Adjutant, who at once called in the clerk. The upshot was that his predecessor was reduced to the ranks and gaoled for six months for stealing government property.

Small's brief was first of all to ensure that nobody in his gaol escaped or committed suicide; other improvements were desirable but of subsidiary importance. This was not easy; there were no suicides while Small was in charge but several attempts were made, including that of a man who tried to choke himself by forcing a sheet down his throat. As for the escapes, these were desperate men. Several were murderers, awaiting execution or knowing that they were unlikely ever to be released. Among them were five former soldiers from the Christmas Islands. When Japanese invasion seemed imminent, their British officer had told them that there would be no surrender and that they must be prepared to die to the last man in defence of their homeland. They had found the prospect unappealing and instead had murdered the officer and the sergeants in their sleep. Their death penalty had been commuted at the last moment, but as they were all anyway in the advanced stages of syphilis the reprieve was not likely to do them much good. There were civilian murderers too, with nothing to lose and a reputation for violence; no one would venture into their cells unless at least one other armed member of staff was present.

Small set about tidying up the shambles he had inherited. Nineteen Indian employees were hanging around, doing almost nothing; he got rid of all but one or two of them. Lax discipline was tightened, new procedures introduced, the appearance of the prison improved, morale among the staff was transformed. But the responsibility which he bore almost single-handed and the oppressive surroundings in which he worked gradually wore him down. It helped when his family, now supplemented by a second child, arrived from England. It might have been better still if he had taken advantage of the possibilities to go away with them to the hills or the sea on local leave, but the work always seemed too pressing, there was no one whom he fully trusted to take charge during his absence. He grew moody and withdrawn.

He did all he could to conceal from his wife and daughter the strain under which he was labouring but it was very obvious to them that he was nervous and found it hard to live a normal family life. 'I couldn't bear to hear my children crying,' he says. 'I'd run out of the house, go and sit down under the trees, just sit around the house sobbing, stupid stuff like that.' In the end he had to admit that he was suffering something close to a full-scale nervous breakdown. He appealed to the Army psychiatrist, who told him that he should imagine himself as a thrush which had been singing on a bough and suddenly found itself put inside a cage. Small had been in one cage already, now he found himself back inside another and subconsciously he was rejecting his incarceration. Small's immediate reaction was to dismiss this as fanciful nonsense but the more he considered the matter the more truth he felt there was in it. He experienced nothing but relief when he was told that he should not set foot in the prison again. Better still, the General commanding the British forces in Malaya was so pleased with the work which he had already done that he decreed Small should not lose his rank as a warrant officer first class in his next posting.

With the prison safely behind him Small was able to put the Military Police behind him too. In February 1948 he reverted to the Northamptonshire Regiment. It was good to be wearing the old cap badge again. It would have been better still to go back to regimental soldiering in the United Kingdom, but the Army wanted to keep him in Singapore. There were consolations in the posting. By now he had a third child; a large, comfortable house and excellent schools were advantages not to be ignored. The family was thriving. Small always told his children that they were never to discuss his rank with their contemporaries. Officers' children might make them feel inferior, with those of other ranks they might believe that they belonged to a higher caste. Both attitudes would be equally unjustified: 'It's what you are yourselves that counts,' he told them. For his own part, superficially at least, he had now fully recovered from his nervous breakdown; on the psychiatrist's advice he took up embroidery and stitched an elaborate village scene. He was still producing rugs for members of his family when he joined the Royal Hospital.

His new job should have been considerably less stressful. He was Sergeant-Major at the garrison camp, some miles out of Singapore, responsible for matters of discipline and administration. In theory there were few problems, but Small's restless determination to put right anything that seemed to him improper or defective landed him in trouble once again. When he was almost due to return to England he noticed that, when the troops were being paid out, the names of twenty-eight Gurkhas were on the list, all of them unknown to him. He suspected that the Gurkhas were mythical and that someone was perpetrating an audacious fraud. 'Has some mistake been made?' he asked the Camp Commandant. The Commandant was dismissive of his doubts: all was in order, those responsible were fully competent to perform their duties. Small still felt deep unease, so he approached a major in the Pay Corps. 'I've a terrible problem,' he said. 'It may sound disloyal to my own officers, but I know something's wrong and I can't do anything about it.' An investigation was mounted, and the next thing Small knew was that two junior officers were in serious trouble and the Camp Commandant had been reprimanded.

Once again, it seemed, justice had been done and Small had triumphed. But the Camp Commandant felt that he had been pilloried and betrayed, and it was he who had to prepare Small's 'employment sheet', the report on his conduct which every warrant officer took on with him to his next posting. Traditionally the reporting officer would read over what he had written to his subordinate so that the latter could defend himself if he thought it necessary. In this case, however, the Camp Commandant refused to tell Small what he had said in his report. Small read it all the same and was outraged to find himself accused of being disloyal, untrustworthy and a troublemaker. He took the letter to his Colonel: 'I don't deserve this, sir,' he protested. The Colonel at once added a paragraph saying that in his view the criticism was unjustified and did not reflect Small's career or character. Once Small got back to England he appealed to the General Officer Commanding, Eastern Command, and eventually had the satisfaction of learning that the report had been expunged from his records.

But this process took three months. In the meantime Small was posted to the regimental depot. The Adjutant, for reasons that he no doubt found compelling but were never explained to Small, chose to accept the Camp Commandant's strictures and to ignore the Colonel's later comments. There could be no place for such an unworthy element in the Northamptonshire Regiment. Small was banished to Thetford in Norfolk where he was Ranges Sergeant-Major in the training area; an uninspiring assignment which was made no more attractive by the fact that the nearest married quarters were in Bury St Edmunds. Small would leave home each morning at 4.15 a.m. and not get back till 7 p.m., hardly seeing his children except at weekends.

In June 1951, the job at Thetford was downgraded. Small hoped that he might now be received back into the regiment but instead he was posted to the Embarkation Establishment at Harwich. He claims that he felt no bitterness over this neglect – 'I took things as they came. I didn't allow myself to get hassled' – but he would have been superhuman if he had not felt some resentment at being, as he saw it, unfairly rejected. His dejection increased when he was told he might get a commission in the Military Police; and then, when he took the plunge, discovered that his application was forty-eight hours too late. 'I was a "nearly" man,' he reflects sadly. He was on the point of being promoted and then missed out because he was taken prisoner; he was in line to receive a Distinguished Conduct Medal but was sidelined for reasons unconnected with his behaviour; now another opportunity had gone to waste.

He resigned himself to completing the rest of his service at Harwich. The work was light, the company congenial – it could have been a great deal worse. His fourth and last child was born while he was there and the family settled in well in their new home. He had been concerned lest Blanche should find it painful to exchange the easy life of Singapore for the rigours of married quarters in Britain, but she seemed positively to thrive on the housework, and never complained about the drop in her standard of living. She was 'a very tranquil soul,' remembers her daughter, 'so quiet, she was an angel.' Small attached great importance to his family and played with the children whenever possible. 'It would break my heart if you ever quarrelled,' he told them. He was a strict father, though, insisting on high standards in the home. When his elder daughter, aged fifteen, first put on lipstick, he thought there was too much of it and made her go and wipe it off.

He was not to see out his career so uneventfully, however. The regiment decided that they needed reinforcements and at last called him back. The situation was not entirely satisfactory – he had to drop a rank to company sergeant-major and was anyway posted to what was for him the wrong battalion, but it never occurred to him that he might try to evade the summons: 'You see, if you're a Regular soldier and your regiment wants you, there's no use arguing. I was still under contract to the Army.'

The 1st Battalion of the Northants was based at Wuppertal in Germany. Small felt that he was once more in his element and he quickly re-established his position in the regiment; his experience in accounts in Singapore ensured that his papers were always in immaculate order and his company regularly got top marks in the inspections. When it became known that the Northants were to go to Korea, Small was promised that he would accompany them as a regimental sergeant-major. It was the appointment of his dreams, the proper culmination of every regimental soldier's career. But once again he turned out to be a 'nearly' man; only two days after he was told of his new assignment his wife fell ill, was rushed to hospital and had to undergo a major operation to her womb. The gynaecologist reported that it would take six months for her to recuperate.

With what seems to the outsider somewhat brutal haste Small was placed on the ERE2 List – the Extra-Regimental Employed list, Grade 2 – which carried with it the strong probability if not certainty that the man concerned could never serve with his Regiment again nor hope for promotion. He was posted to Movement Control in a job which would require him to spend a large part of his life on a train and enable him only to see his family at irregular intervals: 'At this I was distraught.' His Company Commander, who felt that he had been badly treated, sent him off to see the Brigadier. 'The Brigadier's first words were "How is your wife?" something which the Regiment had never asked.' He cancelled the posting and installed Small as Camp Sergeant-Major, a job which still did not involve promotion but was infinitely preferable to what had previously been proposed. His own wife, the Brigadier promised, would keep an eye on Blanche. 'He was a real English gentleman and she was a lady. It makes my eyes moist now when I think of her. She was so homely . . . ' He could not help feeling that the regiment had betrayed him. 'They say there are no trade unions in the Army,' he told his Colonel. 'Well, there is: the Officers' Trade Union. They would never let each other down.' Only when boiling with resentment could Small have spoken thus to a man who, *ex officio*, enjoyed semi-sacred status in his eyes.

In spite of this unfortunate start Small spent a happy eighteen months at Wuppertal. He brought order to a camp where previously there had been little, got rid of superfluous and ill-disposed personnel, and won the ardent approval of his Commanding Officer. At the end of 1955, his job completed, he was transferred to a lorried infantry brigade at Lüneburg. Here too he got off to a rocky start. He arrived just before Christmas, and by a combination of indifference and incompetence on the part of the quartermaster involved, found himself living in five different houses within the space of a week. At the Christmas party for sergeants in the Officers' Mess his new Commanding Officer asked him whether he was settled in. Small explained his problem, on which the Colonel exploded in rage and made sure that permanent accommodation was found within a couple of days.

Bad led to worse. It was at Lüneburg that Small came as close to disillusionment with the Army as was possible for a man of his disposition. Arriving one morning at his office he found a man weeping despondently outside his door. He told him to have his cry out and then come in. When he did so, the man produced a telegram from the police station nearest to his home in England telling him that his mother, whose only son he was, was dying in hospital. Small went at once to the Company Commander's office. Since it was only 9 a.m., he was surprised to find the Major already at his desk. Small knocked and went in. 'Fuck off!' said the Company Commander, who was obviously drunk. Small stood his ground, and explained what the problem was. 'Fuck off!' repeated the Company Commander. Small stormed out of the office and appealed to the Brigade Major. By two that afternoon the soldier was on an aeroplane for London. That same evening the drunken Major followed him. Small was assured that a new company commander would soon arrive.

But it was one trial too many. Like Evelyn Waugh's Guy Crouchback in the great *Sword of Honour* trilogy, Small had expected too much of both Regiment and Army, and was proportionately distressed when all turned out not to be as he had imagined it. 'Inwardly, I felt so hurt and upset. Recalling everything that had happened before in Singapore, I thought this must now be an accepted thing within the British Army.' He had the option to end his term early rather than to serve out his full twenty-five years, and this he decided to do. The Brigadier asked him to reconsider his decision and stay on. Small refused. 'When you've gone through all that, sir,' he told the Brigadier, 'you can't take no more. It's my duty to get out of the Army because I don't feel I can do my work as I have been accustomed to.' Nine months later, on 10 December 1956, he became a civilian.

Northamptonshire was the county both he and Blanche knew best and it was there that they decided to settle. The first task was to find somewhere to live. His wife and children had been installed by the Army in cramped rooms in a hostel in Blackpool, not something that could be endured for long. Small called on a senior employee of the council who told him that, in his opinion, the city owed nothing to former members of the regiment. He could see no prospect of Small getting a house in the foreseeable future.

Fortunately, not all members of the council were of the same mind. A retired lieutenant-colonel for whom he had once worked was in a position of some authority; Small made his problem known and almost at once a house was found for him at Milton Malsor, three miles or so south of Northampton. On retirement he had been given a gratuity of £348; he took it to a furniture store in the city and asked them to supply as many of the essentials as could be provided for this amount. They would have been happy to install more on hire-purchase terms but the idea of being in debt alarmed and repelled him. Nothing, he ruled, was to enter his house unless it had first been paid for.

He put his name down for the Corps of Commissionaires, an organisation that specialised in finding responsible security work for ex-service personnel, but though he was exactly the sort of man for whom they catered, they had a waiting list and could not promise a vacancy for several years. In the meantime he worked as a metal polisher, doing work mainly on motor car components. His salary barely paid for the upkeep of his family. To earn extra money he moved over to night shift, working from 6.30 p.m. to 6.30 a.m. It was drudgery, and he found the lack of responsibility frustrating and depressing, but there was nothing to be done about it. 'I quickly learnt to forget that I had been in the Army. I truly did make an effort not to throw about what I had been in the Army. Believe me, I bit my lip on several occasions. It wasn't easy.' Finally the Corps of Commissionaires came up with a job in security at the Northampton firm of Travis and Arnold. It was nothing magnificent but a great deal better than what he had done previously. He accepted promptly. After some years he managed to move from security to credit control; the change involved severing relations with the Corps of Commissionaires but the work was both more interesting and better rewarded. He kept at it until retirement in 1972.

Meanwhile, as their circumstances improved, life at home gradually became more comfortable. Soon after they moved to

Milton Malsor their elder daughter got a job in Woolworth's and their elder son, aged fourteen, joined the Royal Electrical and Mechanical Engineers as a boy soldier. The younger children were both at school. Once Small came back from night shift to find his wife in tears. Margaret, the youngest girl, had been awake and crying all night, complaining that she was being bullied and that the other children, knowing where she had lived for the last few years, jeered at her for being a German. Small stormed round to the school and saw Margaret's form mistress; he would not tolerate this, he said, she must put a stop to it. The teacher was sympathetic but proved ineffective. Small then went to the parents of the children who Margaret said were the ringleaders; from them he did not get even sympathy. Undiscouraged, he approached the police. Here at last he inspired some action; a policeman called on the parents concerned and told them that unless the persecution stopped there would be prosecutions. Immediately Margaret was left in peace.

By the time that Small retired he was having problems with his breathing. It seemed sense, especially since the family was now so much smaller, to move into a bungalow. They chose the village of Kislingbury, north of Northampton, since their daughter Rita was living there. Retirement was pleasant, if uneventful; Small felt that he had already spent enough of his life travelling around the world and that he now was content to vegetate in peace, doing his embroidery, reading, gardening, sharing his life with Blanche. Looking back on their life together he wondered sometimes whether he had done enough to help her with the house and the family: 'Could I have done more? I loved her so much. She was wonderful.' Then, in the late 1980s, she tripped on the cobbles outside the bungalow, fell heavily and broke her thigh bone. The fracture was complex and took a long time to heal but the aftermath was far worse. Whether coincidentally or partly as a result of the accident, Blanche was affected by Alzheimer's disease. Her mind deteriorated at alarming speed. For two years Small nursed her at home; Rita did what she could to help but she had her own children to look after. Blanche not merely required constant attention but was a danger to herself and others. Once she turned on the gas jets in the kitchen and wandered away; Small had to have special safety catches fitted in case this exploit was repeated. Finally, after more than two years, the doctor said that this could not go on; the only result would be that Small would have a stroke and that then both he and his wife would be incapacitated. Blanche was settled in a nursing home and Small moved into a nearby flat so that he could visit her more easily. At this point she could still recognise her daughter and her husband but within a few months she forgot first one and then the other.

Blanche died in Sam Small's arms in June 1992, and he was left feeling 'lonely as hell'. He spoke of his wife constantly to his children. Rita says that, whenever her name was mentioned, tears came into her father's eyes.

Since his retirement from the Army Small had occasionally met old friends who had served with him but he never went near the depot nor had anything to do with the regiment as an institution. He made no effort to attend the various reunions, nor did anyone invite him: 'I'd put them out of my mind,' he says. 'I can honestly say with my hand on my heart that I never at any time let down the Regiment. They let me down.' But he still had fond memories of his life as a soldier and hankered for the good order and comradeship that he had found during those years. He was determined too, not to be a burden on his children: 'I'm not going to have you worrying about me as I did about your mother,' he told them. He knew about the Royal Hospital at Chelsea but had never talked of it to his wife or considered the possibility that he might end his days there. Now the attractions became more obvious. He summoned his children and told them what he had in mind. They made no attempt to dissuade him. 'Well, Dad, it's your life,' said

Rita. 'I can understand why you're doing it.' 'There was a tear in most of their eyes,' says Small.

Once the decision was taken, he moved fast. He wrote at once to the Hospital and got a hopeful reply; the berths in which the Pensioners slept were in the process of being enlarged so there would be some delay but in principle he was welcome to make his trial visit. He went there in March 1994, 'fell in love with the place on sight', and had no hesitation when told three months later that a place was vacant if he still wanted it: 'I couldn't get in quick enough.' Nor has he ever seen any reason to doubt the wisdom of his decision. Life at the Hospital did not involve retreating into monastic seclusion; Small has determinedly kept open all his lines into his former life. He enjoys visiting the various members of his family and gets a lot of fun out of his frequent excursions. When he first went to stay with Rita at Kislingbury she took him to the local branch of Sainsbury's. His scarlet cloak and black cocked hat caused a sensation. One customer touched him and said: 'Oh, you're a real one! I've only seen one on the telly before.' As he and his daughter left the store the supervisor said: 'I want you to know that you've brightened our day.' Small lapped it all up and will be saddened if the time comes when he must restrict his activities. But he feels no regrets when the excursion is over and he returns to Chelsea: 'This is now my home and I've enjoyed every minute of it.'

THOMAS PARNELL

Corporal Parnell, *c* 1938

Thomas Parnell

WHEN Tom Parnell was born in Bolton on 23 March 1918 he was the third child of a family that was eventually to number five. It is often said that to be in the middle of a line of children is something of a disadvantage. The elder children enjoy the status and perquisites of seniority, the younger the pleasures of irresponsibility. The pig in the middle has the worst of both worlds. Tom is convinced that he was denied the attention lavished on his seniors yet not consoled by the liberties granted to his juniors; he was fobbed off with clothes and toys already well used by his elder siblings, yet these were replaced by new when it came to the two younger children.

This preamble might suggest that Tom was prone to self-pity. The opposite is true. He would never deny that he enjoyed an exceptionally happy childhood. The Parnells, though far from rich, were reasonably well off – 'comfortable', in the words of Tom. There was no tradition of soldiering in the family, though Tom's father, also Thomas, had been called up in the First World War and had won the Military Medal with the King's Own Royal Border Regiment. Then he secured a place in the Lockheed Aircraft Company, while his wife Emily worked part time in one of the many cotton mills to be found at that period in Bolton. They lived on a small council estate where there were forty houses; to be philoprogenitive seems to have been the norm in the neighbourhood; even with five children the Parnells had one of the smaller families: one household boasted fourteen. Mr Parnell was a passionate and successful gardener; he won the prize for the best-kept garden three times in a row and finally had to be asked not to enter for a year or two since he was discouraging others from competing.

Tom was big for his age and strong, a disciplinarian, in the eyes of his younger brother, Harold; indeed, something of a bully. Harold got his own back once, however. He was skilled at putting together crystal sets and making electrical gadgets, and he devised an electric-shock machine. He asked Tom to hold it, then turned the current on at full voltage. His brother could not let go, and eventually had to rip the machine out of the wall. He was not amused. The two brothers in fact got on well, though Tom remembers experiencing some resentment when the battered old bicycle he had inherited from an elder child was replaced by a brand-new model for Harold's benefit. Harold for his part is equally clear that Tom was the favourite child and that it was *he* who suffered in comparison.

Tom went to the local council school and found it agreeable if not exciting. He abhorred mathematics but enjoyed history and geography. As in most schools of the 1920s and 1930s, the teaching of history revolved around the greatness of the British Empire; Tom found the subject enthralling and never thought it in the least surprising that so small an island should govern such large portions of the globe. 'As a young boy I was taught to be proud of it,' he remembers; he honoured the King, too, though the Parnells never paid much attention to their corresponding duty to fear God. His father always voted Conservative, 'because he was a working chap'; politics was not a subject which bulked large in Tom's childhood but he would certainly have thought that Socialism was close to Communism and that both were to be deplored.

Though Tom took his education seriously his activities outside school can have left room for little homework. Every morning and often in the evening too he would deliver newspapers in the neighbourhood, work 'which I thoroughly enjoyed because it gave me an insight into what things were about'. At weekends he accompanied a milkman on his rounds. Best of all, when he was twelve years old, the family moved to the outskirts of Bolton and Tom helped on a local farm. This he loved, particularly when he had anything to do with horses, animals for which he felt a strong and immediate affinity. He learnt to ride, taking to it with relish, and found a pastime which, at the age of eighty-three, still provides him with enormous satisfaction. He was intelligent enough to go on to grammar school and the matter was debated by his parents, but conditions in Bolton were depressed and money was short. If he had been desperately anxious to continue his education his parents would somehow have scraped together the money but, though he would have liked to go to grammar school, he was too concerned about the family's need to press his case.

At the age of fourteen he left school and got a job in a mill. He hated it: the work was boring, the surroundings gloomy, the damp and heat intolerable. The temperature varied between 98°F and 108°F; the rule was that if it touched 110°F work would stop but, to nobody's surprise, this magical cut-off point was never reached. Because of the oily floor employees were always expected to be in bare feet. Tom worked from 7 a.m. to 5 p.m. weekdays, and from 7 a.m. to noon on Saturdays for 14 shillings a week; sometimes he was laid off when orders were short but it was almost always possible to find a vacancy in another mill. Tom would spend his days dreaming of the evenings and weekends, when he would go to the local Rotary Club for boxing, basketball, swimming and long-distance running.

Whenever he had a chance he would visit the farm near his

home to work with the horses. He made friends with the farmer, who belonged to the Duke of Lancaster's Yeomanry, a cavalry unit which was part of the Territorial Army. Tom asked whether there might be a place in the Yeomanry for him. He was told he was too young – eighteen was the legal minimum and he was only sixteen and a half – but he went on pestering the farmer until he got invited to a drill night. He went again, then again, and finally plucked up his courage to ask the Squadron Commander – a man called Eades from a well-known cotton family – whether he might join the unit. Again he was told he was too young; then Eades asked him to stand up. 'You're a big boy, aren't you?' 'Yes' 'Can you tell a lie?' 'Yes' 'Then you're eighteen and you're in the Yeomanry.'

The permanent staff of the Yeomanry were regular soldiers, and over the next eighteen months Tom got a taste for the military, still more the cavalry way of life. The depression had got worse in Bolton, and even if he had fancied a lifetime in the mills future prospects seemed increasingly bleak. Several of his friends had joined the Navy and others the Lancashire Fusiliers; by the time he was eighteen Tom Parnell had decided that for him too the armed services offered the best chance of a career that would be both enjoyable and secure.

He knew exactly what sort of service he wanted to do. Bolton, as well as being the heartland of the Lancashire Fusiliers, was also a traditional area of recruitment for the Guards. When Parnell arrived at the recruiting office he was told there was no vacancy in the cavalry and advised instead to apply for the foot guards. No, said Parnell, for him it must be the cavalry or nothing. He began to walk out of the building. 'Just a minute,' said the recruiting officer, looking through his books: 'As it happens, there's a chance of a vacancy in the Household Cavalry.' 'But they never go abroad,' said Parnell; he wanted something more adventurous. Once more he began to walk out. The recruiting officer saw the fee which he got for each enlisted man disappearing through the door. 'Just a minute,' he said again, turning once more to his books. The Royal

Dragoons were shortly coming home from Egypt; would they be suitable? 'Is that a cavalry unit?' Parnell asked suspiciously. Assured that it was, he accepted gratefully, and on 14 May 1936, Trooper Parnell began his life in the ranks of the British Army.

He did his basic training at Hounslow. He had been told that he would be wise to show some diffidence when questioned about his experience as a horseman and congratulated himself when he saw the treatment meted out to those who were more boastful or self-confident. 'They made their life hell!' he remembers. After two months the Dragoons returned and he joined them in their depot at Shorncliffe. A large number of the senior non-commissioned officers were due for retirement after their period abroad so Parnell, obviously one of the most promising of the young recruits, was quickly promoted to lance-corporal. Life was good, and his only regret was that it would probably be several years before the regiment went overseas again. Then volunteers for India were requested, to join the 16th/5th Lancers who had just gone out there and were short of men. His Sergeant-Major wanted to keep a young man who was not only doing well in his new role as lance-corporal but was also one of the best swimmers and boxers in the regiment, but Parnell insisted that he had joined the Army to see the world. Once a man had volunteered to go abroad it was difficult to stop him. Reluctantly, the Sergeant-Major allowed his name to go forward. There were four others ahead of him on the list so his prospects still seemed dim but for one reason or another his rivals all dropped out.

Early in 1938 he set sail for India. In fact, if he had stayed with the Dragoons he would have got his foreign travel anyway, the increasing threat of an Arab revolt in Palestine led to the Regiment heading back to the Middle East only a few months after Parnell left them.

The 16th/5th Lancers, to their great relief, had just been transferred from what was known as the 'sloth belt' in Southern

India to the North-West Frontier, where there was always the chance of action. The Munich Crisis had occurred when they were actually in transit and for a time it seemed they might be diverted back to Europe to take part in the seemingly inevitable war, but Chamberlain reappeared bearing peace with honour and the Regiment continued on their way to what they hoped would be war with honour in the north. Parnell joined them at Risalpur, a name which translated literally means 'full of cavalry' and which, in 1938, lived up to its name. It was a relatively modern station twenty-five miles or so east of Peshawar. It had been completed just before the First World War; its bungalows had thick heat-resisting walls and fireplaces for winter use, there were good gardens and sports facilities. To Parnell it seemed close to paradise.

He had been promoted to corporal shortly after his arrival. He was unusually young to be given such a rank but he met with no resentment from the older men over whom he had been advanced, most of whom anyway disliked responsibility and were happy to remain as troopers. Almost at once he was sent out on training exercises, 'picqueting the hills', an operation in which a troop of cavalry would occupy the high ground on both sides of a pass before the main body ventured into it. The temperature by day was perfect but by night it grew very cold and in the hours before dawn, when it was below freezing, the horses had to be led around to keep them warm.

Then in December the whole regiment moved out on a march through tribal territory, showing the flag in areas where it was felt unruly elements needed to be reminded of British might. When they were in the depths of the wildest country they received a warning that raiding parties in search of arms were in the neighbourhood. Sentries were doubled and every man slept with his rifle chained to his wrist. At night the Pathan soldiers who served with the Lancers gave a display of tribal dancing accompanied by local bagpipes. (It was a striking feature of life on the North-West Frontier that Pathans recruited by the British Army served with total loyalty during their period with the Colours but reverted instantly to marauding enemy when they were discharged and returned to their villages.) For an impressionable twenty-year-old on his first tour abroad, the atmosphere must have been almost indecently romantic.

In 1939 some of the romance wore off. As war in Europe became more inevitable the War Office decided that cavalry regiments, which would have been out-dated even in 1914, could no longer be left unreformed. Mechanisation became the vogue and in April it was the turn of the 16th/5th. There was as yet no question of sacrificing the horses altogether but officers and non-commissioned officers were sent on courses to prepare them for the change. Parnell was packed off to a Tank Corps regiment in the vicinity to learn about armoured cars and tanks and to practise his driving; he found the work interesting, accepted that the change must come, but dreaded the day when he would part from his beloved horses.

At the end of August 1939, he set out with the Regiment on what would turn out to be their last exercise as a traditional cavalry unit. They were on their way to the Khyber Pass when they stopped to feed and water the horses. A despatch rider on a motorcycle was seen hastening up the track behind them. 'What does he want?' speculated the Troop Officer nervously. He soon found out: war had been declared, the Regiment was to return at once to camp. By the time they had got there the camp had been struck and they moved on by train to Peshawar. They crossed the River Jhelum one hundred years to the day since the 16th Lancers had forded it at almost exactly the same spot on their return from the First Afghan War. On that occasion an officer and ten other ranks had been drowned; this time they fared better. At the barracks at Peshawar they packed up for the last time and handed over their horses to the Indian Army. 'It was very, very painful,' Parnell remembers; perhaps the saddest day of his life so far.

In spite of his sorrow, it was exciting to be on the move and to be destined to take part in what – provided German resistance had not collapsed before his regiment could join the battle – promised to be a war in which glory could be won. Parnell had enjoyed his time in India but he was more than ready to leave it. He was young and vigorous. He had expended his energy in hard work and violent sports – riding, swimming, boxing. These had given him much pleasure, but he would have been exceptional if he had not from time to time hankered for rather more. Any sort of homosexual relationship would have been completely contrary to his instincts and his concept of what was right and wrong. The only European girls around were the daughters of officers and warrant officers, who were pursued by innumerable admirers and elaborately protected. Brothels were strictly out of bounds and not to Parnell's taste: 'It wasn't my scene. I was always too frightened.' He had one near romance. On Thursday afternoons he was charged with taking the Squadron Leader's wife for rides in the countryside around Risalpur. She was young, attractive and bored; he was strikingly good-looking. 'I got pretty close to her,' he admits. 'A situation like that could have led to an affair.' She made it plain that she was there for the taking but he held back, partly out of loyalty to his superior officer, partly out of fear of the possible consequences – again 'I was always too frightened.'

On 9 December 1939, the 16th/5th Lancers embarked at Karachi for the United Kingdom. They stopped in Egypt for Christmas and some of them were detached to reinforce the existing garrison, but Parnell was among those who went back to England. He spent almost a year there, witnessed from a distance the fall of France and the evacuation from Dunkirk, and trained in armoured cars and tanks. He tried to re-establish contact with the various members of his family but travel was difficult in wartime and his siblings were widely scattered; in the event he saw little of them. He stayed with his regiment in Britain until it seemed that the danger of invasion was over and then set off back to Egypt, travelling by way of New York and the Cape of Good Hope – a route which made the celebrated journey to Birmingham by way of Beachy Head seem a short cut in comparison.

It was the first voyage of the *Queen Mary* as a troopship, she had been painted grey but the rest of the conversion had been left until she reached Australia. All the civilian stewards were still on board, food was of almost peacetime quality, the sheets on the bunks were changed each day: for Parnell it was a glimpse into another world. The expedition to New York was to pick up a group of American engineers; no shore leave was granted while the liner was there and it was intended that she should spend only forty-eight hours in port. However, some republican or souvenir-hunter managed to filch the Royal Standard that was displayed in a showcase on the boat deck. The Captain refused to sail until the flag was returned; then an American soldier was observed leaving the liner in handcuffs and the Royal Standard was restored to its proper home. The journey was resumed. In spite of this incident there was no ill-feeling between the British and American contingents, merely the mild curiosity to be expected of two groups of men who knew virtually nothing about each other.

The *Queen Mary* deposited Parnell at Suez. He had hoped that he would rejoin his old regiment but instead was told that the 10th Royal Hussars were urgently in need of reinforcements and that it was to them that he had been assigned. It was his final transfer, he remained with the Hussars until he left the Army.

He was now promoted to troop sergeant, commander of a tank with a crew of five, and fought with the regiment in the hectic campaigns that led up to El Alamein, shuttling 'to and fro across the desert like a yo-yo' as the balance of power shifted first one way, then the other. For most of the time that he was there, the British had the worst of it and the 10th Hussars suffered heavy losses in men and equipment. Parnell believes that neither the courage of the men nor the skills of the officers were to blame; it was the superiority of the German guns and tanks that time after time put the British at a hopeless disadvantage. He himself lost tanks in several engagements but survived this period of the campaign without a scratch. Some might have congratulated themselves on this good luck and wondered how soon it would run out. Parnell gave hardly a thought to the matter. The idea of being killed or injured, he says, never crossed his mind: 'One just gets on with the job.' Sometimes he was sorrowful, sometimes happy: 'You lost comrades, then you got depressed, but you never thought it was going to be you, somehow. I was frightened, there was no doubt about it,' but he had confidence in his officers and enjoyed remarkable tranquillity of mind.

Until just before Alamein the Commanding Officer was Roscoe Harvey; he was 'absolutely wonderful,' Parnell remembers, 'mad as a hatter'. In battle he would habitually sit on top of his tank and direct the battle from this exposed position. Once his tanks were short of ammunition and signals were flooding in demanding fresh supplies. 'Get in with your fucking jackknives,' responded Harvey. His junior officers worshipped him and imitated his insouciant approach to danger. Out of action, they would set up their mess and dine as graciously as if amidst the regimental silver in England, but they always first made sure that the men were fed. 'They were a different breed,' says Parnell admiringly; the comradeship between officers and men, based originally on their mutual love of and respect for horses, was close and profound.

Increasingly, during the Second World War men were being commissioned as officers from the ranks but no one ever suggested this as a possibility for Parnell. 'It was difficult in those days in the cavalry, very difficult.' He felt no resentment at the fact that in other, as he saw it, inferior arms of the service – the Royal Artillery, for instance, or some of the line infantry regiments – men with no greater ability than he possessed, perhaps with less, were made officers; he was content with things as they were. It was not till the late 1950s that the cavalry adopted the practice of sometimes making the Regimental Sergeant-Major a quarter-master-captain, and by that time it was too late for Parnell: 'I think I could have made it,' he reflects, but with barely a trace of regret.

Parnell's loyalty was to his squadron and its commander, more remotely to Colonel Harvey and the Regiment. This was the peak of his military pyramid. He knew the names of Wavell and Auchinleck, would probably have recognised them if they had suddenly appeared before him, but they were infinitely distant figures who had nothing to do with him personally. Winston Churchill, indeed, seemed as close as they did; a heroic figure in whose hands the soldiers felt secure, even though they cursed him when he weakened the forces in North Africa in an ill-fated effort to help the Greeks: 'What the hell's he playing at?' they asked. The first senior commander who impinged on Parnell as an individual was Montgomery. Like most of the men of the Eighth Army he felt that Monty was an exhibitionist, with his two cap badges, his martinet behaviour, his determination to seize every moment of the limelight, but he also saw his qualities: 'He made you feel better, he made you think things were going to be done.'

In retrospect Parnell feels curiously nostalgic about those distant, torrid days. 'In a way I enjoyed the desert. I used to like to sit in the evening when it was all quiet and look at the stars; the desert had a fascination for me.' There was sand in everything, there were flies, there was searing heat, there was a constant lack of water; but there was also tranquillity, the huge moon, 'the stars above you that you almost felt you could touch'. There was a comradeship in the desert that he never experienced so intensely anywhere else: 'Everybody had to look after each other, everybody relied on each other, it was a complete team.' Even the enemy seemed to be bound into this strange unity; in those early days, before the infiltration of the SS into almost every echelon of the German Army, it was a hard but chivalrous war. The fact that the battlefield was barren waste without a civilian or a house in sight made it easier to maintain certain standards. If Parnell disabled a

German tank and saw its crew running away he would not fire on them; if they were near enough he would take them prisoner, if not he would let them go. They did as much for him. For a long time he never told himself that he had killed a *person*, only that he had knocked out an enemy tank or gun position.

In the months before Alamein reinforcements poured in and the troops trained for what they knew would be a great and, they hoped, decisive battle. 'We got this sense of elation,' says Parnell. 'You could see the Army around you building up, you could feel that something was happening.' About two weeks before the battle, any last doubts were dispelled: security was tightened, tracks left in the sand had to be carefully obscured, sometimes even the sacred rite of brewing up a cup of tea was prohibited on the grounds that the smoke might betray the presence of reinforcements. With twelve hours to go the troops moved into their forward positions. At dusk the Sergeant-Major came round collecting cap badges and any personal papers so that, if they were captured or their bodies fell into German hands, there would be no clues given as to which units were taking part. They were advised to get some sleep, since they were unlikely to have many opportunities in the next few days. Parnell settled down beside his tank but he had hardly dozed off before, at 10 p.m., the barrage began and any thought of sleep was banished. 'I never dreamed anything could be so intense; it was shattering even to be behind it.' None of those present had ever heard a noise more devastating.

At first light, with the barrage at its height, the 10th Hussars moved forward through the line of guns, through the British minefields, where tracks had been cleared and taped by the engineers and Military Policemen waved them through as if directing traffic round Piccadilly Circus, on to the area between the two front lines where they spread out in order of attack. Then, suddenly, the guns stopped and everything went very still: 'That's when you get frightened. I must say I said a few prayers.' He was about to participate in some of the most sustained and bloody fighting which British troops engaged in during the Second World War.

For forty-eight hours they were continually in action, often tied down by enemy fire for hours at a time, sometimes manoeuvring to the left or right, but on the whole fighting their way remorselessly forward. It seemed there could be no escape from their metal carapace. Parnell saw rather more of the outside world than the rest of his crew, but even for him most of the battle was passed in semi-darkness and intolerably stuffy heat. At last the Squadron Leader took advantage of a brief lull to allow the men to leave their tanks and make a cup of tea. It had just brewed up when the Germans reopened fire. The men scrambled to get back aboard the tank. Parnell's driver, Ernie Hopton, picked up his mug and walked round the side of the tank. As he did so, a piece of shrapnel removed the mug from his hand and took two of his fingers with it. He looked incredulously at what had happened and exclaimed: 'First bloody cup of char in two days and the bastards take it off me!'

By the third day the 10th Hussars were still battering at the two key ridges, heavily fortified by the Germans, which were blocking the regiment's advance. They had suffered severely: six Sherman tanks had been destroyed and many more seriously damaged, one officer and five other ranks had been killed, six officers and nineteen other ranks wounded severely enough to put them out of action. One of the nineteen was Sergeant Parnell. He had his head out of the top of his tank, observing what was going on, when a shell hit the armour plating a few feet ahead of him. A foot higher up the superstructure and it would undoubtedly have killed him; as it was he got the blast full in his face, had his throat lacerated by shreds of shrapnel and was completely blinded.

For two days, except when heavily sedated, he felt as if his face was being consumed by fire. The driver of his tank had been killed, the others escaped and did what they could to succour him. He could see nothing and was convinced that he had lost his sight for ever. In hospital back in the Canal Zone the surgeon examined him thoroughly and told him that no serious harm had been done; he would have to take care not to expose his eyes to the sun for some time but in the long run his vision would be as good as ever. Parnell believed him, but when the bandages came off and he found that he really could see again, his relief was immeasurable. His first reaction, however, was to laugh. During the days of darkness he had been struck by the fact that the surgeon spoke with the fruity mellifluousness of the actor, Alistair Sim; when his vision was restored he was delighted to find that the surgeon looked just like Alistair Sim as well.

His injury provoked one of his few crises of faith. Though his parents had never made much of formal observances of Christianity, their faith was unquestioning, and they had passed their conviction on to their children. In the train travelling to hospital Parnell prayed that his sight would be restored to him but he also asked himself: 'Why has this happened to *me*? What have *I* done to deserve it?' With his sight his faith also returned. That first evening, when he could see the canal, the sand, the water, 'the moon so huge that you could touch it', he said to himself with total confidence: 'There must be something there.' He was fortified in his belief by his memories of a clever boy from the East End of London in his Squadron, whose name was Ledger. Ledger was a vociferous atheist who took pleasure in tying in metaphysical knots the well-intentioned but not particularly intellectual padre. On the second night of the Battle of Alamein he was hit by a piece of shrapnel and fell fatally injured to the ground. He asked for his mother, said the Lord's Prayer aloud and died.

It was five weeks before Parnell left hospital and was allowed to rejoin his regiment, and even then he was forbidden to venture forth without specially prepared sunglasses with leather sides. He wore these cumbersome objects for the next two years. The regiment, when he finally caught up with it, had advanced some way across North Africa, and though the rains were slowing progress, the opposition, by the standards of Alamein at least, were being forced back without too much difficulty. By the end of 1942 they reached Timini, a patch of desert south-east of Derna, where they remained inactive for several months in one of those abrupt transitions from hectic activity to tedious immobility which is a feature of wartime life for the soldier. Towards the end of February the regiment was ordered to rejoin the Eighth Army around Tripoli. For three days and nights, almost without pause, they sped along the coast, arriving in time to help repel a fierce German attack. Then the advance continued towards the enemy redoubt along the Mareth Line. At El Alamein the 10th Hussars had been in the thick of it; at Mareth they were in reserve.

Soon they were detached with the rest of the 1st Armoured Division to join General Freyberg's New Zealand Division in an outflanking movement to the south. The route was believed by the Germans to be impassable to vehicles, and anyone less resolute than Freyberg might have shared their view. Pockets of deep sand alternated with savage rocks that threatened to tear the tracks off the armoured vehicles; almost continuous sandstorms reduced visibility to a few feet and made conditions in the tank even more hideously uncomfortable than was usual. It seemed to the men inside that they would never emerge from the Gabes Gap, but somehow they kept going. Within a few days they were attacking the startled enemy at the oasis of El Hamma.

In the closing stages of the African campaign a German colonel called Pieters ordered his men to fall back but himself elected to remain with those who were too badly injured to be moved. A British Sherman tank lumbered up and lowered its gun, as if about to fire. 'The bastard's going to kill me,' thought Pieters. Then out jumped Tom Parnell, who took the officer's number, accepted his surrender, looked after the wounded and, for five days, 'treated us as gentlemen'. The German retained a fragment of an old map on which Parnell had written his name but on which the details about his regiment had been obliterated.

For forty years he asked every Englishman he met whether he knew this elusive sergeant. In the end a major from the Manchester Regiment, who each year led a delegation to an Afrika Korps reunion, offered to help track him down. By good luck the secretary of his local golf club had once been an officer in the 10th Hussars and recognised the name. Parnell was traced and invited to come with the delegation the following year to Darmstadt. Parnell took up the offer, met Colonel Pieters and was greeted as a long-lost friend; he cut the 10th Hussar badge from his blazer and gave it to Pieters with his regimental tie. The following year, when the reunion was at Stuttgart, there was a ceremony at Rommel's grave; Parnell would never have believed in 1942 that so complete a reconciliation would be possible. At Stuttgart he met an Afrika Korps man who had fought at Alamein and had commanded 88mm guns on the ridge in front of Parnell's unit. 'You're probably the bastard who shot me up!' exclaimed Parnell with feeling; he probably was, but the thought did not mar their evening and the two kept in contact. He was present at the Founder's Day Parade described in the Prologue to this book.

Now the end in North Africa was almost in sight. For the final push the Regiment painted its tanks green, to conform with the practice of the First Army, and joined in the pincer movement that was crushing the Germans in Tunisia. After the final surrender they reverted once more to being part of the Eighth Army. With a startling lack of consideration the authorities settled the regiment in Azizia, an unprepossessing spot on the fringe of the desert south of Tripoli where the hottest temperature on earth had been recorded a few years before. There they roasted discontentedly until Montgomery chanced upon them towards the end of June, berated those responsible for their folly and insisted that they be moved immediately to a more temperate station on the coast.

Back at Algiers they began to train for the Sicilian campaign, but the Canadians protested that they had been starved of action so the 1st Armoured Division was left in idleness while Sicily was overrun and the Italian mainland invaded. Such periods of respite were welcome but they could also be damaging to morale. When there was time to take stock the men began to feel how far they still were from home and how much they were out of touch with all that was going on there. It was worse for those with wives and children but Parnell found himself missing his family and childhood friends and wishing that he was once more in Britain. As it happened, his brother Harold was also in North Africa and at one point they must have been within a few miles of each other but they never corresponded and had no idea that they had come so close. Their only point of contact was through their mother in Bolton; they both wrote to her with reasonable regularity and she wrote to them, but since they were neither of them allowed to reveal their whereabouts she was unable to do more than pass on the most generalised picture of their activities. 'There never seemed much to say,' is Parnell's answer, when asked why he did not try to establish more direct contact with his sibling.

Rome had fallen and the Germans had fallen back to the Gothic Line across the Etruscan Appennines before the 10th Hussars came back into battle. At the end of August 1944, 35 officers, 600 other ranks and 63 tanks assembled at Senigallia, due east of Urbino, to join in the battle. In support of the King's Royal Rifle Corps they led the attack across the River Conca. The operation was a shambles: 'Based as it had been on faulty information,' commented the regimental history dryly, 'with insufficient time for preparation, over ground unsuitable for tanks . . . and from a start line which had not in fact been secured, it could scarcely have ended in any other way.' The two leading squadrons came under heavy artillery and mortar fire, the Commanding Officer was injured and three sergeants with him. One of them was Tom Parnell. The Troop Corporal in the tank immediately behind him had warned him by wireless that his tow rope was hanging out and risked becoming entangled in the tracks. Parnell climbed out to secure it and a shell landed nearby. He 'flew through the air like a rag doll' and woke up in hospital. Once again his eyesight had been affected but no other serious damage had been done. This time he managed to discharge himself after little more than a week and was back with the regiment before it settled down in winter quarters on the line of the Naviglio Canal. There were still several months of hard fighting before the ceasefire in Italy, when Kesselring surrendered to Alexander at Caserta, but Parnell survived unscathed.

The war in North Africa had been toughly fought, had involved privations and much discomfort, had given Parnell many moments of distress and fear, but it had also been exhilarating and mercifully uncomplicated in the sense that one side had faced the other with nobody in between. Italy, where a civilian population was intimately involved, was more depressing. The sight of women and children being killed or chased from their homes outraged Parnell's sense of propriety. His reactions would have been much the same wherever he had been but were made more acute in Italy by the fact that he felt considerable affection for the inhabitants and found it hard to remember that they had recently been numbered among the enemy. Even when the Italians had been at war he had felt that they did not have their heart in the fight and were not to be taken too seriously. This feeling had been reinforced when the regiment had retained some of the Italian prisoners taken in battle in North Africa to serve as mess orderlies and miscellaneous entertainers. They had quickly become part of the family. When the Hussars landed in Italy they told these camp followers that they were free to go. The Italians made it clear that this was the last thing they wanted; if they went home they would have to fend for themselves and, worse still, would risk being called back into the Italian Army and might even find themselves under German command. Far better, they thought, the devil they knew and could get on with. A dozen or so of them stayed with the regiment until the end of the war. Left to themselves they might well have continued the association even longer and accompanied their new friends to Austria and eventually back to Britain, but the Commanding Officer regretfully concluded that enough was enough and they must be left behind at the frontier.

At the end of the war the regiment found itself near Trieste at Sagrado, holding a line between the Italians and a belligerent Yugoslavia which felt that the area should rightfully belong to it. Parnell was well briefed on the issues involved – the Army by 1945 was rather more conscious of the need to keep the men informed of what was going on than had earlier been the case – but found it no easier to decide where his sympathies should lie. He knew and liked the Italians, yet the Yugoslavs had been Britain's allies and the victims of Italian aggression. His job was to police the demarcation line and to discourage the Yugoslavs from taking by force what they felt to be their just entitlement. Tom Parnell would never have supposed that his private views about the rights and wrongs of this issue should in the least affect the way he carried out this duty. His most earnest hope was that he would never have to turn his gun on one side or the other. His prayer was answered, but once or twice it was a close-run thing.

The relationship with the Yugoslavs was an odd one, friendly on the surface but with a marked undercurrent of resentment and hostility. The British troops occupied one half of what had been a prison; the Yugoslavs, women as well as men, were in the other half. Certain facilities were common to both, a British trooper might well find himself squatting on a toilet a foot away from a Yugoslav woman with her feet wrapped in rags and an ammunition belt – mercifully empty – around her waist. Outside the prison was a river; each morning the British would mount a machine-gun on the western bank to discourage intruders. The two groups would play football together, but the threat of the machine-gun was a real one. At one point relations were so strained that the Hussars drove tanks into certain strategic positions and the Yugoslavs dug slit trenches alongside them. Only once was there violence, however. The Yugoslavs used from time to time to hold a dance in the village square in the course of which the political commissar would make a speech, always ending with a cry of what, to the British troops, sounded like 'Viva La Tito!' Once a drunken British soldier followed this with a stentorian shout of 'Bon appetito!' The Yugoslavs did not take kindly to what they saw as an affront to their national hero, and the fight that broke out took some quelling.

In October 1945 the regiment moved on from the powder keg of Trieste to a more peaceful posting at Graz in Austria. Here Parnell experienced one of his proudest hours as a cavalry man. The famed Lippizaner horses from the Spanish Riding School in Vienna had been secreted in caves near Graz to protect them from the Russians. To Parnell fell the privilege of conducting six of them back to their home, a task which both gave him enormous pleasure and won him many friends among the local inhabitants. The Austrians, anyway, were anxious to be as hospitable as they were allowed to be and greeted the British troops as liberators rather than conquerors. Unlike in Germany, the British were allowed to fraternise and did so with enthusiasm; one of their main activities, Operation Woodpecker, consisted of cutting down trees to provide fuel for the local population.

Between Trieste and Graz Parnell had been on leave to the United Kingdom. He refused 'Python', which in the arcane terminology beloved by the military mind would have meant that he signed off and went into civilian life, but instead opted for 'LILOP' – 'Leave in Lieu of Python'. He did in fact play with the idea of leaving the Army and joining the Mounted Police but was discouraged by an uncle who was himself a mounted policeman and said that the service was dwindling by the year, if not in terminal decline. With this possibility dismissed, he put the idea of retirement out of his head; he would have liked to work with horses but regimental life suited him admirably and he could think of no other career which would give him the camaraderie, the stimulation and the fulfilment which he had found in the Hussars.

In fact, though he was unaware of it, he had already taken the first tentative steps down a path that was to lead him away from his military career. When very young he had wanted to marry his first cousin but had been dissuaded by his parents, who thought the relationship too close. Since then he had had nothing approaching a serious love affair. Now, while on leave in Bournemouth, he met another holiday-maker, Pearl Lee Robinson. Pearl was a strikingly attractive blonde, the daughter of a farmer from near Ely. She was much younger than Parnell; had never done any work except to help out from time to time on the family farm, was lively, energetic and determined to enjoy herself. Parnell found her alluring but had reservations; she knew nothing about the Army and he was not sure that she would fit in well with the pattern of regimental life. He was about to go abroad again and told himself that it would be unfair to a young girl to marry her and then promptly disappear overseas. Secretly, he had some doubts whether he was ready to restrict his own liberty in such a way. He was in love, he enjoyed being in love, but he was not so much in love as to put himself very far out to attain his ends. The relationship was put on hold – for the time being at any rate.

The 10th Hussars moved from spot to spot in Germany, in the spring of 1947 ending up in Lübeck, the northern port on the borders of the Russian zone. Theoretically the Russians were his allies, the Germans his vanquished foe, but like most British soldiers in the area Parnell found that he had much more sympathy with his former enemy than his former friend. He was billeted near Lübeck with a family called Müller and became attached to them. When he next went to England he visited his girlfriend at her Cambridgeshire home. A German prisoner-of-war was still working on the farm, awaiting repatriation. Parnell mentioned to him that he was based in Germany, near Lübeck. The prisoner-of-war said that he came from that part of Germany himself. How interesting, Parnell went on; he was billeted with a family called Müller at such-and-such a village. 'My parents!' said the German. So Parnell returned to Lübeck bearing messages and photographs as well as the customary coffee and cigarettes. He found no difficulty in making friends with the Germans with whom he came in contact. Most British soldiers had found that the rules about non-fraternisation made little sense once the immediate bitterness of war was over; by 1947 a man as good-natured and easygoing as Tom Parnell was likely to make himself very much at home if the family on which he was billeted showed any disposition to be welcoming.

By now he had convinced himself – and had found little difficulty in convincing his wife to be – that marriage was the proper step to take. What finally made up his mind was the fact, by 1950, that only four members of the Sergeants' Mess were still bachelors. 'I must be missing something,' he concluded. He saw marriage as a desirable step in his military career; his Commanding Officer, Colonel Archer-Shee, liked his senior warrant officers to be married since he felt it lent stability to the regiment. Parnell would not have married just to please the Colonel, but the fact that the Colonel would be pleased if he married was certainly a factor to be taken into account. They married in 1951, to the surprise of his parents, who had regretfully decided that he was not the marrying kind.

Parnell soon found, however, that as a career move his marriage proved less than a total success. Pearl quickly decided that the traditions and shibboleths of military life were unappealing. She was unused to any kind of hierarchy and to her the significance attached to rank, particularly as regards the gulf between commissioned officers and the rest, was irrational and somewhat galling. 'Our officers' wives were very good,' Parnell considers, but this did not stop his wife finding them patronising and supercilious. She did not demand that her husband should leave the Army, indeed she did her best to come to terms with his regimental life, but her discontent was palpable.

They came back to England in August 1953 and after a brief stay at Tidworth on Salisbury Plain Parnell was detached to do a tour with the Wiltshire Yeomanry at Devizes. The Yeomanry regiment was affiliated to the 10th Hussars, so Parnell had known he was likely at some time to be appointed to them as an instructor, but the timing seemed to him particularly unfortunate because while he was there the regiment was despatched to Jordan. This was a part of the world he had never visited and his wanderlust was so far unsatisfied that he bitterly regretted missing the chance to go there. Apart from that, however, he found his work with the Yeomanry congenial enough. He was by now a sergeant-major, the accommodation was comfortable, training the volunteers in the use of tanks, for which he was responsible, was interesting without being too onerous. His son, Nigel, was born in Devizes in 1955 and in the same year he told his Colonel that he would like to sign on for another five years. Regretfully the Colonel replied that this was not on the cards: it was a time for cutbacks and the most that could be offered was an extension of a year with the probability but not the promise of another extension after that. In fact Parnell, who was valued highly by the regiment, secured two further extensions of a year each and could have made it four in all if he had wanted it. By that time, however, he was back at Tidworth, a town that he disliked; there seemed little chance that he would serve overseas again; his wife was far from reconciled to military life. He was now nearly forty years old; sooner or later he would have to look for a job outside the Army that would see him through to retirement. In the circumstances it seemed that sooner would be better than later; on 29 October 1958, he left the Army.

Civilian life was a disillusioning experience. He was taken on by Shell and after a period of training was put in charge of a centre at

Evesham, teaching people how to run filling stations, lubrication bays and other such facilities. He enjoyed the work, getting to know people was always a pleasure for him and he made many friends among his pupils. The job, however, involved visits to stations in the south of England and he was horrified by what he found there: 'I almost lost my faith in human nature when I saw how much fiddling went on.' He hankered after what he remembered as the straightforwardness and probity of Army life. There was no going back to the 10th Hussars but he wondered whether he might not take on a military career in some other form. He saw an advertisement in *Soldier* magazine for warrant officers to go to Zambia and on an impulse put his name down. The next thing he heard of his application was when he met a young officer at a regimental dinner, who said: 'I believe you are joining me in Zambia in September. I'll be your squadron leader.' Left to himself he would have taken up the offer but his wife made it clear that she disliked the prospect, and Shell, rather than lose him, offered better pay and improved terms of service. With some regrets he abandoned Zambia – the subsequent history of the region has left him thankful that this was his decision.

A year or two later, this time with his wife's cautious blessing, he looked into the possibility of joining the Canadian Mounted Police. He went so far as to have an interview in the Canadian High Commission in London and seemed to have reasonable prospects of getting a job, then once again decided to stick by Shell and England. Shell, as it turned out, did not stick by him, or rather, when Shellmex split with British Petroleum, he felt some uncertainty about his prospects and moved to Elf Petroleum. They sent him north, by now doing an accountant's work, and he was transferred to Doncaster where he stayed until retirement.

When their son was twelve years old, Parnell and his wife went for a skiing holiday to Switzerland. After a few days she complained of pins and needles in her right arm. By the time they got back to England she was experiencing the same sensation in her left leg as well. The doctor was baffled but sent Pearl to hospital in Sheffield for tests. The surgeon diagnosed a brain tumour, but after a cursory examination said that he did not think it would be difficult to remove. The following day, on reaching the hospital, Parnell was asked to call on the surgeon before going in to see his wife. The tumour, he was now told, was inoperable; it was too big and too close to the brain. His wife could not expect to live for more than a few months. By the time their son reached the hospital she was already in a coma. Nigel was horrified by the sudden transformation of his lively and youthful mother into a bald and wizened crone who could only babble incoherently, and shrank from going to see her. Parnell, for his part, spent every evening by her bedside. He was not there, however, the afternoon her Uncle Arthur visited her. She did not know her uncle particularly well and he had been told that there was no chance she would recognise him. To his surprise, however, she emerged from the mists of semi-consciousness and greeted him by name. A few minutes later she was dead.

Nigel Parnell had learned to expect no show of emotion from his father. Only once did he see his reserve crack, and that was when he witnessed a bad road accident in which people were trapped in a burning car. The incident vividly recalled the deaths of friends during the war and he had to take two days off work to recover from the shock. While his wife was dying he had seemed numbed and incapable of expression. He made no attempt to talk to Nigel about anything except the most routine matters and when Pearl died he asked a friend to break the news to the boy. Tom Parnell for his part says that he was disconcerted by his son's failure to show any emotion; only years later when Nigel himself was about to get married and was telling his future mother-in-law about his mother's death did he break down in tears. The failure of father and son to communicate or to share their grief was characteristic of their race, their sex and their generation, but Parnell's military background can only have reinforced his natural reticence. For six weeks, anyway, he had no opportunity to gauge his son's reactions; he despatched him to stay with his aunt and himself retreated into stunned seclusion. When Nigel did come home his father sent him to boarding school, the Gordon Boys' School for military children. It cost him £700 a year, which he could ill afford but he saw no alternative. His work involved much travel and even if he could have coped emotionally he would have found that his duties stopped him giving his son the attention that he knew was needed.

The Parnells had been planning to move to York or Harrogate but now any such ideas were put aside. For six months or so Parnell did no more than survive. He performed his job competently, he went through the motions of living, but nothing seemed to matter. One day he was in the lavatory at his office and heard a colleague ask the managing director what he was going 'to do about Tom?' 'I'm going to give him that much work he won't know whether he's coming or going,' was the reply. 'It doesn't matter how well he does it, but he must be kept at it.' Little by little the therapy worked. For Parnell, the seeping back of life into his paralysed emotions was almost as painful as anything that had gone before – 'it was shattering, absolutely' – but he began to take an interest in his work, to follow the doings of his son.

There were times when that son thought he could have done with rather less attention. Parnell was a thoughtful and conscientious father but he had high standards and found it difficult ever to say 'Well done!' Nigel was a successful pupil, but if he came second his father would say: 'Pity it wasn't first.' Parnell was emphatic about the need for tidiness and punctuality, to this day his son feels uneasy if the backs of his shoes are not polished as thoroughly as the toes. But in spite of a disciplinarian streak he was strikingly tolerant of views that were not his own. He himself had always voted Tory, his wife was a Labour supporter, debate was constant, sometimes heated but never acrimonious. He urged Nigel always to be true to himself and make up his own mind, not to go with the tide. If his son had announced himself Communist he would have been distressed and tried to argue him out of it, but he would not have seen it as a reason for quarrelling. He accepted the vagaries of teenage fashion with resignation if little enthusiasm; almost the only time Nigel can remember any strong protest was when he bought and proudly wore a pair of blue and silver platform shoes. 'Makes you look like a tart! Bloody stupid!' snorted his father, but he did not try to ban their use.

If things about him were going wrong, however, he saw it as his duty to put them right. It was not only in his own house that he sought to impose good order and decorous behaviour. Nigel remembers once being taken by him to a football match. A group of boys were being particularly foul-mouthed and obstreperous. To his son's alarm, Parnell told them to shut up and mind their manners. Amazingly, they subsided. The authority of a former sergeant-major could evidently still make itself apparent – and, anyway, Parnell was a formidably large and stalwart figure.

When his wife died Parnell was only middle-aged and still fine looking. For several months he carried on as if still a married man, every night he would place his slippers exactly where it had been her habit to put them. Gradually the physical evidence of her existence was eliminated and he began to admit that there were other women in the world. From time to time he would bring one to the house. At one point his son thought that he was going to marry the widow of an old friend. Nigel at first was disturbed at the thought that anyone should take his mother's place, but later decided that his father's happiness was more important and taught himself to welcome the idea of remarriage. Finally he asked whether his father planned to do so. 'I'll never find anyone like your mother,' said Parnell, and he never did.

Nigel remained a boarder, though each time that he left home to go back to school it was clear that his father found the parting painful. Though he made his own strong faith very evident Parnell made no effort to coerce or cajole his son down the religious path.

He put off Nigel's christening until he was twelve years old so that he could decide for himself whether or not he wished to join the Church of England. Similarly, he would have liked his son to become a soldier but never brought any pressure on him to do so. When Nigel at last made it clear that his father's dream of having a son who would pass out at Sandhurst was never to become reality, Parnell was disappointed but merely remarked that his wife had never liked the Army either.

Parnell retired from Elf Petroleum at the age of sixty-five and for three years lived more or less contentedly in Doncaster. He loved his garden, got on well with his neighbours, found no problems in keeping himself active and usefully occupied. Nigel married and bought a house in the street where his father lived. Since he was often away from home, he handed over to his father the management of the garden. To his mild dismay Parnell ripped out all the sprawling shrubs which Nigel had liked and substituted ranks of marigolds and wallflowers, standing stiffly to attention as in a well-ordered municipal garden. Old age did not make Tom Parnell any more tolerant of sloppiness or untidiness; he deplored the way his grandchildren left their toys lying around the house or garden, though they did not find him in the least intimidating and paid little attention to his strictures. Occasionally Nigel would ask his father to tidy up the garage or workshop, tasks which kept him contentedly occupied for hours.

Even while his wife had been alive Parnell had occasionally wondered whether he might not finish his days in the Royal Hospital. After her death and his retirement the idea was always at the back of his mind; he used occasionally to visit his old Sergeant-Major, who was now a Pensioner, so he knew well what was involved. There always seemed to be good reasons, though, for deferring a decision. Then several of his friends in Doncaster had strokes and were to some degree incapacitated. Who would look after *him* if he were ever to be in such a plight, he wondered? His son insisted that, of course, *he* would, but Parnell had no intention of being a burden on anyone and knew that Nigel's work and family commitments already made more than enough demands on his time. Early in 1986, at the age of sixty-eight, he announced that he planned to move to Chelsea. His son remonstrated with him but was secretly relieved that he would never again have to worry whether his father was being properly looked after. Nigel's only stipulation was that Parnell should not sell his house for at least twelve months in case he found life at the Hospital did not suit him.

It seemed at one time as if this had been a wise proviso. Parnell at first found that the accommodation was cramped, that he missed his own house, that time hung heavy on his hands. After two weeks or so he telephoned his brother. 'I think I've burnt my bridges before I've crossed them,' he said. 'Would you like a lodger?' He probably knew that there was no danger his suggestion would be taken up; his sister-in-law was arthritic and his brother fully occupied in caring for her. For several months, however, he did wonder whether he had made the right decision. Then gradually a new pattern of life imposed itself. 'I wasn't well-educated by any stretch of the imagination,' he says, 'but I educated myself through life.' He began to read a lot more: travel books, biographies, never novels. He taught himself wood-carving in the workshops. After he had been at Chelsea for a few months he began to be offered responsibilities within the Hospital and took them on with alacrity. Within a year, eighteen months at the most, he felt that he belonged: 'It was a new lease of life.'

The old urge to travel has not left him. He still rides whenever he gets the chance, though now he cannot use one leg fully and has to have recourse to a mounting-block. Several times he has visited a ranch in California where he goes for a seven-day trail on horseback, sleeping each night under the stars. Aged eighty-three he sees no need to renounce such pleasures and hopes soon to be back in California. He goes to Doncaster once a month or so to visit friends, his only sorrow is that the owner of his old home has cut down the two silver birches which he planted in the garden: 'Savages! Philistines!'

He is a contented man. 'I've enjoyed life to the full,' he says. 'I've met all sorts of nice people.' He intends to go on living life to the full and meeting nice people until his health finally fails him. The remarkable preservative qualities of the Royal Hospital make it seem likely that this time will be far distant.

DOUGLAS WRIGHT

Lance-Sergeant Wright, *c* 1941

Douglas Wright

Who is the happy Warrior? Who is he
That every man in arms should wish to be?

WORDSWORTH endowed his happy Warrior with an improbably long list of qualities, but if to earn the title it is enough to relish the actual business of fighting, then Dougie Wright comes close to it. There was nothing in his parentage to lead one to expect it. His father, John Arthur, had found the First World War a deeply disagreeable experience. According to his son, his principal task had been to collect bits and pieces of dead bodies and bury them; unsurprisingly, he spoke of this period of his life, if at all, with distaste. It left him deeply restless. He never had a regular job and was out of work for a large part of the time. When he was employed it was in such odd jobs as cleaning cars, selling tripe from a basket around the village, gardening, understudying as a pig auctioneer; whatever the work, he was as likely to spend the money he earned in a pub on the way home as to pass it on to his long-suffering wife.

With the man who should have been the breadwinner bringing in so little in the way of a settled income, the Wrights were almost always short of money. Their plight was not helped by the fact that there were nine children. The total had been increased pretty regularly every two years; more by habit than volition, Dougie believes: 'It was just the way of it in those days.' Their house in the Cheshire village of Poynton was damp and cockroach-ridden, a traditional two-up, two-down, with all the children except the latest baby crowded into one bedroom. It had water from the mains but only one cold tap, and the lavatory was a shed in the garden. It only cost 3/6d a week but even that modest rent was hard to find and their payments were frequently in arrears. The children had little in the way of clothing – just what they stood up in; Dougie never wore underwear before he went into the Army. On their feet they wore clogs or rough boots. They had no proper pram, only a box on wheels, and there was no electricity or gas in the house. A couple of paraffin lamps were the main source of light, the children were given a candle when they went to bed. Food was always short, the children lived largely on bread and potatoes. When their father had a boiled egg he would sometimes cut off the top and give it to one of the elder children. This was indeed a treat.

There were virtually no books about the house and the family did not take a newspaper and boasted no wireless; Dougie's uncle, who lived nearby, was the proud owner of a crystal set with earphones, the only one in the street. Dougie had one or two tattered cowboy stories and occasionally laid his hands on comics such as the *Wizard*, but even if he had had the inclination to read more there would have been little time or opportunity. The children were sent to Sunday School, but rather to get them out of the house than for any more serious purpose. Dougie's father had no time for religion; his mother might have been more enthusiastic but had no trace of energy left after keeping her family alive and functioning; as for Dougie himself, 'it never meant a lot to me'.

Some of the neighbours were as badly off but most of the men worked down the nearby coalmine and got a wage which, to the

Wrights, seemed princely. The mine and all the houses in the village belonged to the local grandee, Lord Vernon. Dougie cannot remember ever feeling that this was in any way unfair: 'We just took it as a fact of life.' His father felt that working down the mine would be altogether too arduous and declined even to consider it. Poynton also boasted a silk mill and a clothing factory; Dougie's mother, Annie, used to work part time in the second, making shirts and trousers and often bringing home scraps of material out of which she would conjure rough clothes for the children.

There was a reasonably good primary school in Poynton – needless to say called Lord Vernon's School to complement the village pub, the Vernon Arms. Dougie did not actively dislike it but he took little pleasure in his education. His chances of doing well at school were anyway not improved by the fact that he was left-handed but, as the culture of the times demanded, was dragooned into writing with his right. Even without this handicap, however, he would never have made an academic: he was ill-disciplined and his attention span was brief, he was quite good at arithmetic but felt no desire to study it above an elementary level; reading and writing left him cold. What he wanted above all was to be in the open air. The school had a large garden and Dougie much preferred to work in it when he would otherwise have been in class. The vegetables which he grew were sold to the benefit of school funds and the headmaster, with a realistic assessment of his pupil's potential, was happy to settle for this compromise. Even if Dougie had had the makings of a scholar his education would not have progressed much further; there was no convenient grammar school in the neighbourhood and in recorded history no boy or girl from Lord Vernon's School had ever won a scholarship into further education.

His main preoccupation was to spend as little time as possible at home. He was not unhappy but there was a tension in the air, a sense of oppression, which filled him with discomfort. His mother was under constant strain, the effort of keeping up her work in the factory and running a home for a large family on inadequate funds wore her down. 'I didn't realise till later in life that my mother was really badly treated,' Dougie Wright recalls. His father did not hit or even verbally abuse her but he neither considered her needs nor appreciated her labours. He would lurch home from the pub, having spent the money that she needed so desperately for the children, and then demand sex: 'My mother would be saying "no" and you could hear all that was going on.'

Dougie devised a multiplicity of activities, which brought in a little extra money to help his mother but also ensured that he did not have to witness too much of the strains of life at home. Every morning he would leave the house early so as to do a newspaper delivery to twenty or so farms in the neighbourhood; school over, or in the holidays, he would go back to one of those farms to milk cows or to help with the ploughing. Whenever he could contrive it he would be paid for such work in kind rather than cash. Once, when aged thirteen, he asked a farmer if he could have half a sack of potatoes for his family. 'No,' said the farmer, presumably with some malice, 'you can have a whole one, though.' He had thought there was no possibility that the tall but skinny Dougie could tote a hundredweight of potatoes a mile across the fields to his home, but the boy was lacking neither in strength nor in determination. Mrs Wright did not have to buy potatoes for several weeks. Dougie was fond of his siblings in a generalised way but felt no particular affection for any of them. With the brother nearest to him in age he fought continually. He was the bigger and stronger of the two, but his brother was tall for his age, and naturally combative – a future Royal Marine. 'I only had to touch him and his nose would bleed,' Dougie complains today; his mother saw only big brother brutally attacking little brother and came to the rescue of the latter.

Unlike his father, Dougie would not have been frightened by the hard work involved in going down the mine, but by the time he left school he was well over six feet tall, far from ideal for labours underground. Anyway, his heart was in the land. As soon as he could he began to work full time on one of the farms where he had helped out in the past, and gave half his earnings to his mother. His experience and physical strength made him a valuable recruit but he was headstrong and did not take instruction kindly. It was a violent society. The farmer, if he did not like what one of his hands was doing, would 'give him a good smacking'. Dougie observed, noted, and assumed that this was the proper way to register disapproval: 'I thought it was the right thing. I know in later life it's not, but at the time I think I must have.' He had not needed much encouragement to reach this conclusion. At school he had enjoyed the reputation of being one of the roughest of the boys. He was never a bully, he protests, but he was quick to take offence and relished a fight: 'I was rather wild as a youth. I'd strike out at people.' When he struck out at other schoolboys or farmhands little damage was done except sometimes to his opponent's features, but he was almost as likely to turn on his employer. He hit the farmer for whom he worked and soon worked for him no longer: 'I'd have a go at the boss – fisticuffs. I lost several jobs through this.' He moved on to another farm, then another; finally he got a job at a riding stable where he loved the horses so much that he managed not to quarrel with his employer for more than a year.

But pleasant though this was, he knew that it was not what he wanted to do with his life. He hankered after something more exciting, which would take him far from home and the landscape which he loved but knew too well. He played with the idea of becoming a policeman and took advice about the possibility. 'Go into the Army and smarten up for a few years,' he was told. 'Come out, and you'll make a good copper.' The idea seemed sensible; he had never thought of a military career before but it would be something new and likely to lead to travel. It was the time of the Munich Crisis and someone had told him there was bound to be a war; that sounded promising. If war did come, he would end up in the Army anyway, so it made sense to get a start on his contemporaries; if it didn't, he could easily return to civilian life. 'I've always been very changeable, liked change. I wouldn't stop at one thing very long.' With hardly a pause for reflection, still less any discussion with his father, he presented himself at the recruiting office at Stockport. The Sergeant in charge happened to be recruiting for the Guards. Dougie explained that he loved horses and had been considering the cavalry. He was too big, he was told, he would do better to settle for the infantry. There were openings in the Grenadier Guards. That sounded all right to Dougie, he signed on, told his family what he had done and was on his way. He left home with a minimum of fuss: 'We were never taught to kiss in my family; my mother did when we were babies, like, but in later life she never did.'

Guardsman Douglas Wright enlisted on 9 December 1938. He did his twenty-two weeks of basic training at Caterham. The first months of a new recruit to the Guards were always difficult and sometimes found by the victim to be intolerable. Physically Wright did not find them particularly arduous: he was stronger than the average recruit and well co-ordinated. The fact that he was naturally left-handed posed problems with the drill but he overcame them without too much struggle. He was already a good shot through the experience given him by the various farmers for whom he had worked, and though here too his left-handedness was a disadvantage he learnt to be ambidextrous; an attribute which was to serve him well at certain stages of his Army life. What was more difficult was to adjust from the dirt and squalor of his home to the clinical neatness and cleanliness of a Guards barracks. Folding up sheets and blankets in the required patterns, polishing equipment, shaving scrupulously, ensuring that both his body and his clothes were meticulously presented were concepts new to him and hard to comprehend, let alone to master. To compound his problems, he had joined three weeks later than most of his squad and so was always likely to be among the least proficient.

Each group of recruits was assigned a 'trained soldier', a man who was not a non-commissioned officer but who had enough experience to act as mentor to the new boys. Often such men allowed their little ration of authority to go to their head and made themselves disliked. Wright's 'trained soldier' seems to have been exceptionally obnoxious. Anyone whom he took against got 'scrubbed' – thrust into a bath and scoured with coarse brushes. Wright avoided this fate but made an enemy of the older man: 'He tried to duff me up one day in the washhouse.' Wright got his own back, though. He found the trained soldier looking out of the window, crept up behind and pulled down the sash violently so that his victim was trapped with his head outside and his body inside. 'I've got you now, you bugger!' said Wright exultantly. To add to his woes, he was perpetually hungry. The food proved to be little if at all better than it had been at home; for tea there would be twenty-four slices of bread for twelve men, with twelve lumps of margarine, twelve spoonfuls of jam, twelve lumps of cheese and a mug of tea. Sometimes he found himself wondering why he'd joined the Army.

But as he became used to the way things were done, life became easier. He soon found that he was as good as or better than most of the other recruits. By the time he was due to move on from Caterham to the King's Company of the 1st Battalion of the Grenadier Guards at Chelsea Barracks, he felt fully competent to join the Regiment; better still, at Caterham his squad had been the first to learn the newfangled art of drilling in threes, so that he found himself actually a jump ahead of the longer serving Guardsmen whom he was now joining.

Between Caterham and Chelsea he was given a weekend off. He much enjoyed his appearance at home, swaggering around in his red tunic with his cane under his arm. 'I was the king pin then.' His younger brother was vastly impressed and resolved to join the services as soon as possible. Wright's main problem was keeping his kit clean and together while he was with his family; the slovenliness which he had taken for granted a few months before now seemed alien and unpleasant, he had grown away from his background with disconcerting speed.

Certainly there was no room for slovenliness in the life that awaited him at Chelsea Barracks. The Guards in London were not merely in the public eye, they were a showpiece of imperial pageantry and military might in the heart of the Empire's capital. Life was a series of glamorous parades: mounting guard at St James's Palace, Buckingham Palace, the Bank of England, Trooping the Colour. The sergeants and sergeant-majors were fearsome beings, but provided a man was meticulous in his appearance and brisk in his drill there was no need for him to get into hot water. Wright enjoyed the parades and took some pleasure in flamboyantly saluting all those whom he encountered, even when it was patently unnecessary. At Buckingham Palace the ten-year-old Princess Margaret Rose delighted in walking up and down in front of the sentries, extracting a salute on each occasion; Wright was more than pleased to relieve the monotony of sentry duty by obliging.

But though strutting up and down in London had its amusing side, it was not what he had joined the Army to do. Given his temperament, it seems unlikely that he would have put up with it for long. Luckily for him he did not have to. The battalion was on manoeuvres at Tidworth in September 1939 when the news came through that Britain was at war. 'We all cheered' – war was, after all, the point of being a soldier. Within weeks they were on their way to France. They took it for granted that they would be pitched immediately into battle, that victory would be theirs in a few months. Instead the battalion moved forward to an area which Wright vaguely assumed to be near the borders of Belgium, hung about for three days living off biscuits and bully beef, then began to dig in. What they hoped to achieve by this exercise was not divulged – to those in the ranks at least: 'Nobody ever told you what was going on,' complains Wright. 'I found this very bad about the British Army.' In fact they were based in the village of Amappes, constructing the 'Gort Line', a belated extension of the Maginot Line to the south. They spent six months digging, draining and revetting while behind them the Royal Engineers constructed reserve lines with concrete pill-boxes and an anti-tank ditch. 'The autumn was terribly wet, the winter bitterly cold,' recorded the regimental history, 'yet their spirits remained extremely high.'

This was hardly adequate as a description of Wright's state of mind. He was bored and discontented; he had come to France to kill Germans, not to dig holes of doubtful usefulness. Inevitably he got into hot water. He had spent the whole day digging trenches and in the evening marched back to his billet with his only set of clothing soaked through and muddy. On his return he was confronted by a corporal who had not been with them on the working party because he was awaiting promotion to lance-sergeant and transfer to another platoon. Without even giving him a chance to dry off, the corporal ordered Wright to carry his equipment to his new quarters a few hundred yards away. 'And he'd been sitting there all day doing nothing. I just told him to fuck off!' Telling a corporal to fuck off is even less well received in the Brigade of Guards than in other sections of the British Army. Wright duly got all that he had expected – twenty-eight days' Field Punishment – and accepted it without argument or a trace of rancour. 'I just took it for granted because I'd done wrong, in a temper as you might say. Always in my life if I came across something I thought unfair I'd bash straight against it; no matter what it was I'd bash straight against it. And it's always got me into trouble. Probably still does.'

Life in France had its compensations. The brothels, Wright found, were legal: 'Very nice, they were. You didn't have to go with women, just sit around and drink.' He noticed that on the whole the men who used prostitutes were the older ones, men of thirty or thirty-five who were missing their wives and wanted consolation. The younger men felt less need: 'We were all a bit backward those days, women-wise.' But he managed to amuse himself all the same; he used to go rabbit shooting and found that his trophies were useful for barter, whether for champagne, rum or other favours. In November a hundred men from his battalion went to Paris. It was the first time he had ever worn battledress. Each group of four men was allotted a French soldier to lead them around and show them the city. 'They took us to all the posh places. We said we wanted to go round the brothels. That was the first good one I'd been in.'

They stayed where they were, perfecting their defences, until the end of April 1940, by which time they had still not heard a shot in anger, still less fired one themselves. Then came the German invasion of Holland and Belgium. Immediately all their laboriously constructed fortifications were abandoned: 'The daft thing was that as soon as the trouble started we went into Belgium.' There was hardly an officer or man in the 1st Battalion who would not have agreed wholeheartedly about the daftness; the political arguments for going to Belgium's rescue perhaps outweighed the military disadvantages but the results were disastrous. The British troops pushed forward to the line of the Dyle Canal, were outflanked, fell back, were exposed by the collapse of the Belgian Army, fell back again: 'We did nothing but run, dig in, run, dig in, right back to Dunkirk,' remembers Wright. He slightly oversimplifies the course of the retreat – there were some quite fierce engagements fought along the way – but the unwelcome truth was that the Guards found themselves running for dear life in front of the German advance without having been given any real chance to prove that they could fight. It was 'a terribly long and tiring march', wrote the Company Commander. 'I have never seen the men more exhausted, and it was only by sheer will-power that they reached their positions.' Those positions were back at the Gort Line, which they had been at such pains to construct during the previous winter, but by the time they reached them they had already been outflanked once again. The men were on half rations, they only had ammunition for a further four days, on 27 May they were told to abandon all but the most essential equipment and make their way to Dunkirk.

The first violent death Wright witnessed occurred when a man in the section next to him was shot through his tin hat by a German sniper. He died a few hours later: 'It didn't give one much confidence in tin hats,' says Wright drily. Otherwise he saw relatively little action during the greater part of the retreat. But any sense that he was being left out of things was more than put right in the final stages. The Guards Brigade made up the rearguard and Wright was in the rearguard of the Brigade. Once he was on sentry duty when a big dog came up and sniffed him. He made a friendly noise and it moved on. Immediately behind it came a patrol of forty or so Germans who were within a few yards of him but passed on oblivious.

When they reached Furnes, on the fringes of the Dunkirk salient, the Guards found themselves plugging a gap left by the disappearance of the Belgian Army. The 1st Battalion occupied the southern outskirts of the town for a final rearguard action, they held it for three days, then on the third night Wright and a handful of other men were given all the Bren guns the company still possessed and what was left of the ammunition and told to blaze away all night in the hope that the Germans would think the town was strongly held. Whether this deception operation in fact deterred the Germans or they had their own reasons for not pressing home an assault, the little band of Grenadiers survived till morning and then set off on the march to the coast, with little idea of what they would find when they got there.

They reached the seashore at La Panne, just out of sight of Dunkirk itself, a town that to this day Wright has never seen. His unit was almost the last to arrive and the beaches were more dense than at Margate or Blackpool on the most popular bank holiday. Every so often a Messerschmitt would strafe the closely packed troops: 'It reminded me of when I was on the mowing machine taking a swathe out of a field.' A few soldiers blazed away hopefully at the attacking aircraft but no effective defence was possible. The only hope of escape was by boat, but though vessels could be seen in the distance, they were unable to get close enough to the shore. Wright had never felt so helpless in his life but, having not slept for virtually three nights, he was at least too tired to feel afraid.

In fact he was on the beaches less than two hours. One of his platoon saw a capsized rowing boat floating in the distance; they secured it and baled it out with their tin hats. It had already been used in an attempted escape but too many people had clambered aboard, with disastrous consequences. This time a sergeant-major was on the spot; he allowed only a dozen or so to enter the boat and then gallantly refused a place himself. They paddled out to the nearest ship, struggled aboard and were given bully beef and cocoa. Wright then went below and collapsed into sleep. The ship put into Dunkirk, was attacked from the air and had its bridge severely damaged, but for all Wright knew they might have been on a pleasure trip round the lighthouse. The next thing he heard was the sound of cheering as the ship entered Sheerness.

Though Wright did not know it, the plan had been that the Guards Brigade would pause only briefly in England to re-equip and re-form and would then go back to France. The French surrender put an end to that. Instead, the battalion trailed off to Liverpool to get new battledress, was moved briefly to Salisbury Plain to put itself in order and then was based at Swanage in Dorset to form part of what was optimistically described as Britain's coastal defences. By this time, rather to his surprise, Wright had been made a corporal (the Guards, as the result of a whimsical ruling by Queen Victoria, knew no such animal as a lance-corporal). The King's Company, to which he still belonged, was slightly detached from the rest of the battalion. Given his recent promotion this was just as well, for the other companies revolted against the intolerably strict discipline to which they felt they were being subjected, marched on the headquarters and protested noisily. If the King's Company had been on the spot they would almost certainly have been involved. In fact the authorities briskly transferred the Colonel, Adjutant and Sergeant-Major and took no action against the demonstrators, whom they felt had been ineptly handled. Non-commissioned officers who took part in the incident, however, were left with a black mark against them, and it is hard to imagine Wright remaining demurely in the background.

As it was, by the time he was posted to the 6th Battalion at Caterham, he had become a lance-sergeant. Neither the rank nor the job appealed. The battalion seemed to him to be made up of the dregs of other battalions, the recruits were badly trained and were being asked to undertake tasks beyond their abilities. They were 'nice people, good friends', but they knew little about making war, and to send them into battle, in Wright's opinion, could only prove catastrophic. He wanted no responsibility for what would follow and at his own request reverted to the ranks. He got the reputation of a troublemaker, being on one occasion confined to barracks for the unusual offence of having his hair cut too short. He was still with the battalion when they set out for Singapore, a journey which was truncated when the city fell to the Japanese. They hung about for a while in Durban, where Wright created mayhem and had several unfortunate brushes with the non-commissioned officers who had so recently been his colleagues, then were dumped with the rest of the Guards Brigade in Syria.

The journey from Durban to Syria was made in a small and grossly overcrowded troopship, through rough seas and with the temperature below decks 100°F or more. The camp in Syria was in a stretch of rough country at the foot of Mount Hermon, hot, sand-blown, infested with flies, remote and bleak. There was little to do, nobody even seemed to know for what they were supposed to be training. For a man who found doing nothing the most painful of experiences, it was a penitential sentence: 'We never looked like going into action or anything. Just messing about there.' Wright was bored, discontented, and would undoubtedly once more have run foul of the authorities if salvation had not unexpectedly arrived.

It came in the form of a recruiting team for the Special Boat Squadron, a highly irregular unit whose function – always ill-defined – was to conduct raids on enemy-held territory, disrupt communications, destroy shipping, blow up installations, spread alarm and despondency among the German and Italian garrisons and, perhaps most important, ensure that the six German infantry divisions in the Eastern Mediterranean were not withdrawn for more fruitful work elsewhere. When Wright was approached the Squadron was only just emerging as an independent unit from the maw of the Special Air Service. Recruits were urgently needed, the team was looking for volunteers who were young, strong, brave and preferably had no family ties; most of all they wanted men who were not hidebound by military tradition and were ready to undertake any initiative, however harebrained or extravagant it might seem. For the most promising material they turned to the 'guardroom types', those who were consistently in trouble with the authorities, rather than the 'good soldiers', who might be more dependable but were also less likely to respond well to the unexpected challenges the new service would offer them. Though this particular team was recruiting primarily for the Boat Squadron, volunteers would be expected to train as paratroopers as well. This deterred many, and even of those who persisted in their application only a quarter were finally accepted.

Wright put himself forward without hesitation. He did not much like the idea of parachuting but was prepared to do so if needs must; for the rest the job offered extra pay and the near certainty of adventure, both tempting though the second incomparably more so. To the men from the Squadron he must have seemed ideal material, especially since he was a strong swimmer.

Within a few days he was at Kabrit, near Ismailia, training for his new work. Commanding the Squadron was George Jellicoe – the 'Belted Earl', his men called him – a dashing twenty-five-year-old who was himself a Guardsman, though a Coldstream rather than a Grenadier. Jellicoe was elusive; nobody ever knew whether he would be present for a particular operation or transacting mysterious business elsewhere. Wright was usually under the immediate command of Anders Lassen, a former cadet from the Danish merchant marine who had the reputation – probably justified – of having personally killed more Germans in the Eastern Mediterranean than any other two men put together. He was entirely fearless and driven by a fanatical urge to revenge the downfall of his homeland. 'He volunteered for anything and everything,' Wright remembers, and usually volunteered his men along with him, assuming that they would be delighted to join him in apparently suicidal ventures. He was eventually killed in Italy and was awarded a posthumous Victoria Cross. If he had survived the war his intention had been to buy a launch, cruise down the African coast and pillage the diamond fields. Wright would probably have gone with him.

The first operation in which Wright took part was a raid by submarine on Sardinia, to destroy German aircraft on the ground and thus prepare the way for the landings in Sicily. It could easily have been his last. The operation was a disaster: there were no aircraft on Sardinia and, worse still, the Germans seemed to be expecting the attack and repelled it bloodily. The unit was almost wiped out. Fortunately for Wright he was struck down by malaria on the way out, and though he insisted that he was fit enough to join the assault it was obvious that he could hardly stand, let alone go ashore.

After that things went better. He took part in a series of raids on the Greek islands, blowing up installations, killing or kidnapping German personnel, keeping the garrisons in a state of constant disquiet. Lassen was as resourceful as he was reckless. From Lemnos they escaped by kayak with a vastly superior German force in hot pursuit. They ended up in Turkey, where Lassen somehow talked the Turks into not interning them but instead putting them on to a train for Syria. On Amorgos they captured a German wireless operator who had a dog and a Greek mistress; Lassen took the dog and Wright the mistress. The German loved his dog and offered to hand over the codebooks in exchange for an assurance that it would be well looked after; no such stipulation was required in the case of the mistress. Lassen kept his word and the dog was still with him when he was killed. It was alleged to be a Maltese terrier; its habits, says the historian of the Boat Squadron, 'which Lassen encouraged, were lubricious and obscene'. When they returned to Amorgos the German presence had been substantially reinforced – a tribute, no doubt, to their previous exploit. Wright, by a judicious and extraordinarily courageous deployment of explosives, was personally responsible for 'bumping off most of the German garrison'. He was awarded the Military Medal. 'It was nothing,' he says. 'It was just handed out with the rations.'

It was under Lassen that Wright took part in his only operation on the mainland of Yugoslavia. The objective was to destroy the railway bridge at Karasovic. This they did successfully; 'That was the easy part,' says Wright; the Germans had already prepared the bridge for demolition, all that was left to do was to 'stuff in the explosives and blow it up'. But then a force of four hundred Germans and Ustachi – Yugoslav supporters of the Germans – chased the raiders into the hills. Even Lassen saw the time was not appropriate for heroics, ten against four hundred were hardly acceptable odds. They took to their heels and 'we ran too fast for them', says Wright, though they managed to kill quite a number of their pursuers as they fled. Lassen's report on this operation was so terse that Jellicoe told him to rewrite it at greater length. 'But vat is it you vant me to say?' grumbled the Dane. 'Ve landed. Ve reached ze bridge. Ve destroyed it. Zat is all no?' Wright would not have put it any differently.

Hearing Wright talk, one would think that life in the Squadron was a series of lighthearted escapades mingled with bouts of revelry. When they raided Eos they 'liberated' a group of Greek girls who were serving members of the German Officers' Mess. The commander of the raiding party persuaded the young naval officer in whose ship they were travelling that the girls were an important source of military intelligence and must be taken aboard. All went merrily, but when they reached Cyprus he lost his nerve, gave the girls some money to buy clothes, put them ashore and abandoned them. There was a sequel some twelve years later, when Wright found himself back in Cyprus at the time of the Suez Crisis. To his dismay he was roundly abused by the madam of one of the larger brothels and accused of lack of chivalry. Eventually he realised that it was one of the girls from Eos; since she had done very well for herself in the meantime and had settled down happily in her new home, she bore him no lasting grudge.

One must not let innumerable such cheerful anecdotes obscure the fact that Wright and his companions were subject to pressures, both physical and psychological, which most people would have found insupportable. They were repeatedly in imminent danger of death or serious injury, prey to what must have been agonising tension as they ventured into the unknown, pitted against unreasonable odds and never knowing who, if anyone, could be relied on to help them in case of trouble. It was not all rollicking adventure and fun with the girls. But on the whole Wright enjoyed himself immensely and those years in the Eastern Mediterranean were the most fulfilling of his life. He was sometimes bored, he was sometimes frightened, but as he now puts it: 'It was lovely. Shooting, wine, women and song. When one was with Lassen . . . Oh dear!'

Whether the job was worth doing is another matter. Some hold that operations of this kind were a waste of resources and distraction from the serious business of winning the war. The more commonly held view is that they were justified by the effect they had on enemy morale and the disposition of his forces. But worthwhile or not, for men like Wright these adventures provided an unparalleled opportunity to prove themselves and display their abilities in a way which otherwise would have been denied them.

The fun was not to be repeated. As the British Army slogged up Italy and the centre of attention turned to France the Boat Squadron had a steadily diminishing part to play. The Chiefs of Staff decided to send it to the Far East, to join in the closing stages of the war against Japan. To prepare for this its members were transferred to the United Kingdom. The smaller men were sent to Scotland to train for service in midget submarines; Wright, who was no midget, was considered unsuitable and he was still wondering what was going to happen to him when the atom bomb fell and the war was over. He assumed that he would now return to the Grenadiers but soon discovered that, though he had been considered fit to take part in potentially gruelling operations in the Far East, the malaria which he had contracted in the Middle East was deemed to make him unfit for peacetime service in the Army: 'It was "Get 'em out", then, "Get 'em into civvy street".' In fact the Army was not being wholly unreasonable; for the next three years he suffered from frequent bouts of fever and it was not until 1949 that a doctor tackled his malaria successfully and he was given something close to a clean bill of health.

Dougie Wright left the Army in 1946, convinced that his wandering, restless days were over and that he wanted nothing but to make a home and settle down. For a home, he felt, you needed a wife; and he rapidly fell in love with almost the first girl he took out. She was Adrienne Jones, with a Welsh father and an Irish Catholic mother, and as urban by background as Wright was rural; but her first ambition was to have a house of her own and when

Wright proposed and told her that he would find it easy to get a place on a farm with a tied cottage going with the job, she accepted both husband and country-living with barely a second thought.

He was right in supposing that his farming experience, strength and wartime record would always make it easy for him to find a vacancy, but badly wrong in supposing that he was ready to settle down. Over the next ten years he changed jobs five or six times, got bored in one place, quarrelled with his employer in another. During the same period he had three children, two daughters and then a son. His wife found the nomadic country life increasingly irksome; she was a difficult, discontented woman but Wright did not make life easy for her. He was 'not good marriage material', says someone who knew him well; he was fiercely individualistic, found it hard to compromise, and paid little attention to what other people said. He had a gentler side, and a wiser and more patient woman could have established a relationship acceptable to them both, but Adrienne had neither the wisdom nor the patience. She nagged him to earn more money but then complained bitterly that he was neglecting her when he worked unsocial hours. In 1956 he was responsible for six hundred or so pigs on a large farm and was frequently called out at night. Once he came in late and, he says: 'She went crazy with me. I grabbed her by the arm and started shaking her. I really got hold of her and shook her, but I never struck her.' It would have been out of character if he had; Wright was short-tempered and quick to violence, but hitting a woman was not his style. He was certainly rough, though, and for his wife it was one affront too many. Next day she stormed out and placed the children in a Catholic home. Wright visited them there a little later: 'It was pathetic really to see them, to see your own children in misery.'

Meanwhile he had rejoined the Army. His malaria seemed a thing of the past, the Grenadiers were in need of experienced personnel, he was welcomed back enthusiastically. After a brief period for retraining he found himself posted to the Mediterranean

where the Suez Crisis was brewing up towards its ignoble
conclusion. Shortly before he sailed, his wife reappeared and said
that she wanted to come back to him. With some hesitation he
agreed; but never again, he insisted, if she left him a second time it
would be the last. There was no question of her immediately
accompanying him but he agreed that if, as seemed most probable,
the Grenadiers ended up in Cyprus, she should join him there as
soon as the authorities agreed.

The 3rd Battalion, of which he was destined to become Pioneer
Sergeant, charged with the repair and maintenance of equipment,
contained a large number of Reservists who had been called up
because of the possibility that Egypt would have to be invaded.
They were deeply displeased at this disruption of their lives; if they
had been flung straight into battle they might have reconciled
themselves to their lot but when they were deposited in Malta and
left to stew while the politicians decided what to do, they went
berserk and vented their rage on their own officers and the local
population. Wright sympathised: if he had been a Reservist
himself, he would probably have been in the forefront of the
trouble. Since he was in Malta by his own volition, however, and
had no other life to return to, he sensibly lay low. As in Dorset in
1940 the authorities believed that the main responsibility for such
discontent must rest with those in charge; once again Colonel,
Adjutant and Regimental Sergeant-Major paid the price and were
transferred.

Wright felt that the Suez Crisis was a tragedy of mismanage-
ment and cowardice. His personal solution would have been to
smuggle six tons of explosive up the Nile, detonate them and divert
the course of the river into the Red Sea – a venture which he and
his Boat Squadron colleagues might well have carried through,
though probably without the dramatic consequences he believed
would follow. Like most of his fellow soldiers he attributed the
fiasco more to the attitude of the Americans than the irresolution

or irresponsibility of the British or French: 'You've got to do as the Yanks say,' he comments regretfully.

As a Pioneer Sergeant in Cyprus Wright possessed skills and exercised responsibilities that made him almost indispensable. This turned out to be just as well for him, since, true to form, he was soon in trouble again. He had been required to build a cricket pitch for which half a ton of cement was needed. As holiday time was approaching he asked the Quartermaster whether he could go ahead and buy the materials. No, he was told. Then, the following weekend, he was ordered to go out and procure the cement. 'I'm sorry, sir. I can't get any today.' 'No such thing as "Sorry" in the Guards! You'll go out and get it.' All the Turk and Greek merchants were by now shut so Wright did the rounds of the other regimental stores. Everyone said that they had closed for the weekend but sought to console him by offering him a drink. Wright, by now in a thoroughly bad temper, refused the offer on the first few occasions but when he got to the Pioneer Corps and was told that there *might* be some cement available but that they would need a little time to make sure, he had a glass of brandy while he waited. Then he had another. By 2 p.m. he was unequivocally drunk. At this point he was told that his quest had been fruitless; the cement was inaccessible. He lurched to his truck and ordered the driver to take him back to his bungalow. Instead, the driver deposited him at the guardroom, where his condition was noted with some disapproval.

Wright now decided that he should make one last hunt for cement at the company stores. When he got there, he found himself confronted by a hostile Alsatian guard dog. The dog went for his throat but Wright punched it, kicked it and threw it out of the stores. Then he staggered on towards his bungalow. By now the duty sergeant-major had been alerted and Wright found himself interrupted and led off towards the guardroom. He went along with docility, then baulked at the last minute. 'Sorry, mate,

I'm going!' he announced, rushing out of the camp with the picket guards, who had no wish to get into a violent brawl with a well-liked sergeant, in cautious pursuit. He knew that if he went home he would be arrested, so he hitched a lift into Nicosia and 'went on the booze with the Turks'. He remained there until Monday morning, then tottered back to camp. Now his qualifications served him well: 'They needed a Pioneer Sergeant and if they'd reduced me to the ranks they'd have had a job to find one.' He got away with a severe reprimand.

Adrienne and the children had joined him in Cyprus before this episode; on the whole they got on well enough, though Wright wished that his wife would take his side rather more wholeheartedly in the various altercations in which he became involved: 'When I got into trouble it was always my fault,' he complains. 'Admittedly it was, but still . . .' Then she fell ill from some mysterious malady which was never properly diagnosed. She went to hospital and Wright accepted without demur the responsibilities of a single parent. The children were well fed, properly turned out and felt entirely secure. His technique was not always up to his intentions. Once he cooked apricots into which he put so much sugar that they became a sickening syrup. The children refused to eat the resultant mess; he was most indignant but made no attempt to force it down their throats.

His wife's illness presaged the end of their marriage. She went back to England for further treatment and Wright followed with the children. She discharged herself from hospital – in her husband's view before she was ready for it – and rejoined him in Blackpool. Within twenty-four hours she accused him – unjustly, and largely on imaginary grounds – of having an affair with another woman. Once again she flounced out, to stay with her brother. This time Wright was determined that it should be final. Some months later she again asked to be taken back but he refused – even though his commanding officer urged him to agree to a reconciliation. By the time they met again she was pregnant by another man. In spite of this she still wanted to come back to him. He remained determined, whereupon she obtained a quick divorce and remarried. They never met again and she later died.

The divorce was in 1959, by which time Wright had become a regimental police sergeant at Wellington Barracks in London. The appointment was made, presumably, on the time-honoured principle of poachers making the best gamekeepers. Wright, however, still had more than a touch of the poacher about him. Once he was detailed to take a man to the military hospital at Millbank for examination by a psychiatrist. He was waiting in the corridor when 'a little old fellow in a white coat' came along, spotted the Italian Star on his tunic and asked him where he had served. Bari, mostly, Wright replied. 'Really!' said the other man. 'Santa Claus was buried there.' St Nicholas's remains were indeed interred in Bari, but Wright decided that a joke was being made at his expense. '*He's* the fucking patient, not me,' he retorted, pointing at his charge. When he got back to his barracks he was put in close arrest for insubordination toward somebody who turned out to be not merely the head psychiatrist but also a brigadier. Once again he escaped with a severe reprimand.

In 1961 he was posted with the 1st Battalion of the Grenadiers to the Cameroons, a British colony on the verge of independence. It faced division between Nigeria and its francophone neighbour to the south and the situation was uneasy. There were sporadic skirmishes with disgruntled tribesmen and one or two British soldiers were killed. Wright saw no action, however; indeed, he remembers the posting with pleasure. 'We had a lot of fun there. I used to go and inspect the brothel girls every day. I'd take my stick and lift up their skirts and say "Dirty! Dirty!" All in fun. They'd have a big giggle about it.'

But he remained unregenerate. From the Cameroons he came back with the 1st Battalion to Tidworth and in 1962 went up to London for the ceremony of Trooping the Colour. The Colour-

Sergeant, in what seemed to Wright unnecessarily brusque terms, told him to move his kit from one barrack room to another. He replied that he had no time to do so before the parade. When he got back, having 'had a few drinks in the mess', he found that his kit had been thrown unceremoniously into the other room. He stormed out in search of the offending Colour-Sergeant, found him, as he thought, alone, and attacked him. Unfortunately the Company Sergeant-Major was in the background; he intervened, whereupon Wright attacked him too. The price he paid was court martial and demotion to the ranks. 'It was my own fault,' he observes philosophically. 'If you do something wrong you're punished.' In fact he got off lightly. The Colour-Sergeant whom he attacked had been generally disliked, so Wright made few enemies. He was sent to Pirbright as a butcher but was made a corporal after a few weeks. He was back in the Sergeants' Mess within the year.

He had remarried within twelve months of his divorce, this time to a girl nineteen years his junior whom he inherited from a friend who had been posted abroad. He was paying alimony to his first wife, which meant that, when he was posted to the Cameroons and left his new wife to have their first child in his absence, she was decidedly short of money. She endured this with equanimity and was equally unperturbed when her husband descended abruptly to the ranks and, in due course, rose again. He was once more regimental police sergeant by the time the battalion was sent to Germany; she went with him and they settled into married quarters. By the time they left Wuppertal in 1964 two more children had been added to the family. He was there for nearly three years, one of his longer postings. Soldiers can expect to move around the world at short notice and in unexpected directions, but Wright's career seems to have been exceptionally itinerant. After Germany he went to Cyprus, where the battalion put on blue berets and did a peacekeeping job for the United Nations. They were near the partition line between Greek and Turkish Cyprus;

Wright felt no real sympathy for either side and could see no good reason why they should not be able to establish a basis for co-existence without outside assistance. On the whole he preferred the Greeks, though he admits regretfully that they seemed to have little in common with the warriors at whose side he had fought more than twenty years before.

He had still one more posting abroad and that proved to be as depressing as any of them. After a brief return to Caterham he was despatched to Sharjah, in the Persian Gulf. Conditions in the camp were bleak and the stay was likely to be short so no wives were allowed to accompany their husbands. There was little to do and nobody seemed to have any clear idea why they were there in the first place. It was 'boring. Rubbish, really.' After nine months he was back in England. He was more than fifty years old and the time had come to make decisions about the future. He went on a course to become a recruiting sergeant, work which would have kept him employed for another ten years. He was not selected; not, as he saw it, through any fault of his own but because the Army wanted 'somebody modern'. A younger man was preferred to him. He could have continued with the Grenadiers for two or three more years but he was not sure that he would any more feel at home there. Besides, the Army was in one of those periodic points in the cycle in which numbers are reduced and redundancy terms are favourable. Wright decided to get out while the going was relatively good and before any fresh indiscretion jeopardised his pension. In 1970 he was discharged and began life as a civilian.

More for want of other ideas than from territorial loyalty he moved back to Poynton. With his redundancy money and the help of a small mortgage he managed to buy a house – a fortunate accident of timing since the property boom of the next few years would have put anything comparable beyond his reach. But he did not find that advancing years had made it any easier for him to settle down. His first job was as a steward of a club, a job not unlike that of an innkeeper. He could manage the conviviality well enough but he disliked the late hours and soon moved on. Next he found a place with an American firm where he worked as a shot blaster, removing rust from old machinery. Here new trouble arose. The unions operated a closed shop in the factory and Wright, who was, in his own words, 'a bit of an old Tory', stoutly refused to pay union dues. He offered, instead, to donate the money to any charity that they cared to nominate. That was not good enough for the union leaders, who called the two hundred employees out on strike. The manager was in despair; he sympathised with Wright and thought him a good worker, but his first concern was to get the factory back to work. 'OK. Give me a month's wages and I'll sod off!' Wright offered. His boss accepted immediately. 'That was me,' says Wright resignedly.

After that, he reverted to the trade he had learnt at Pirbright while in disgrace, and became a butcher. He moved from job to job, sometimes because he was offered better pay, sometimes just because he got bored. His wife, who seemed to grow more easygoing with the years, saw nothing to protest about, and he was never out of work. Then he did a two-year stint at Styal Prison in Cheshire, working as a gateman. He enjoyed the job and might have stayed on if his contract had not expired. Instead he was offered a similar job at Strangeways Prison but decided that he did not like the set-up. Styal had been in the country while Strangeways was in town; he would have had to work at nights; worst of all, 'it smelt to me; old lags, you know'. He got a job in security at the Co-operative but this too lasted only briefly. The families of the security men were being mugged; Wright was more than happy to take on any number of muggers himself but he was not prepared to put his wife and children at risk. Again he moved on, for a final stint of butchering.

When he was almost sixty-five he retired, settling in a bungalow in Scarborough. But now it was his wife who proved the restless one. Wright was content with what they had got, but time after time she insisted that they should move. Each time there would be a row, each time he would mutter threats about leaving her and retreating to the Royal Hospital, 'It got on my craw,' he says. When it came to what he hoped would be the final move Wright decided to avoid any possible problem that might arise if, as seemed most probable, he predeceased his wife. The new house was placed in her name. To his dismay she then decided that she wanted to move south to Plymouth. Their daughter had married a sailor who knocked her about unmercifully and had now deserted her; her mother wanted to be near her. Wright would have preferred to stay in Scarborough but because of his ill-judged generosity had to agree to the move: 'I couldn't do nothing else.' They bought the largest house they could afford, 'a rough old thing', and spent endless time, energy and money doing it up. At last everything was to Wright's satisfaction. Then his wife decided she wanted to move again. It was too much. 'I'm stopping here,' Wright said. 'If you don't like it you can get a divorce. I'll go to Chelsea.' She proved as obstinate as he was, so he signed a paper admitting to a mythical adultery and the divorce went through. He was sad about it – 'She was a very good person' – but both of them believed they would be happier apart.

Wright duly applied to the Royal Hospital, was accepted and took up residence. His motives, says his daughter, were at least partly unselfish. He realised that his wife was far younger than him and did not want her to spend too much of her life looking after an old man. Nor, less unselfishly, could he stomach the idea of becoming dependent on her. But when it came to the point he discovered that it was still difficult to settle down. He found no serious problems at the Royal Hospital. He had a few quarrels, but none that ended in blows: 'You'd get thrown out tomorrow if you did, which is only right.' He did not feel intolerably restricted or cramped in his new surroundings. His wife was still living in Plymouth, unable to find a job and subsisting – because she was not yet old enough for a pension – on £48 a week. She was having a hard time and he felt a sudden surge of pity. He left the Royal Hospital and went to share his life with her.

It did not prove a success. Within a few weeks, he says, 'she was laying down the law again'; he found her impossible to live with. His daughter has another explanation: he found life in Plymouth boring, there was nothing to do except play bowls and spend occasional evenings with the British Legion. At least at Chelsea there had been conviviality and the company of his peers. Whatever the reasons, he knew within six months that he had made a bad mistake. He swallowed his pride and applied for re-admission to the Royal Hospital. They took him back with the same equanimity as they had let him go. In March, 1998 he rejoined for the second time. 'I don't think that I'll ever leave again,' he says, and then adds thoughtfully, 'though you never know . . .' With Wright you never did know and you never will.

LEONARD PEARSON

Lance-Corporal Pearson, 1940

Leonard Pearson

LEONARD Pearson was descended from a line of tenant farmers who had occupied the same land in North Yorkshire for several generations. The link with the farm was severed shortly before the Second World War when the site was requisitioned for conversion into a bomber station but, even if it had remained in the family, Len's father, John, as a younger son, would have had no place in it. John hankered after a life on the land, however, and after surviving the First World War with the Royal Engineers and then spending an unhappy period as a building labourer, he found a job on a farm near Marton, the village where he had been brought up just south of Middlesbrough. Shortly after Len, his eldest son, was born on 8 August 1921, he moved away from Marton and for a few years shifted from place to place, finally settling on a farm at Croft-on-Tees, a mile or so south of Darlington on the borders of Yorkshire and Durham. Len was brought up, and still feels himself, a Yorkshireman.

His mother, Catherine, was a Roman Catholic of Irish stock whose family had come over from Cork some twenty years before. She does not seem to have felt any urge to proselytise for her religion; the children were brought up in the Church of England and when her husband, after several years of married life, suggested that he might convert to keep her company, she replied discouragingly: 'It's too late now.' Len today feels that this was just as well. In later life he found it increasingly hard to stomach any form of organised religion and if his mother had pushed him into the Roman Catholic faith, 'I don't think I could have remained true to it because of a lot of the dogma I couldn't go along with. I think I would have ended up a lapsed Catholic.' There was a strong Roman Catholic presence in the neighbourhood, however. The Hospital of St John of God's was not far away and acted as a kind of non-denominational community centre; the Pearson children would go there at night to see old Charlie Chaplin films.

As with so many working-class families of the period, the father had his time and energies more than absorbed by the effort of making enough money to feed, clothe and house his family; the effective running of that family was left to the mother. But though this meant that she was required to be a strong and resourceful *materfamilias*, outside the home she preferred to play an overtly subsidiary role. If her husband went into a pub she would wait on the threshold, however cold or wet the weather; in public at least she would defer to his views with becoming modesty. Catherine was a strict disciplinarian, who made sure that each child contributed to the working of the household and was quick to point out any shortcomings. She preferred to remonstrate rather than beat, but when Len's younger brother stole an orange from a fruit shop, Pearson recalls, 'he was nearly dead when she'd finished with him. I bet he remembers that to this day.' The children were not afraid of her, however: 'All the time she was so approachable.' Her anger, though formidable while it lasted, was quickly dispelled; her love was unfailing: 'There were occasions during the hard times when she would starve herself so that we would have enough.'

Such hard times came all too often. Len was the eldest of six, and to bring up six children on a farm labourer's wages was no light task. The cottage was cramped and uncomfortable, with two large bedrooms – into one of which the children crowded – and a living area in the centre with a kitchen leading off it. There was no inside bathroom, just a zinc tub that once a week was taken off the wall, and an outside hut that served as a lavatory. The cottage was cold and damp in winter, stuffy in summer. Food was sufficient, but only just. The Yorkshire farmers were 'very, very canny', both over the wages they paid and the extras they permitted; a labourer's pay traditionally included a pint or a pint and a half of milk a day but the farmers never threw in a few eggs as a bonus. Mrs Pearson grew her own vegetables and kept a few chickens; her husband usually kept a pig or two as well, though when it came to sending them to market he had to rely on somebody else to do the dealing. In lieu of overtime during the harvest season he would sometimes be given a piece of farm-cured pork. It went into the stockpot which Mrs Pearson kept permanently on the simmer – she was skilled at producing palatable meals out of very little.

But though always short of money, the Pearsons could always afford a paper, either the *Northern Echo* or the *Darlington and Stockton Times*. They took it for the local news; national politics and international news largely passed them by. Unusually in the neighbourhood they also had a wireless – 'Oh gosh, that was a problem!': it was powered by a wet accumulator which had to be taken to the nearest garage to be recharged whenever it ran low – but they used it mainly to listen to popular music. The area was strongly Labour in its political allegiance, especially after the family moved when Len was twelve or so to Rushyford, a village on the edge of the coal mining area ten miles north of Darlington. His parents played no part in politics though Len thinks they probably voted Labour; the Irish element of the family was mildly anti-royalist and sceptical about the merits of the British Empire. Len's Irish grandfather told fearful tales of the Black and Tans and denounced the iniquities of the English in Ireland, one of his aunts was a staunch republican who 'said the most terrible things about the Royal Family'. He noticed, however, that if any royal traveller passed through the area she was always to the forefront waving a flag. There was a vague assumption in the neighbourhood that everything would be much better under a Communist government; Len remembers people saying: 'Of course, in Russia they've got hospitals and everything.' The local landowner, Sir Timothy Eden, was so irritated by what he felt to be ridiculous naivety that he once offered to pay the fare of anybody who would like to go to Russia to see this paradise for himself. One young man took him up; unfortunately for him he was there when war broke out and had the greatest difficulty in getting back. Sir Timothy would no doubt have been vastly amused at his predicament; he was 'a real Tartar', Len Pearson remembers. 'If you went over his wall scrumping for apples a blast of shotgun pellets would fly over your head.'

Len went to several village schools, ending up at Rushyford. The frequent changes cannot have helped his education but he would anyway not have shone academically. A few of the children from Rushyford went on to Richmond Grammar School. Len took the exam and came near enough to passing to be given a second chance, but 'I wasn't bright enough, obviously,' he recalls regretfully. Even if he had passed he would probably not have taken the offer of a place; his mother, he believes, would have 'felt let down' if he had not at once gone out to work, to bring a little extra money into the straitened family budget. At the age of fourteen he could read and write English with facility, knew a bit of history and geography, had a few words of French and a grasp of the principles of arithmetic. It was not much, but it could have been a great deal worse.

At the time he had no regrets at leaving school. For the last few years his ambition had been to join the Royal Navy; he didn't know exactly why, 'it just seemed to appeal'. Then a neighbour who had been in the Marines during the First World War warned him that if he once joined the Navy he would never be able to escape from it. He did not feel inclined to tie himself up for a long period when he knew so little about the life that would await him;

whatever he tried, he wanted to keep open the possibility of changing his mind. But if he was not going to be a sailor, what should he do? His father would have liked to see him follow family tradition and go on to the land, perhaps one day taking on his great-uncle's farm near Rushyford. Len knew that this was the last thing he wanted; his experience of farming was that it involved endless uncertainty, gruelling hard work and, even at the best of times, inadequate rewards – 'It was always hand-to-mouth, everything.' He still liked the idea of joining the armed services – 'perhaps the uniform appealed, I don't know' – but was too young to do so straight away. He followed the line of least resistance, as did most of his fellow pupils, and went down the mine.

'Down' the mine was in fact not yet a possibility – a minor could not be a miner. Instead he worked above ground; one week for six days on a shift from 1 p.m. to 9 p.m., the next week for five days on a shift from 5 a.m. to 1 p.m. For the long week he got paid 9/6d, for the five-day week only 8/5d. He handed his pay over to his mother who gave him back 5d as pocket money; he didn't resent this: 'I could see her problem.'

He did go underground once, as part of his introduction to the job. As he got out of the cage at the foot of the shaft a jet of cold water cascaded all over him – 'that was as far as it went' and he was not sorry for it. For the rest of the time he worked in the lamp-room, topping up the oil lamps, cleaning the mud off the electric lamps, recharging the batteries. The last was a messy job; with acid bubbling from the batteries, a new set of overalls was necessary nearly every week. Most of his friends, who were destined to go underground in due course, worked on the screens picking the stones from the coal. They were no better paid than Len but counted as underground workers and as a result qualified for a free delivery of coal each month. With coal at 30 shillings a ton this was not worth a fortune, but it was still a useful bonus. Len felt no jealousy of their good fortune – 'mining didn't appeal to me in any way' – and longed for the day when he would be able to escape and start what he was now convinced would be his real life as a soldier.

That day came in January 1937. It was a good time to join the Army; after nearly twenty years of cheeseparing, Baldwin's government was realising that Britain was ill-equipped for a war which seemed every day more likely. Len had no firm idea what branch of the service would suit him best; the fact that his father had been in the Royal Engineers gave him a slight predilection in that direction, but if he had been told he must be a gunner or an infantryman he would have accepted the ruling with equanimity. Since he was not yet sixteen years old the decision would anyway be deferred for some time. On 20 January 1937, Leonard Pearson enlisted as a boy apprentice and was designated for the Army Technical School at Chepstow. First he had to pass an entrance examination, which took place at the depot of the Northumberland Fusiliers in Newcastle. A few days of suspense followed after which he was accepted and sent on his way. After three years at Chepstow and a final examination, his role in the Army would be decided. If he had become a boy soldier in an infantry regiment he would from the start have known what his military career would be; as an apprentice at the Army Technical School his future was much more questionable. Some of his contemporaries would end up in the infantry, others might be assigned to one of the Service Corps. Only a handful would become Engineers. The uncertainty was mildly disturbing but, at least, whatever the outcome, he would have learnt a trade along the way.

In January the camp at Chepstow was a cheerless sight. It has now been swept away to make room for the new Severn Bridge, but in 1931 it was still little changed from the prisoner-of-war camp which it had been in the First World War. The accommodation was in huts and 'very, very basic, no hot water, no baths'; the fare was equally austere, 'I was always hungry while I was a boy apprentice, always.' To some such privations might have seemed almost intolerable, but Pearson was used to nothing better and bore the discomfort without complaint. The important thing was that he had made a start in life; he would cheerfully have put up with much worse for that. The boys worked school terms, with a long holiday in the summer and three weeks off at Easter and Christmas. The pay was only 11d a day – 6/5d a week; of this they were given 2 shillings a week for pocket money and the rest was accumulated until it was handed over at one of the three 'Big Pay Days' at the beginning of each holiday. There was never as much as they had hoped, since the boys had to pay for their own socks and other incidentals, but with the addition of a ration allowance for the holiday, Pearson went home with a princely total of £7 or so. This he dutifully handed over to his mother; when it came to the turn of his younger brother some years later no mention was made of the ration allowance and the family budget suffered by that amount. 'Very fly,' Pearson comments, in mingled admiration and disapproval. 'He got away with it.'

Pearson was a success at Chepstow; he was soon appointed a boy corporal and became boy sergeant-major after eighteen months, the earliest moment at which such promotion was a possibility. To be put into a position of authority over one's peers always creates problems and Pearson did not find it easy. 'You thought that as soon as you were promoted you would say "Jump!" and everyone would jump,' he remembers, 'but being with boys of your own age you more or less got the thumbs-up sign.' Patience, tact and determination were all called for; luckily Pearson had them all and found the experience an invaluable grounding for later life. There was much emphasis on games and promotion was related almost as much to athletic ability as to other qualities. Pearson's forte was long-distance running; he won the cross-country race three years running and found himself, willy-nilly, selected to represent his section of the school in the mile, the half-mile and the quarter-mile. 'That was ruddy hard, to keep up your end at all those distances,' especially since one race often followed immediately after another and there were no extra rations for the contestants.

The education was not entirely technical; the staff from the Army Educational Corps thought it their duty to teach the apprentices a range of more general subjects and required their pupils to study books and be examined on the contents. Pearson had to read Thackeray's *The Virginians*: 'I must confess, it was an effort to keep reading' – a temperate judgement on one of the most ponderous of Victorian novels. A few of the really bright boys from Chepstow went on to become officer cadets at Sandhurst but this was most exceptional; none graduated in this way from Pearson's year. They were a mixed bag, however, both socially and intellectually; the boy who slept in the next bed to Pearson, 'my very first pal', was the son of a colonel in the Indian Army. Because of his background he knew all the ropes and helped Pearson lay out his kit for inspection. Twenty-seven years later this young man ended his military career as a major.

Pearson enjoyed wearing his uniform and showing it off at home when he went back for the holidays. He would have liked to have kept rather more of his hard-earned money but at least he was treated with some deference by his siblings and was not expected to work on the farm. By now he had decided that he would not be satisfied with anything except the Royal Engineers. A high level of achievement in the various examinations was essential if this end was to be achieved. Fortunately he had shown considerable aptitude for machine drawing and fitting and had no trouble in reaching the necessary level. On 8 August 1939, he began his man's service. He was still at Chepstow on 3 September, getting ready for the compulsory church parade. They assembled, were dismissed, assembled again, were dismissed again, clustered around the wireless and heard the plaintive voice of Neville Chamberlain announcing that Britain was at war. At least church service was cancelled, so something good came out of it. Pearson and his friends knew little about the issues involved. Poland, it seemed, had been attacked by a bullying Germany, and Britain and France were going to its rescue: 'The injustice of it appealed to us, I suppose. We had to do something about it.' They went in to lunch in a state of high excitement: 'All the boys were singing the First World War songs.'

Len spent a few more months at Chepstow before, in January 1940, he was assigned to his chosen unit and posted to Shorncliffe, the Royal Engineer depot near Folkestone. His pay was not increased above the basic 6/5d a week but at least 6 shillings of this was paid to him direct instead of the 2 shillings pocket money which he had hitherto received. A handful of the trainees were former boy soldiers who had experience similar to his own but the majority were 'Belisha boys', recruits so christened in honour of the then Secretary of State for War, Leslie Hore-Belisha. They believed that they had been conscripted for six months but were in fact to serve for six years or more.

Pearson felt himself immeasurably superior to these raw novices, but that did not stop him 'sweating blood' to make sure that he passed out among the leaders at the end of the three months' basic training. His efforts paid off – 'Once I'd become a sapper I never looked back'; he graduated directly into a cadre destined to become non-commissioned officers. When he emerged from this second stage he had still only edged away from the very bottom of the military pile – lance-corporal, local, acting and unpaid – but he was now a qualified tradesman and 'life bucked up' because he was paid 2/6d a day: 'I thought I was a millionaire for a couple of months.'

He was still at Shorncliffe when France fell and the British Expeditionary Force was evacuated from Dunkirk. Pearson would have liked to be over there himself, blowing up bridges and railway lines and otherwise covering the retreat of the defeated Allies. Instead he stood on the cliffs and saw the billowing clouds of smoke from the burning oil tanks across the Channel at Calais. The Engineers were at the docks to meet the men returning from Dunkirk and shepherd them on to trains for London. More grimly, Pearson found himself on a burial party for those who had died of their wounds on the journey back. 'That was a very basic affair': the dead arrived in coffins heaped on a furniture van with a medical orderly sitting on top, swinging his feet and smoking a cigarette. Most of the bodies were unnamed and, British and French alike, were piled into a collective grave. It might have been still worse if there had been grieving relations to cope with, Pearson reflected.

At Shorncliffe the Engineers were in the front line against the invasion which was expected daily. Caesar's Camp, a flat-topped hill overlooking Folkestone, was excavated to become a defensive strongpoint, set with 'thumping great tank traps' twelve feet wide and eight feet deep. Digging in the chalk in wet weather was oppressively hard work; no machinery was available, it was just brute force. Pearson and his fellow Engineers worked alongside two elderly navvies who were employed by the local council. The soldiers 'tore their guts out', the navvies 'just pecked away, taking it far easier than we did', but the professionals still made a bigger hole than the amateurs.

Early in 1941 the unit moved to Clitheroe. After a period training new recruits, Pearson was posted to Derby to educate railwaymen in the techniques of the Royal Engineers. He was billeted with a local family and for the first time in his life found himself with free time and a little money to spend. Most of his friends turned their attention to the local girls but Pearson did not yet have any aspirations in that direction. Instead he would go roller-skating with his landlord, an occupation he at first found intensely painful but which soon became a source of real pleasure. Life was agreeable enough, but he hankered for something more adventurous and close to the enemy. His wish was soon gratified. The rapid advance of the German armies into the Soviet Union in the late summer of 1941 and Russia's weakness in industrial production made it essential to send as much help as possible. The northern sea route was difficult at any time and hideously precarious in winter; roads and railways across Persia provided a possible alternative but were inadequate to bear the burdens that would be put on them. A railway works unit was assembled at Woolmer, in the Hampshire countryside north of Liss, whose orders were to proceed to Persia to put the line into better order. To this Pearson was assigned.

He soon found that he had to tread carefully. Most of the men were railway workers from Derby and Crewe who belonged to the supplementary Reserve. They had gone to France with the Expeditionary Force but, after evacuation, had been sent back to their civilian work. Now they were once more dragged away from homes and families, and were not best pleased about it: 'They were bolshie as hell,' remembers Pearson. Nor did they take kindly to instruction from a twenty-year-old tyro – 'They knew it all, and that was the end of it.' To add to the complications there was ferocious rivalry between the contingents from Crewe and Derby. It was never resolved, but Crewe scored heavily when the Derby team was required to put in order an old but immensely powerful locomotive called a Garrett, which had been originally designed to haul heavy loads over Shap Fell. It had two engines and the process of reassembly was somehow bungled so that one engine worked against the other – a mechanical push-me-pull-you. 'Typical bloody Derby men,' said the team from Crewe with satisfaction.

They reached Basra, at the head of the Persian Gulf, in November 1941. Their arrival was made less impressive by the captain managing to run the ship on to a sandbank. For twenty-four hours they were stuck there in the searing heat while the local inhabitants performed their ablutions on the waterfront and looked with some amusement at the sorry spectacle. When they belatedly landed they expected to set to work at once putting the railway line from Basra to Teheran in order. They found that the job had been done already. A company of Gurkhas lined up to greet them when they disembarked with a cheery: 'All done, Johnny. It's all yours.' In some irritation the Engineers moved immediately to Teheran and installed themselves in the railway workshops. From there Pearson, now a lance-sergeant, made expeditions to the north, mining bridges and ravines and generally preparing a hostile reception for the German armies which it seemed might break through from the Caucasus and seek to link up with the Afrika Korps in Egypt.

Pearson was struck by the terror which the Shah inspired in his people; it was the first time he had encountered a police state and he did not like it. The poor were very badly off and short of food. Once, when near-famine threatened, there were serious riots. The main preoccupation of the British was to ensure that order was restored; Pearson was sent out with a platoon to quell the crowds. 'Be prepared to shoot but, if you have to, first shoot in the air,' he was told. Left to himself he would have preferred to shoot the police, but he saw the dangers of letting the situation drift out of control and would have turned his fire on the rioters if those had been his orders. He thought that the Persians had no particular enthusiasm for either the Germans or the British; they probably felt more afraid of the former but the British were on the spot and 'were a crust of bread for them' so the locals treated them with outward deference.

On the whole relations between the races were reasonably harmonious, though inevitably the two cultures clashed from time to time. The British deplored and tried to put a stop to the system by which anyone in work paid a proportion of his wages to the person immediately above him in the hierarchy; the Persians considered this the normal way of doing things and resented attempts to change it. Socially there was sometimes friction too. Pearson remembers an incident in a nightclub when a British soldier wanted to dance with a woman who was in the company of a Persian officer. The officer protested vigorously, whereupon the Briton pulled the Persian's sword out of its scabbard and tried to wrap it around his neck. A general affray might have begun, but fortunately the police arrived and sorted it out before things went too far.

At first Pearson found the night life of Teheran exotic and exciting – 'I was so green in those days, I'd never been in a nightclub before' – but he soon discovered monotony set in. The cabaret was provided by a group of Russians who had got stuck in Teheran; they never moved on and their performance never changed. The cinemas showed mainly old Russian films, no teams from ENSA ever came to Persia; if the British troops wanted variety in their entertainment they had to provide it for themselves. In practice this consisted of little more than a concert show on Christmas nights – 'Everybody making a fool of themselves for the benefit of the rest,' Pearson describes it. He himself did no more than help arrange the chairs; 'I was an ignoramus,' he admits ruefully.

From Teheran he was detached to Ahwuz in the deep south, to liaise with the Americans. The latter were possessed by the spirit of hustle; their original intention had been to run trains between Teheran and Ahwuz at hourly intervals, then it was pointed out that, since there was only a single line for the greater part of the distance, this would be likely to involve numerous collisions. 'That calmed the Yanks down a bit.' But they were very generous to the British troops, whose camp was run on much more austere lines – hurricane lamps for instance, while the Americans enjoyed electric light. The Americans invited their poor relations to cinema shows and sent them back laden with Lucky Strike cigarettes, cookies and other rare delights.

Ahwuz was technically a 'town', but very much within inverted commas, it was a 'nothing', a bridge, a collection of tents and shabby huts, and then the end of the line in both the literal and metaphorical sense of the phrase. It nearly put paid to Pearson. While he was there Stalin surprisingly decided to release some of the Poles who had been taken prisoner at the beginning of the war. They were sent down by train through Teheran to Ahwuz where they were to catch a ship for Kenya. Their condition was deplorable: undernourished and dressed in lice-ridden rags. Pearson was responsible for getting them from railhead to dockside and is convinced that one of them infected him with typhus. His parents were sent a telegram warning them that he was on the list of those who were dangerously ill. One of his friends who was infected at the same time was dead and buried within a week. For several days he was delirious; all he remembers is looking out of the window, seeing a tree, and asking: 'What part of blighty are we in, orderly?'

Once he was off the danger list he was sent to hospital in Poona. He was emaciated; five feet ten inches tall but less than seven stone in weight. Between the hospital and Ahwuz, where he was transferred to a ship, he travelled in an ambulance with two victims of dysentery; every time the ambulance went over a bump his companions groaned, vomited and defecated. It was not a pleasant journey. Poona was much better, a former civilian hospital within sight of the racecourse, so that Pearson was able to get much pleasure watching the horses exercising. But after a few weeks he was bored. There was a large British colony in Poona, but though they might have put themselves out for an officer they had no interest in a convalescent other rank. He once tried visiting the Indian Army mess but 'they didn't want the British in there. The atmosphere was electric, so hostile that you didn't hang around. We disturbed their peacetime routine.' All he could do was wander disconsolately around the hospital and get on the nurses' nerves. It was a relief when he was on the move again; this time to Deolali, a huge reinforcement camp north of Bombay consisting of row upon row of tents and little else.

He had by now been passed fully fit, but the Army seemed to have lost interest in him. The monsoon was in full fury and Pearson found himself more or less permanently acting as orderly officer, 'and I wasn't very happy, I can tell you that, mud up to the eyeballs'. Then, when least expected, salvation came. He was summoned for an interview and confronted by two officers who told him that they were looking for instructors in demolition work, preferably unmarried. They gave no indication where such work might take him but said that they belonged to a mysterious body called Force 136 – a name that meant nothing to him. Knowing the speed at which military bureaucracy usually operated he expected to be kept waiting for weeks or even months; instead, within forty-eight hours, he was summoned back to Poona to enrol.

At once he found himself plunged into a world of cloaks and daggers, of secrecy so exaggerated that the left hand not only did not know what the right hand was doing but sometimes did not even know that its opposite number existed. On arrival at Poona he was met by an Indian and taken to a secluded villa. There an unidentified Englishman told him that he was free until the evening but must be back in good time because he was leaving the country that night. 'For God's sake don't get involved with the Military Police,' he was told, 'for we'll deny all knowledge of you.'

'Home at last!' thought Pearson contentedly, but instead he found himself heading south for Ceylon. There he found himself on an island called Kinya in China Bay, near Trincomalee, where Force 136 had its base. It was codenamed ME (Military Establishment) 25 and was invested with vast, almost mystical prestige. Nobody outside the organisation knew exactly what it was doing (those inside sometimes seemed almost equally unclear) but its activities were generally held to be nefarious and significant. To conserve stocks of petrol, on certain days nobody in Ceylon except the most lofty of top brass was allowed to use a vehicle, but the mere mention of ME25 overcame all restrictions. Pearson was grateful to be associated with such an elite, even though it did not seem likely that he would play any very active role himself. His function, first at Kinya and subsequently at Horena, near Colombo, was to train a group of Burmans and Karen tribesmen from the jungle areas of the Upper Chindwin River in the use of small arms and explosives. The group was under the command of two Rhodesian officers, Colonel Peacock and Major Poles, and Pearson understood that they would eventually be dropped behind the Japanese lines in Burma to disrupt communications when the final push began. Peacock and Poles were friends from before the war; Peacock had spent some years in the Forestry Department in Burma and thus spoke the language fluently.

It was not long before Pearson found himself accepted as part of the team; not just as a trainer who would be left behind when the real business started but as an active participant. He never actually volunteered, but neither was he recruited: 'It was as natural as breathing. I'd trained these chaps; they were going in to do a job – who should go with them but yours truly?' When the decision was taken the pace suddenly gathered. Pearson had his parachute training at the last moment, back in India at an aerodrome near the delta of the Ganges, within easy reach of Burma. On the morning of the first day he was jumping three feet or so from a veranda, learning how to fall and roll over; that afternoon he practised from a grounded aircraft; the same evening he made his first jump. 'It was a wonderful experience. You feel ten feet high when you touch down.' He did six or seven drops, each time enjoying it more, but the pressure was so hectic that when it came to the final jump of the course, which took place at night, he was told that there was no time and that he would have to get his practice doing the real thing. Pearson was not in the least discomfited by any moment of the training – 'so short and sweet it was unbelievable'. His only fear was that he might break an ankle in landing and be returned to his unit 'as a duffer'.

'Operation Character', as it was called, was launched on 2 February 1945. As the time approached Pearson had been pleasantly surprised how little concerned he was by what might lie ahead – 'What will be, will be', he reflected philosophically. His tranquillity was to be severely tested. There were three P Force groups in six Dakota aircraft. Peacock and his team, including Poles, a Captain Guthrie, Pearson and a number of Burmans and Karens, took off in the second flight. When they reached the designated dropping zone Peacock stood at the open door ready to jump. As the pilot circled the area Peacock remained, staring in some perplexity at the ground. For what was probably only a couple of minutes but seemed to Pearson an eternity the plane cruised around; then Peacock and the pilot conferred and the plane turned back. Only when they were safely home did Pearson learn that what should have been an area of deserted paddy fields in the Karen hills had instead turned out to be set with trees and, even more alarmingly, lit by what seemed to be camp fires. Peacock had no wish to land in the middle of a Japanese force and decided to abort the mission. His caution was justified when it was subsequently established that, by ill luck, a Japanese unit had indeed selected the dropping zone as a place to bivouac for the night.

To salvage something from the fiasco, the aircraft returned by way of the Burmese town of Prome, where it scattered a load of leaflets. Even this proved unexpectedly troublesome. When the door opened the leaflets blew like confetti around the plane. The pilot insisted that all the bits of paper be picked up before the men were allowed to disembark on their return to base, a task performed with much cursing and ill humour.

The following night the pilot tried again at another site. This time there was no Japanese presence, but the ground was a lot rougher and more thickly set with trees and bushes than had been hoped. Pearson landed successfully but one in five of those who jumped with him suffered some sort of injury. Major Poles broke a rib but did not let a little thing like that impede his further progress. Captain Guthrie fared worse. He thought he was falling into a tree, crossed his legs as was the correct procedure in such a case, instead landed in a bush and suffered a badly fractured ankle. It was at once clear that he would not be able to keep up with the rest of the group for a few weeks at least, but what should happen to him in the meantime was an agonising problem. The Japanese must have heard of the landing. Within a few hours there were reports that a substantial force was hurrying towards the area. All that could be done was to entrust Guthrie to the Karen tribesmen who lived nearby and hope that they would be able to secrete him in the jungle until he was able to move again. At great risk to themselves, the Karens agreed to do their best. Guthrie survived and was able to play a useful part in the later stages of Force 136's operations.

For the next nine months the group remained hidden, frequently involved in skirmishes with the Japanese but amazingly suffering no fatal casualties. Peacock established his headquarters on top of a mountain where the RAF were able to make occasional drops of ammunition and other supplies. At first the task was to reconnoitre and to enlist the local Karens in a fighting force that could go into battle against the Japanese when the moment came. Then the pace quickened. The Supreme Commander, Louis Mountbatten, had decreed that the town of Toungoo must at all costs be taken before the start of the monsoon so as to open the way to Rangoon. If the Japanese were able to withdraw their two divisions from the Karen hills and reinforce the Toungoo garrison, this would prove much more difficult if not impossible. Force 136 was given the task of obstructing the Japanese retreat by demolishing bridges, felling trees across the mountain roads, ambushing convoys, and generally disrupting enemy movements and lowering their morale.

Pearson's special responsibility was to lead a small group of Karens in attacks on enemy convoys. Usually he would plant explosive in a pothole in the road and fire it by hand as the first lorry went over; the support team hidden in the bush would then open fire on the Japanese soldiers as they jumped from the vehicles in search of the hidden foe. Sometimes Pearson had time to lob a grenade or two into other lorries towards the head of the column.

The plan was that the group should melt away into the jungle before the formidable firepower of the Japanese had been assembled and the going became too hot. Sometimes the timing was too tight for comfort. Pearson was usually the last person to leave the scene of the action. The first time he attacked a convoy a Japanese mortar opened up on him when he was still lying only three or four yards from the road. He was spotted and chased into the jungle. The Karens had gone ahead to an agreed rendezvous, Pearson knew that if he could rejoin them he would be safe since their superior knowledge of the jungle paths would enable them to get away, but at that moment he had no idea where he was. He saw a man only a few yards away, thought he was a Karen and called out the password. A burst from a Japanese tommy-gun was his answer. Fortunately he was on top of a slight rise and was able to tumble down the other side to safety; he was 'shaking like an aspen leaf', he remembers. Such risks were worth running. On the five-mile section of the road for which he was personally responsible, more than a hundred Japanese lorries were destroyed and innumerable hours precious to the enemy were wasted.

Occasionally the Japanese would make a systematic attempt to sweep an area of jungle in which men from Force 136 were believed to be ensconced. The last thing that Peacock wanted was to be drawn into a serious confrontation with the enemy; he ordered that when a superior Japanese force was advancing the guerrillas should fall back and regroup at some pre-arranged and distant point. If the worse came to the worst and a soldier was surrounded, he should put his back to a tree and open fire. 'I never felt that way disposed myself,' says Pearson drily. His own closest escape came when he fired on a village which he knew to be occupied by a Japanese garrison. The enemy were nearer to him than he had supposed and were on his track within minutes. At one moment it seemed to him certain that he would be taken. He resolved to shoot himself rather than face the protracted torture that he knew would be his lot if captured in such circumstances:

'Whether I would have had the guts to do it when the time came, I don't know.' Mercifully the Japanese were as much lost in the deep jungle as Pearson himself, the pursuit slackened and he was never put to the test.

'It is extraordinary,' wrote Major Poles, 'that a young, inexperienced soldier, hitherto untried in war, and never before faced with tactical responsibilities, could accumulate such experience over such a period. His gallantry and behaviour were always in the best traditions of the service.' It was so obvious to Colonel Peacock that Pearson was doing work far more demanding than anything that might be expected from someone of his rank, that he suggested he should take a commission, with immediate effect. Pearson looked aghast at the idea. It would be a feather in his cap, urged Peacock. If he decided he didn't like it he could always resign the commission and revert to the ranks once the operation was over. 'Well, with my humble background I just didn't dare do it,' says Pearson. 'I couldn't. It frightened me. I'd been in the Army before the war and an officer to me was a man of independent means.'

Even after the Japanese surrendered, operations were by no means over for Force 136; for several weeks individuals or small units among the enemy either did not hear that the fighting had finished or refused to accept their Emperor's decision. One officer from Force 136, prospecting some way ahead of his men, saw a group of Japanese, strode towards them and announced that they were his prisoners. 'He must have been a bit barmy,' Pearson remembers; the Japanese laughed heartily and retorted that they weren't his prisoners, he was theirs. He was roughly handled by his captors but was luckily still alive when this contingent of Japanese was finally convinced that the war had indeed ended.

The moment when Force 136 linked up with the advancing Fourteenth Army should have been dramatic but in fact fell flat; the scout leading the advance patrol merely nodded to Pearson, said 'Wot'cher, tosh' and walked on. Poles told Pearson to take charge of a party of the sick and wounded and get them to where they could receive medical treatment. The first unit he met was the Rajputna Rifles. He asked for food. A British officer looked at him superciliously and said: 'You must realise this is a front-line unit. We can't feed everyone.' Eventually he conceded that, once the officers had dined and if there was anything left, Pearson's men could have it. Pearson stormed into the cookhouse and demanded: 'Feed my men, or else ... ' They were fed. Next day they came across the Welsh Regiment: 'The difference in welcome had to be experienced to be believed. They couldn't do too much for us.'

Pearson had been put in charge of the sick largely because he was sick himself. On the whole he had stayed remarkably well during his nine months behind the Japanese lines. Apart from malaria, which he escaped, there were many others threats to health: snakes, scorpions, poisonous spiders, thorns that caused wounds which would fester and become inflamed. Leeches were particularly troublesome because if pulled off they would leave their arrowhead behind and the spot would soon turn septic. The approved course was to burn them off with a lighted cigarette but this did not avail the unfortunate man who got a leech lodged in his nostril. After much debate, he lay on his back and poured salt water down his nose until the leech released its grip. Drinking water was hard to come by and, though the supply by air was reasonably reliable, food was always inadequate and malnutrition a fact of life. There were wild birds and occasional animals to supplement the rations, but guns could rarely be used for fear of attracting the attention of the Japanese. Pearson remembers once trying to shoot hens with a crossbow; in this case the object was more to deny food to the Japanese than to replenish their own supplies, but the meat would still have been extremely welcome. Nine times out of ten he missed and the chicken jumped into the bushes with a fearful clucking. But it was the mental stress more than the physical which had worn Pearson down: the constant tension, the sleepless nights, the knowledge that the slightest slip might cost not merely his own life but the lives of cherished comrades, the relentless hostility of the environment. 'Sergeant Pearson. Evacuated from Field 18/8/45, exhaustion,' reads the terse record. Major Poles says that he left with extreme reluctance. So no doubt he did, but the reluctance was mingled with relief. Pearson himself remembers that nobody was more pleased than he was when peace came 'as I was absolutely, totally exhausted'.

After making sure that the sick men were being properly looked after, Pearson hitchhiked to Rangoon and made his way to his old headquarters in Ceylon. 'You should have been home months ago,' they told him, and put him aboard a Royal Navy destroyer, HMS *Rapid*, which was about to sail for England. Unfortunately her behaviour did not suit her name; she proceeded at 'economical speed', stopped for a repaint at Malta and, even when she arrived at Devonport, dropped anchor and spent the night just outside the harbour with the street lights of Plymouth twinkling tantalisingly a few hundred yards away. But even the weariest river winds somewhere safe to sea. The following night Pearson was back in London, in a pea-souper fog that convinced him – if conviction were needed – that he was home at last. A brief visit to the Special Operations headquarters in Baker Street was the preamble to a much-deserved period of leave. Once more he found himself in the Yorkshire he had left four years before: 'It was lovely coming home.'

So what came next? He was still only twenty-four and uncommonly resilient. Within a few weeks he felt recovered from the rigours of the war. Once he had a nightmare related to his experiences in the jungle. The rule there had been that, before settling down for the night, one should dig a shallow trench, put one's American carbine inside and sleep on top of it. He dreamt that he was back in Burma and that he woke to find himself surrounded by Japanese. However hard he tried, 'for the life of me I couldn't get my carbine out'. For some survivors dreams of this kind proved to be precursors to a line of interrupted nights;

Pearson somehow exorcised the memories. Burma never figured in his dreams again.

He was ready for anything. But outside the Army he couldn't think of anything much that he would like to do. He still had more than fifteen of his original twenty-two years to serve, and though nobody would have demurred if he had decided to cut his service short he barely even considered the possibility. In a way, he could not lose by staying in. As an Engineer he was bound to acquire greater experience with every job; experience which would enable him to get better employment when eventually he entered civilian life.

He was not left to enjoy his leave for long. Almost before he had settled down he was summoned to join No. 7 Bomb Disposal Unit. There was a desperate need for men of proven courage, a calm disposition and experience of handing explosives to deal with the millions of mines and unexploded bombs which pitted Britain's surface. Pearson was obviously a prime candidate for such a role. It seemed to him a bit hard to be given so perilous a task after surviving the jungle in Burma, 'but you don't dwell on those things, at least I didn't. Anyway, I was with a good crowd of men. It was a good, happy unit.'

After only a few weeks in Bristol he was despatched to the Cornish coast, to clear the minefields which had been planted to meet a possible invasion. It was tricky work: the mines had been sown in haste, few records existed of where the fields had been located, anyway the wind had changed the conformation of the sand dunes and made the problem still more difficult. At their first job, at Perranporth near Newquay, they decided to dig a trench into the area where the minefield was believed to be. All went well until they actually met a mine; it exploded and brought down the walls of the trench on top of them, killing several Engineers and German prisoners-of-war, who had volunteered for the work in exchange for a promise of early repatriation. After that they had recourse to a high-pressure hose, using water from the sea to expose the mines. Once the mines were visible it was Pearson's task to put an explosive charge on them and blow them up.

The locals did not always seem to be as appreciative as the Engineers felt they should have been. The inhabitants of one Cornish resort were anxious to get summer visitors back as quickly as possible. If they did not hear enough explosions from the beaches they would upbraid the Engineers for wasting time, even writing letters to *The Times* and the *Daily Telegraph*, complaining that the work was not being given sufficient priority. The Engineers got their revenge by directing the blast towards the backs of the hotels and boarding houses: 'You'd hear *bang*, then tinkle-tinkle as the windows blew in.' But when the work was done the villagers gave their benefactors 'a marvellous fish-and-chip supper' and presented them with a silver casket and an illuminated address – so the Engineers were left feeling a little guilty about their acts of sabotage.

Apart from his younger sisters Pearson had had little experience of women before he joined the Army and his military career had offered few opportunities to repair the omission. He was not afraid of girls, he explains, but he had 'never chased after them like some of the other chaps did'. Then, at the end of 1945 in Bristol, he met Eileen Roberts. She worked in the sales department of the tobacco company, Wills, and when Pearson met her was pushing her mother in a wheel chair. He offered to help, she accepted gratefully; soon they were going out together. She was an only child and much the same age as Pearson; her mother was an invalid, her father, who had used to run a public house, had died some years before. It was no hurricane affair, they did not formally become engaged until 1947, but neither of them was in any doubt that they were making the right decision. Eileen never objected to the fact that her fiancé was a soldier nor suggested that he might do something else: 'Well, if that's your job we'll accept it,' she would say. They married as soon as the bomb disposal job was over and spent the honeymoon with Eileen's mother in Bristol. It was not, perhaps, the most romantic of arrangements but it suited them both; Pearson had acquired a mountain of photographs over the previous years and his wife spent much of the time sticking them in albums.

As soon as the honeymoon was over, Pearson was on his way to his next assignment, a two-year course at the School of Engineering at Chatham. The married quarters were all occupied, so he had to make do with a bed-sitting-room, where Eileen joined him after a few months. Their first child, a daughter, was born while they were there. Pearson enjoyed the course and found it sufficiently testing to convince him, by the time he had finished, that he knew everything there was to know about engineering. He knew a great deal, but inevitably his skills were specialised and often irrelevant to civilian life. Only when he was finally demobilised did he discover that he needed to take evening classes to qualify for the higher grades of work and become a member of an engineering institute.

Eileen was already pregnant with their second child when, in January 1950, Pearson was posted to Benghazi in North Africa. He was working with a military hospital which was in urgent need of a first-class laundry, and Pearson's main task was to assemble this from a selection of bits and pieces which were in store and, with the help of much ingenuity and resourcefulness, transform it into a working unit. His wife joined him with their daughter and the new baby – a five-week-old son – but though this certainly enriched his life it did not make it more restful. He was working much too hard, often through the night, and sleeping badly when he did get to bed, waking to find the sheets soaked in sweat. He tried to take up long-distance running again and ran the mile in the unit sports, but soon found that his lungs 'weren't big enough to keep me going'. Eventually he appealed to the doctor and said that he thought he must have flu. The doctor sent him to have an X-ray, examined the results and ordered him to hospital. 'I can't. I've got a wife and family, and a job to do,' protested Pearson. 'You're a very sick man,' replied the doctor. He had tuberculosis, perhaps picked up originally in the jungle in Burma. He would recover, but only if he did exactly what the doctors told him. One of the things that the doctors told him was that he should give up smoking. Until then he had been getting through fifty cigarettes a day – though some of these had been distributed to the workmen on the laundry project. Withdrawal pangs added an extra pain to what was anyway a protracted and disagreeable illness.

Pearson was invalided back to England and installed in the Connaught Chest Hospital at Hindhead. At first he was only allowed to get out of bed to pay one visit to the lavatory a day, then the ration was increased to two, finally he was deemed fit enough to withstand an operation at the Naval Hospital at Chatham. After some months he was discharged, as he supposed ready to continue with his military career. The Army was keen to have him back; there were too few men of his experience and qualifications to make them accept his loss without much regret. They felt, however, that they could not run the risk of another breakdown, and the possibility of having a permanent invalid on their hands. They asked the doctors for an assurance that his health was fully restored. To Pearson's dismay, this was something that the doctors were not prepared to give. 'So I was out, much to my annoyance, for the Army had been my life for so long.'

If he had stayed, he would probably have put in for the commission that he had rejected while in Burma. Of the surviving Engineers who had qualified with him from the course at Chatham, most were already officers and the remainder would soon follow. What had once been unthinkable now seemed an acceptable, even a proper, step. He says that the reasons for his change of heart were mainly financial; rates of pay for junior officers had improved, the need for private means was no longer so pressing, 'being a little bit prudent we could have got by'. This is certainly part of the story, but it is also the case that he had matured and grown in self-confidence; when he was offered a commission in Burma 'it frightened me to death', now he would have accepted the extra responsibility with equanimity. To have his career cut short just when such prospects were opening was doubly galling.

During his time in hospital his wife and children had lived with his mother-in-law in Bristol and it was there that the reluctant civilian decided to settle and start a new career. At first he felt 'very lost', the backing of a huge organisation suddenly removed from him. Fortunately it was a period of full employment and, unlike many former soldiers of his generation, he possessed skills that equipped him for a wide range of jobs. At first he did not venture too far from the governmental fold, applying for a job in the Inspectorate of Electrical and Mechanical Equipment in Bristol. The interview was a formality; the man responsible for recruitment was a former chief petty officer in the Royal Navy, who knew exactly what Pearson would be capable of and liked the look of him. But though the work was well within his powers, promotion was painfully slow and the rigid hierarchy of the Inspectorate was irritating for someone who was anxious to get on. After three years he moved to the Ministry of Works, but here too he found that the civil service mentality and the assumption that promotion was related not to merit but to length of service were intolerably stifling. After eighteen months he looked around again. This time he ventured into private industry. Imperial Tobacco was advertising a vacancy that seemed to Pearson to amount to 'the same blinking job as I was doing already, only in different words'. He applied for it, was asked how much he was paid by the Ministry of Works, and was offered the same rounded up to the nearest £100. He knew that it was 'one of the finest organised firms you could ever work for in the Bristol area', and was particularly attracted by the fact that it was energetically diversifying out of tobacco so there would be opportunities in plenty for him to use and develop his engineering skills. He accepted the offer without hesitation.

For the first three months or so after their marriage his wife had gone on working so as to earn the money to get her from Bristol to Chatham where her husband was based. Now that he was out of the Army and settled in Bristol she would have liked to get back to work again. The extra income would have been very welcome but Pearson, so tolerant and mild in most respects, had some curiously conservative ideas and enforced them obstinately. 'I come from the North-East, and it wasn't the practice': men went out and earned the daily bread, women remained at home. In fact Eileen must have had plenty to do at home; by the time they settled in Bristol they had three children and the third, another girl, was little more than a baby. Pearson was a concerned and conscientious father but his work, particularly after he had been with Imperial Tobacco a year or two, kept him often away from home and most of the business of looking after a family rested on his wife. Eileen was much more of a churchgoer than her husband, but he supported her when she insisted that the children should go to Sunday School. He was resolved that they should have a better upbringing than he had enjoyed himself, both in education and in the pleasures of life; he always managed to arrange at least a week's family holiday each year, even if only in Weston-Super-Mare, a mere fifteen miles away.

After some toing and froing they moved into a three-storey house in Bristol where Eileen's mother, now only able to shuffle around on crutches, lived with them for several years. Unlike most parents with military background Pearson was not particularly demanding over such matters as cleanliness or punctuality; he was a perfectionist, however, and it gave him great pain to see a botched job. As a result he ended up doing most of the tasks around the house himself; since he also did all the driving and looked after the finances, Eileen found that her role in the family was largely confined to cooking, cleaning and tending to the children. Outside the home, however, she contrived to have a life of her own. She was a staunch Tory who worked busily on the local committees and canvassed at elections. Pearson himself was moderately to the left but he thought all politicians more or less worthless; he viewed his wife's activities with some surprise but made no effort to dissuade her.

His determination not to delegate but to do everything himself must have contributed to the disaster which was to overtake him. Imperial Tobacco needed people who would do design work. The task called for skills beyond anything Pearson possessed but he resolved to try: 'OK, I'll go back to the drawing board.' He went to evening classes, studied at home, learnt on the job and by 1966 was head of the Engineering Services Department. He was working far too hard, doing several jobs at once – when he gave up two people had to be promoted to take over his various duties. In February 1966, he drove with two of his colleagues to a site near Manchester where work was going on. He had had a headache that morning and was conscious of feeling more tired than usual but thought no more of it and did a full day's work. As they were driving back the man beside him said: 'You've been driving this ruddy car all day. Let's stop for a cup of coffee and then I'll take over.' So they called in at a wayside café. As they were going through the swing doors, Pearson remembers, 'my left side just collapsed. It didn't worry me overmuch for I thought it would wear off in a minute.' His friends urged him to hurry up but, by good luck, the members of an ambulance team were in the queue just ahead of them and they realised that something was seriously wrong. They got on to their radio and arranged for Pearson to be removed to the local hospital. The duty doctor examined him and told him that he had suffered a slight stroke. It would be best if he stayed in the hospital overnight. Even then Pearson was not seriously worried: 'I thought, oh, all right, it'll obviously wear off by tomorrow morning.'

In fact it was ten weeks before he could go home, and then he could walk only with the help of crutches and at a slow shuffle. At least his sight and hearing were unaffected and mentally, too, he survived pretty well, though he noticed that he would suddenly lose a train of thought. In such cases, if he didn't worry about it and took his time, the thought would usually come back 'like a newsflash on TV'; but he found such lapses disconcerting. He was told that he would probably in time recover most of the use of his left arm and leg, though he would never be entirely restored to what he had been before. A quick recovery was not to be expected nor, indeed, desired; the prevailing doctrine at the time had it that those who did get better rapidly were the ones most likely to have a second stroke, and the second stroke would probably be fatal, or at least far more destructive.

As a man accustomed to being intensively active and to doing everything for himself, he found his incapacity almost impossible to bear patiently. He now had to rely on his wife to do the driving, to look after the bank account, to take over responsibilities which he had previously assumed only he could manage. When he wanted jobs done about the house his children had to be enlisted; he knew he could have done them far better himself and fretted helplessly at what he felt to be their inadequacy. In his mind, says one of his children, 'he was still doing all the things himself'. But if he was sometimes cantankerous and unreasonable it was primarily because he hated to be a burden on other people. He in no way wanted his family's lives to be affected by his illness; when his son asked if he should leave school and get a job Pearson insisted that he should continue with his studies.

Imperial Tobacco were exceptionally good employers. They gave his wife a first-class railway ticket to visit him every week while he was in hospital and provided a chauffeur-driven car to take him home when he was discharged. But though Pearson worked hard to rehabilitate himself, with daily physiotherapy and swimming sessions, they made it clear that they could never take him back for fear of possible claims for compensation. 'We wouldn't even employ Len as a liftman,' the personnel officer told his wife. Anything else within reason they would do. They paid him an immediate pension, continued it without demur when he got another job, increased it in the period of galloping inflation. Pearson appreciated their generosity and bore no grudge but he could not endure feeling himself useless; what he wanted was a serious occupation. His doctor passed him as fit to work: 'You can do another job, *if* you can find one.' The note of scepticism infuriated Pearson: 'It really got the hell in me.' He knocked at every door, approached every engineering concern in Bristol. Finally the Regional Health Authority said that they were looking for someone to set up a reference library of design: 'If you're prepared to have a go, we might be able to fit you in.'

Pearson was at first suspicious that this might be a non-job, something thought up by a benevolent employer who anyway had to fill a quota of disabled employees. He soon found that there was a real need for such a library and that he was exceptionally well qualified to organise it. To start with, indeed, the work was only part time; but once they were convinced that he could handle it the Health Authority appointed him an administration officer and took him on full time. He stayed with them for fifteen years.

Then came a moment for decision. While he was in the job Mrs Thatcher introduced a system under which anyone registered as a disabled employee had the right to take retirement at the age of sixty. Left to himself he would not have taken advantage of the offer but his wife urged him to do so. She herself had got involved in voluntary work running the shop at the local hospital and had had enough of it; if he retired, she pleaded, it would make it easier for her to do the same. He agreed, and in 1982 they began retired life together.

They had a few happy years. Their previous holidays had been spent with the children in a seaside caravan, enjoyable enough but hard work for Eileen. The only real holiday for her would be a cruise, Pearson decided, and off they went in the *Canberra* on a tour of the Mediterranean: 'Oh, it was lovely! She enjoyed it so much.' The trip was so great a success that, even though they could not really afford it, they decided to repeat the adventure. This time it was to be the Norwegian fjords. They made the reservation, and then came disaster. Eileen felt ill enough to consult a doctor, went into hospital and was diagnosed as having stomach cancer. A large part of her intestines had to be cut out but the doctors were resolutely cheerful. There was another patient in the ward, they said, who had endured even worse cancer of the stomach, and she was alive after eleven years. Eileen could hope to do better than that.

There followed a period of remission. For several years she lived at home, well enough to look after her husband. They went on their cruise to Norway and enjoyed it greatly: 'That was the last real holiday we had together.' They had bought a bungalow, which was more convenient for Pearson after his stroke, but they had barely moved in when it went up in flames – probably because one of the workmen had left an unextinguished cigarette on the joists in the roof. Their son was living with them at the time and managed to save the cat and dog, the neighbours rallied round and pulled out much of the furniture, but a great deal was lost and for several months the Pearsons were homeless, camping with friends and neighbours while the bungalow was rebuilt. Finally they moved back in, and till 1991 life seemed to be on an even keel. Then Eileen began to feel ill again; it became increasingly clear that the cancer was taking hold once more. The final stages were quick but not too agonising, the worst pains controlled by a cocktail of drugs which left her dazed but at least able to communicate until the end. She died on 27 November, the birthday of their eldest child.

His wife's death devastated Pearson; he was never able to come fully to terms with it. Only after she had gone did he realise how heavily he had depended on her. He had always been asking her to fetch a book from the next room or to make a cup of tea; now he had to do it for himself. He managed, but the effort was sometimes painful. As he could not drive he had to rely on neighbours to do the shopping, but he hated to impose on them and often went without things that they would have been happy to procure for him. His children took it in turns to visit him at weekends, but here too he was reluctant to be a burden. The dog, a mongrel which his daughter had brought home when she was still at school, began to have fits and had to be put down. Sometimes Pearson thought that he should be put down too.

Before his wife died Pearson had sometimes remarked that, if she went first, he would go to the Royal Hospital, but, after she had gone, it seemed somehow a matter of honour that he should hold on and prove he could fend for himself. He did so for the best part of two years. His children were admiring of his resolution and anxious not to distress him by suggesting that things might soon become too much for him, but they viewed the future with trepidation. Without ever putting it to him directly they hinted that he might give some thought to a move to Chelsea. He knew that their advice was wise; life at home was week by week becoming more arduous and even if he had been prepared to live with one of his children, it would have been physically impossible for them to accommodate him. But whether the Hospital would be prepared to take him with his still serious disability was another question. Eventually he decided that he might as well try: 'I was cussed enough to think that if I didn't get accepted I'd be no worse off.' He would have been a great deal worse off – he suspected it then and he was certain of it within a few weeks of his acceptance and installation in the Hospital.

Life at Chelsea suited him admirably. The only thing he would have changed was the attitude of a few of the ward non-commissioned officers, Pensioners who had been selected to take certain responsibilities looking after their companions in their section of the Hospital. They were there to help the other Pensioners, considers Pearson, not to boss them around, but a few of them seemed to feel that they were back in the Army in charge of a squad of recalcitrant recruits, ordering 'Do this! Do that!' That had never been Pearson's way: 'I tried to lead by example.' He himself, anyway, has been lucky in his ward NCOs, who were always happy to do anything to help and never let a little authority go to their heads. In every other way it suits him well to be back in the military world where he has spent so much of his working life. 'The Army was the making of me,' he concludes; and, he feels, it might as well see the end of him as well.

That end he contemplates with philosophical resignation. His wife was always keen to make use of any scraps that were hanging around the house. He used to say that when he died she would have him cremated and use the ashes in an egg-timer. She is not there now to do anything so practical but he would still be happy to be of service in any way.

Len Pearson died at the Royal Hospital on 3 April 2001.

ARTHUR JEFFERY

Private Jeffery, *c* 1946

Arthur Jeffery

ARTHUR Ernest Jeffery – in youth he was almost always called Peter because his grandfather found it easier to remember children with biblical names – had no connections with the Army. His father, Ernest, had been in the Royal Navy, serving mainly in destroyers, and had fought at Jutland. He came out in 1922, tried a few jobs without much success, and eventually became a pipe-joiner, laying sewers or water pipes across the Devonshire countryside. Assiduous and energetic, he thought little of bicycling twenty miles there and back if his work took him to distant parts of the county. He had high standards when it came to punctuality, cleanliness and good manners, and expected that his children would observe them too.

Above all Ernest Jeffery was obsessively truthful. The only exception he allowed himself was over his age; he found it hard to admit even to his own family how old he really was and had no hesitation in falsifying the records when he sought to rejoin the Navy on the outbreak of the Second World War. Though he frequently spoke harshly to his children and imposed punishments on them, Peter remembers only one occasion on which his father struck him. He had been asked to pick up a new bicycle from the railway station, and also a saw which had been sent for sharpening. Fooling about with the lights of the bicycle Peter got the saw caught in the spokes and ripped out six of them. He borrowed a pair of pliers and managed to put them back into place. 'Was the bike all right?' asked his father that evening. Peter replied that it was, hoping that his repair work had been properly done and that his father would never know about the accident. Next day his father went off on his bicycle and the wheel collapsed, nearly throwing him under a bus. That night he returned, on a 'horrible old bike' that he had borrowed from a friend. 'You told me the bike was all right!' he said accusingly. So it was, replied his son, '– and he hit me. My word, he did hit me. If you told the truth you were all right.'

Money was always short, for Ernest Jeffery was a freelance and if there was no job on offer or the weather made work on the pipes impossible, his income would stop at once. He had learnt to box while in the Navy and used to earn a bit on the side by working as a professional boxer at the fairs in Barnstaple, Plymouth or other not-too-distant towns. There was not much money in it – he was lucky if he made £1 a time after expenses had been paid – but even this amount was extremely welcome and, anyway, he enjoyed it. Peter never went to see him box in the ring but would sometimes watch him train at the back of the local pub. In the evenings Ernest used to coach a group of three or four young enthusiasts. Peter's mother, Anne, hated boxing and tried to stop her son taking up the sport, but his father encouraged him. The first real present that Peter could remember being given was a pair of boxing gloves. They cost five shillings.

He had the sea in his blood on both sides. His mother's father had been a fisherman and had worked in the old sailing ships. Anne's father's house was in the same village and for Peter it was a second home, where discipline was more relaxed and nobody bothered much if his hands were dirty or he was a few minutes late for meals. Anne did not bother unduly either, but she accepted her husband's standards without protest. There was no doubt who made the rules in the Jeffery household and Ernest was inflexible.

Peter was born on 10 April 1922; his mother had married at the age of eighteen and was still less than twenty years old at the time. A daughter was born four years later; then came a gap of nearly ten years before a second son and daughter were added to the family. Their home was in Lympstone, a small fishing port on an estuary of the River Exe. At first they lived in a cottage with only two bedrooms and no bathroom; when Peter was nine his father managed to secure a rather larger council house on the outskirts of the village. The mains electricity and water ran only a hundred yards away but the Council decided it would be too expensive to link up the Jefferys' house, so though they were able to boast a bathroom its usefulness was limited. Still the house had three bedrooms, a lounge and a living-room-kitchen; to Peter it seemed palatial.

Lympstone had an excellent village school, with a headmaster who was dedicated to his work and who demanded and got high standards in the other teachers. Peter began in the nursery class when he was only two and a half and stayed there till he was fourteen. He was a bright child and well able to hold his own at school, but though he never disgraced himself he had little enthusiasm for books or learning and did no more work than was needed to get by without discredit. His father had educated himself while in the Royal Navy, wrote an excellent hand and followed current affairs with intelligent interest; the family took a daily paper – 'which a lot of people in those days didn't' – and discussed the world's events. They chose the *Daily Mail* because it carried more detail of the shipping movements than the other cheaper papers and a brother of Peter's mother was still in the Royal Navy.

Peter's was a church school and there was a short prayer in each class at the beginning of the day but that was as far as religious education went. Peter does not remember the vicar ever putting in an appearance. He found little more enthusiasm for organised religion at home. His parents packed the children off on Sunday mornings – to chapel rather than church – but they rarely did as much themselves; Ernest Jeffery made a point of going to the service on Armistice Day but otherwise felt his Sundays too precious to waste in worship. The children saw nothing odd about this discrimination; they assumed that church, like school, was something you had to attend when young but soon grew out of. But though the Kingdom of God got scant attention, the earthly kingdom below was treated with due respect. Empire Day, which took place on 24 May, Queen Victoria's birthday, was celebrated with much fervour, with flag-flying, pageants of heroes and patriotic songs.

Music was not taught formally at school but it was part of Peter's life. Ernest Jeffery was a versatile and accomplished musician; his son could not remember an instrument which he could not play with a fair degree of competence. He was a drummer in the village and the Territorial Army bands but he also had an accordion, a guitar, a concertina and an upright piano in rosewood. The piano cost £5. This took up so much of the household's disposable income that it was several months before they could afford to have it tuned. Anne Jeffery could tinkle away on the piano and joined in the family music-making, but she could not match her husband's skills. Peter took after his father though with less pronounced ability. He never got anywhere with the piano – 'I lacked the co-ordination of the left and right hands' – but he enjoyed playing other instruments and became particularly adept on the cornet.

The village school had an impressive record for sending its pupils on to the grammar school at Exmouth; indeed, says Peter proudly, it 'turned out several children who got commissions or good jobs in the civil service'. His sister made the transition to grammar school successfully and his father would somehow have found the extra money if Peter had done the same, but he had no such ambitions. He wanted to get on with life, to become independent, to see the world. His headmaster had encouraged the children to devote some time to the school allotment; Peter enjoyed the work and, as a stop-gap when he left school at fourteen, helped his uncle, an ex-marine, look after the garden of a rich neighbour. The job of gardener's boy, however, could not contain him for long. His uncle preached the wonders of the Royal Marines, his father fully supported the idea; as soon as he was of an age to become a band-boy he set off for Exeter to enlist.

It proved an unpropitious start to a military career. At Exeter he was given an educational test and sent to a doctor for inspection; then he was despatched to Bristol to see a second doctor, then to Plymouth to see a third. Having surmounted these hurdles he moved on to the Marine Depot at Deal. The journey took from 5 a.m. to 7 p.m.; he had nothing to eat all day and he had to make his own way to the barracks; his welcome was off-hand and no refreshment was provided; next day he had to parade before yet another doctor. His audition for the band passed off all right but by now he had had more than enough of Deal and of the Royal Marines: 'I didn't like it. I really didn't like it. I felt like a fish out of water.' After a couple of weeks he packed his bag and left, without saying a word to anyone.

Technically, he was a deserter. The thought did not concern him greatly. He was only 'an insignificant little band-boy' and it did not seem to him likely that the majesty of the law would be harnessed to hound him down. But even if the threat had been more real he would have lost little sleep. Perhaps as a result of his childhood, perhaps by genetic inheritance, it took a great deal to worry him. 'I'd learnt to shut things out,' he says. 'I would have accepted the punishment if I'd been caught, if I'd done something wrong. I always accepted the consequences. But I didn't worry.'

He could not help feeling some alarm, however, about the reception he could expect at home. He knew his father would disapprove of his escapade. He arrived on a Friday evening, when his parents were just going out. His father asked him what he was doing in Devonshire when he should have been in Deal. Peter explained that he had run away, that he loathed the Marines and would never go back to them. 'You chose it,' said his father. 'It was your decision. Now you must stick with it. If you're still here when I come home tomorrow at lunch time, we'll go to the police station.' There was no shouting, he spoke calmly, but before he left for work the following morning he went into his son's bedroom and said: 'Now, don't forget what I told you.' His mother was distraught, imagining her son thrown into gaol, but there was no hope that she would argue the matter with her husband: 'There was no shifting Father when he had made up his mind.' Peter Jeffery knew that he had to do something quickly.

He borrowed half a crown from his mother and set out for Exeter. To join the Navy, he knew, would involve the same sort of rigmarole as he had encountered with the Marines and would take more time than he could afford. He thought about the Royal Air Force, but had been told that they expected mechanical skills beyond anything he possessed. So he went to the Army recruiting office and, on an impulse, said that he wanted to join a regiment serving in China. He specified China because he felt no one in England wanted him, it was a long way away, and his sailor uncle had regaled him with picturesque tales about sailing up the Yangtse river.

The recruiting sergeant said that he had just the thing for him, and signed him up for the Devonshire Regiment. In fact the Devons at that time had one battalion in India and the other at home and the Sergeant knew perfectly well that in any case it was highly unlikely Peter would be allowed to go abroad for six months or more, but he got a fee for each new recruit and was not disposed to let a promising candidate slip away. Ernest Jeffery was presumably satisfied by his son's behaviour; at any rate, he appears to have borne no grudge and never referred to the matter when they met again.

And so at the age of fifteen and three-quarters Arthur 'Peter' Jeffery joined the 2nd Battalion of the Devonshire Regiment as a boy soldier. Though he had been designated as a band-boy in the Marines he thought that he had put music behind him when he joined the infantry. Then, after a couple of months, he happened to be in the band-boys' room and laughed at the efforts of a friend who was trying to play the cornet. He was challenged to do better himself and promptly did so. Somebody told the bandmaster, who summoned him for an audition and recruited him for the band. By this time he had discovered that service as a boy soldier consisted of little more than a series of boring chores, so he accepted the inevitable with good grace. A drawback was that the band-boys were always on duty for church parade but otherwise he was no worse off than any ordinary boy soldier.

The life was a good one, with plenty of sport, which he enjoyed. He was soon in the boxing team – he fought as a featherweight at 8 stone 12 pounds – and was undisputed champion until the militia were called up in 1939 and an influx of experienced new talent arrived on the scene. He found the discipline sometimes irksome, but no more so than any other boy of his age would have felt it. There was rather more emphasis on education than he had expected but he was more ready to countenance it when it was the Army, not his school, which made the rules. The Third Class Certificate involved some rudimentary arithmetic and a smattering of regimental history: the former he knew already while the latter called for little more than the ability to read and write. The Second Class was more exacting: as well as map-reading, geography and history the candidate was required to read two books and take a test on them. Jeffery was given John Buchan's *Greenmantle* and *The Thirty-Nine Steps* and enjoyed them thoroughly; they gave him a taste for reading and throughout the war he contrived always to have a book with him. Better still, the hard work brought financial rewards: for passing the Second Class Certificate he was paid an extra 3d a day; in the same year he qualified on the rifle ranges and got 3d a day for that too. Sixpence a day might not seem much, but before Hore-Belisha's reforms of 1939 the basic pay was only 14 shillings a week so the increment added a quarter to his income.

In the summer of 1939 the 2nd Battalion was posted to Malta. The Devons were more flexible than some other regiments over transfers from one battalion to another and Jeffery was offered the chance to join the 1st Battalion in India. He had no strong views about which posting he would find the more enjoyable and decided to stick with the people he knew and with whom he had trained. After twelve months in Malta, it would anyway be open for him to apply for a transfer to India. His mother was less enthusiastic about his destination. There had been a lot of trouble in Palestine recently and to her one part of the Mediterranean seemed very near another. 'This is the result of your chasing him!' she told her husband indignantly. Ernest laughed. 'It'll do him good,' he said. The Devons were anyway only expected to be in Malta for a year; Jeffery would have been incredulous if he had been told that he would be there for nearly five years and not return to Britain till the middle of 1944.

During those years he wrote to his parents perhaps a dozen times. 'I was terrible for letter-writing, terrible,' he admits. He would start with excellent intentions but put off the moment from day to day; even when he got going he would decide to finish it a few hours later, then the following day, then next week. His father wrote to him regularly once a fortnight and sent him the local papers, his mother wrote as well from time to time; they got no reply. Once, after more than a year's silence, his mother became so desperate for news that she wrote to his Commanding Officer. Jeffery was sent for and given a stern reprimand for his idleness and lack of consideration. Over the next few weeks he wrote two or three letters under supervision, but Malta in 1941 was not a place where much attention was paid to such matters and the correspondence soon died out. During the campaign in Sicily his parents, unknown to Jeffery, were sent a telegram to tell them that their son was missing. In fact he was present and correct, but it was several weeks before his parents received a letter which put their minds at rest. Only when he first came home on leave did he realise how much unnecessary anxiety he had caused. After he had been back for a few days his mother said to him: 'You know, son, you may have children of your own one day, and if they're away you'll realise what communication means.' He was abashed, but it was another twenty-five years before he discovered how right she had been.

Peacetime in Malta was 'wonderful, wonderful, truly it was wonderful'. The Devons, together with a battalion of the Suffolks, made up the military garrison but the Royal Navy was all-important and the naval base provided the reason for the Army's presence. The climate was idyllic; food and drink were ridiculously cheap, there were excellent facilities for sport, on Thursdays he would go sailing with friends. He had a local girlfriend, half Maltese, half English, but relationships of this kind had to be handled with circumspection. 'To get to the walking-out stage you had to say you were Roman Catholic, whether you were or not. There were more Roman Catholics in our regiment than you'd imagine possible! But if you started getting too serious, before you knew what was happening the priest was there. You had to know how far to go and when to finish.' Quite a few of the men got married to local girls, especially when the battalion was still in Malta after three years and it began to seem as if it would never move. Jeffery was only just twenty and felt no urge to succumb to such temptations, but his life was not notably chaste. There were no designated brothels but 'there was a street full of bars where you could get a woman' especially during the war when cigarettes or food were in short supply and could be used for barter.

The war, at first, barely disturbed this pleasant existence. The higher echelons of the Army made little attempt to let the rank-and-file know how the war was progressing, and it was not until

Dunkirk that the average private soldier realised that things were not going particularly well in France. Even then it didn't occur to Jeffery and his friends that they might be sent home to defend the United Kingdom – rather they wondered how long it would be before the war came to them. Everything changed when Italy entered the war in July 1940. Suddenly Malta was in the front line, only twenty minutes from the Italian airbases and a vital link in the chain between Britain, Gibraltar, Alexandria and the Suez Canal. The Devons were guarding the airfield at Hal Far, a prime target for Italian bombers from the moment war began. To fend them off there were at first only a handful of inadequate anti-aircraft guns and three ancient Gloster Gladiators, christened Faith, Hope and Charity. The Italians nevertheless preferred to remain at 20,000 feet. 'They were like pinpoints up in the sky,' Jeffery recalls. At such a height precision bombing was impossible but enough bombs fell to make the defenders uncomfortable – on the third day of the bombardment a working party repairing the runway at Hal Far was hit and two privates from the Devonshire Regiment were killed.

Italian bombers reluctant to push home their attacks were one thing; when early in 1942 the Germans took over the assault, things became very different. Now Malta was under full-blooded siege and neither its garrison nor the luckless inhabitants were left in peace for more than a few hours. Junker bombers, escorted by Messerschmitts and operating from bases in North Africa, came over three, four, sometimes even eight times a day. The ancient Gladiators had now been replaced by Hurricanes, but there were few of these, they were outnumbered and outpaced by the Messerschmitts, and their lack of cannons meant that, even if they were able to engage a bomber, they did not often manage to shoot it down. The first Spitfires did not arrive till March 1942; it was a couple of months before they were ready to engage the Germans and even then there were only a dozen or so available. Until mid-May, when a substantial force of Spitfires took to the air, it was almost impossible to keep the German attackers at bay. The Stuka dive-bombers, which descended almost vertically with a fearsome shriek and pulled out only at the last moment after they had dropped their bombs, were the enemy that the British troops disliked the most. 'To be bombed by Stukas was a terrifying thing,' Jeffery remembers. 'I used to feel as if somebody had tied my arms up. You could do nothing back.' In fact you could do something back; machine-gunners who kept their heads and held their fire to the last second of the Stuka's dive quite often brought down the attacker. But for Jeffery and his fellows filling in craters and preparing shelters, there was indeed a feeling of impotence in the face of overwhelming power. Considering the frequency of the attacks, it is remarkable that the nearest he got to a serious wound was not on the airfield at Hal Far but in Valletta, when he was off duty and a German bomb dropped at random almost achieved what the Stukas had failed to do.

The anti-aircraft guns did all that could be expected of them but they were perpetually short of shells and could not afford to blanket the skies as was done in the blitz in London. It was not only shells that were in short supply. The convoys on which Malta relied for its food were not getting through or only reaching Valletta after heavy losses. Stocks of every kind of commodity dwindled: the bread ration fell from eight ounces a day to four ounces, then vanished altogether; a few biscuits and corned beef became the staple diet. A soldier on active service was supposed to need four thousand calories a day, by mid-1942 the ration scale in Malta was two thousand. In theory rations could be supplemented by buying from civilian shops, but on the black market an egg cost 2/6d, a cabbage 3 shillings; a private's pay left little scope for luxuries of this kind. Even the local wine – known as Stuka juice – became more sour and more expensive, costing 4/6d a quart instead of 6d. The Maltese were no better off than the British and for the most part did not even have the consolation of feeling that they were fighting 'their war'. Jeffery had the impression that they would have been happy to see the British go and to be left in peace. They had no intention of doing anything to achieve this end but their sullen resentment added to the prevailing gloom. According to the account of an officer in the Devonshire Regiment, Major R. T. Gilchrist, life in Malta during the siege 'was like a life sentence in prison without hope of reprieve. The resistance which most of us had to put up was not so much against the danger of bombing as against a most morbid depression. In the case of many of the men this feeling was counteracted by the fiction of "the boat". However improbable it seemed to those in the know, these men always expected a boat to arrive to take them home.'

Jeffery did not waste much time dreaming of possible boats, nor was he morbidly depressed, but he was profoundly relieved when the balance of power in the air tipped in favour of the defenders. Until this happened, the authorities did all they could to raise morale and provide entertainment. The Devons in particular made a speciality of swimming contests and boating regattas. They were also the first battalion to experiment with Combined Operations and kept up their training even when the German bombardment was at its height. The future regimental historian, Colonel Windcott, who arrived in the late summer expecting to find a bunch of pallid troglodytes, instead discovered 'men in the pink of condition, bronzed and cheerful and going about their duties with the snap that tells of good training and discipline'.

The siege had effectively been lifted before the end of 1942 and by March 1943, the battalion was on the move. Jeffery's horizon was still confined to the doings of his own platoon, or perhaps company. He had heard about the victory at El Alamein and was dimly aware of Stalingrad but he knew little about the course of the war. However keen his interest, it would have been hard for him to be well-informed. There were few wirelesses available to bring the latest news; if papers arrived from home they were three months out of date or more; the *Daily Mirror* was anxiously awaited – if only for the strip cartoons – but when it came it was in batches of a month at a time. The junior officers were not much better informed and rarely saw it as part of their duties to keep the other ranks abreast of current affairs. Things were slowly improving, but in the middle of the Second World War the average private was still astonishingly ignorant of issues that did not immediately affect him. Jeffery was anyway more concerned about his supply of cigarettes. He was very much the average private and content to remain so. It was not for want of opportunity. 'A couple of times I got made up,' he says, 'but I wasn't really . . . I didn't really bother.' He only got an extra 3d a day for being a lance-corporal, he had nothing much to spend it on except gambling at nap, poker or pontoon, and he disliked the responsibility. Each time he was promoted he reverted to the ranks at his own request: 'I felt a freer spirit.'

He was glad to get out of Malta; quite apart from the privations he had endured he felt that he had been wasting his time while the soldiers in the Western Desert had been doing what they had joined the Army to do – fighting the enemy. Now, he hoped, he was on his way back to England where, no doubt, he would take part in the invasion which must surely come that summer.

The battalion embarked on an old mail boat; its afterdeck crowded with sheep, goats and chickens. Jeffery's berth was far down below; he quickly decided it was too stuffy to be tolerable and volunteered to man a bren-gun on deck. The gun proved superfluous, they had a peaceful passage to Alexandria and, once arrived, 'ate like we never ate before'. Two eggs for breakfast, to a soldier who had not had an egg in his rations for nearly a year, was a feast of Lucullan splendour. The Malta Brigade – the Devons, the Hampshires and the Dorsets – went into camp for twelve days' rest at Sidi Bishr where they did little except gorge, sleep and receive new clothing and equipment; 'no more boots held together by bits of old car tyres'. It was a pleasant break, which would have been even more so if it had not coincided with a rare spell of bad weather, with cold winds and driving sand almost making them wish that they were back in Malta.

Once they were deemed ready to get back to work the Devons were packed off to Kabrit on the Bitter Lakes near Suez to continue training in Combined Operations. They thought that this was just a stage on their journey home and entered into it with zest, though the work was punishing compared with their earlier exercises in Malta: it was 'hard, hard, we really did get fit'. Suspicions about their destination began to form when they found themselves training in pegged-out areas the size of a landing craft and carrying out landing drills. Surely, if they had been destined for the coast of Europe, they would have been doing this work in Britain? Rumour had it that they were going to invade the Andaman Islands in the Bay of Bengal, a suggestion that struck gloom in people who had already been away from home for the best part of five years and had no wish to venture still further afield.

Finally the brigade moved back to Alexandria and embarked. Jeffery found himself in the flagship of what was evidently to be an invasion fleet. Most people still thought that they were heading east, and it was not till the following day, when the course was clearly north-west, that the truth began to dawn. Then maps came out, briefings began, and they were told that they were to take part in the invasion of Sicily.

The immediate reaction was relief; they were heading in the general direction of the British Isles, and though they were being taken by a pretty circuitous route, at least every mile would bring them nearer home. Everything possible was done to keep the men occupied during the journey, with cinema shows on deck, water polo matches, boxing contests. Each man was issued with a booklet called *The Soldier's Guide to Italy*. Oranges, lemons, almonds and pistachios were plentiful in Sicily, they were told; wine, especially Marsala, was the most popular drink. There was also a warning: 'The Sicilian is well known for his extreme jealousy in so far as his womenfolk are concerned, and in a crisis still resorts to the dagger.' The prospects of wine and women raised the men's spirits greatly – as for the daggers, they thought they could cope with those if the threat arose.

When the convoy was still a few miles off Sicily the weather took a sharp turn for the worse, so much so that there was talk of the landings being aborted. The Devons were the reserve battalion and so had to hang around at sea while the Dorsets and Hampshires went ahead and secured the beaches. Jeffery was a good sailor but most of the others were violently seasick and so miserable that they would have gone ashore against any opposition rather than spend another hour in the boats. Nor was seasickness the worst peril; Jeffery was watching one flat-bottomed landing craft with ten or so tanks aboard: 'One minute it was going along, the next minute it was in two halves, gone.' In such circumstances there was little chance that anyone could have survived. Jeffery himself was a strong swimmer, but he was wearing heavy equipment and would have found it almost impossible to disentangle himself from it if his boat had gone down. Compared with such perils the possibility of enemy resistance seemed a minor consideration.

They finally went ashore at 5 a.m. The Dorsets and Hampshires had met scarcely any opposition; indeed, so uneventful were the landings that it was generally felt the final exercises on the Bitter Lakes had been more realistic. The Devons moved through the Dorsets' lines and, as arranged, pushed on into the interior. Within thirty hours they had advanced fourteen miles: 'We were marching in our sleep,' Jeffery remembers; they had been sixty hours virtually without rest by the time they were given their first break on Sicilian soil. They met some Italian troops and took prisoners but the resistance was half-hearted. The peasants, for their part, seemed positively to welcome the invaders; they lined the streets of the villages, clapped as the British troops marched in and asked the new arrivals for food and cigarettes. How genuine the enthusiasm was, Jeffery never knew, but certainly the Italians were more hostile to the Germans than to the newcomers.

As in Malta when the Junkers and Stukas arrived, things changed when the opposition was German. Soon the resistance was growing stiffer and during the six weeks or so that the Sicilian campaign lasted the Malta Brigade suffered almost 40 per cent casualties. Its advance was in theory supported by armour, but in fact the large sector in which Jeffery was operating never saw more than two troops of British tanks. The Germans ahead always seemed to be ensconced on the high ground and to have taken up strong defensive positions; they fought with courage and tenacity. One of the few advantages the attackers enjoyed was in the air; Jeffery saw only a handful of German aircraft during the advance across Sicily.

He survived the campaign unscathed but several times was left wondering how he had managed it. The fiercest fighting the battalion saw was in the foothills in front of Agira, a picturesque small town some thirty miles west of Catania. Its houses were clustered on the steep slopes of a hill which led to a rocky pinnacle, itself surmounted by a medieval tower. The Germans were only just beginning to dig in when the Devons had their first view of the town; but for a failure in wireless communications the British troops would have called down an artillery barrage and rushed the half-prepared defences. The failure to do so cost them dear. For several days of tenacious fighting the brigade forced its way forward, hill by hill, almost rock by rock. In the end the town fell only when British forces advancing on both flanks finally made the German position untenable.

Jeffery's platoon, under Lieutenant Scott, had to lead a battalion attack, advancing over open ground and up a steep slope towards a crest heavily held by the Germans. 'You realise your mates are to the left and right of you and yet at the same time you're on your own,' he remembers. If the man beside one was hit one could not disrupt the attack by stopping to help him: 'That's the most hurtful thing.' While one was in headlong advance one had no time to feel afraid: 'You don't worry so much when it's happening; if you hear a bullet whistling by you know you're all right.' He was anyway running through an olive grove that seemed at the time to offer acceptable cover. Only when he reached the top of the first ridge did he look back and realise just how inadequate the protection had been. 'Then the reaction sets in. You think: "Jesus, I could have got killed coming up there!" I think you shut things off, because if you dwelt on it all the time you wouldn't want to get up once you'd lain down. I think this is when the discipline comes in, the leadership.' Jeffery reached the top alongside his Lieutenant, whose twenty-first birthday it was that day. The ridge was taken, the Germans were in retreat, it seemed as if the skirmish was over. Then a sniper fired and Scott was hit; he spoke two words, sat down and died. Jeffery stayed alone with him for ten minutes until the rest of the company came up. Five or six other men had been killed in the assault: 'God, how easy it is to die.'

They had secured the crest that was supposed to open the way for the next phase of the advance. They spent the night there, listening to the Germans busily at work in the hills opposite. When they resumed the attack they came under heavy mortar fire: 'Terrible things, mortars. The Germans were very good with them.' There were more casualties, more deaths, then the concept of a direct assault was abandoned. Nobody stopped to wonder whether the lives had been well spent; when in battle there is no time and precious little inclination to indulge in such speculation.

Once the campaign was over the brigade was given a fortnight to rest and absorb reinforcements before the assault on Italy. They sailed for the mainland on 5 September. This time they were only a few hours at sea; apprehensive, because they had no idea what opposition to expect, but grateful that it would all be over quickly. As in Sicily, the landings turned out to be remarkably trouble-free. The 5th Division had gone ashore further up the coast at Salerno and had drawn the brunt of the German resistance; the Malta

Brigade landed in the Gulf of Santa Eufemia and found only a handful of troops to oppose them. These they brushed aside and pushed on towards Naples. Gradually the resistance grew more intense. After three days Jeffery's platoon came under fire. He jumped over what he thought was a low wall, fell fifteen feet on to rocky ground and knocked himself out. By the time he came to he was in a casualty station.

Now came one of those curious episodes which can occur in any large organisation but to which the British Army seems particularly prone. Jeffery fell into an organisational black hole. If he had known the right questions to ask or strings to pull he could no doubt have extricated himself, but private soldiers are not encouraged to ask questions or pull strings and instead he waited to be told what to do and, when no orders arrived, drifted with whatever tide there was. By the time he had been treated in the casualty station, patched up in hospital in Sicily, sent to Alexandria to convalesce and returned to Italy, his brigade had been pulled out and sent back to Britain to prepare for D-Day. He assumed that he would return to join them but instead found himself hanging about a transit camp in Italy. He had no idea what was going on and was offered no explanation. He felt frustrated but 'there was no point in arguing' – he and a group of other men in the same plight were just 'a load of soldiers waiting for something to happen'.

What did happen was that he found himself attached to the United States Army and landing with them at Anzio, south of Rome but well ahead of the Allied forces. How or why this came about he never knew. Jeffery suspected that it was the result of some bureaucratic muddle but could see no way to remedy it. The Americans seemed to be equally baffled by his presence but made him welcome with characteristic generosity. In many ways he enjoyed the experience, it was 'like living in a land of plenty; whatever you wanted you could get, there was no shortage of anything'. But he was uneasy about the relationship between officers and men in the American Army. In the system to which he was accustomed 'you always knew where you stood'; a sergeant or even a corporal might possibly address a junior officer by his first name but it would only be in the stress of battle, 'there was no familiarity between us'. Discipline could be relaxed, there did not need to be overmuch formality except on the parade ground; but an officer was an officer, a sergeant a sergeant, a private a private. In the U.S. Army a private might easily call his colonel by his first name. Jeffery didn't think that the American attitude helped, nobody ever seemed to be sure who was in charge: 'They are so friendly that they become contemptuous, you know.' He found the contrast between the two styles particularly marked on the occasions when he went out with an American patrol: 'They were a funny lot, really. They all had lots of guts but it wasn't like going on patrol with our blokes. We never really knew what they were capable of.'

The actual landing at Anzio was 'a walk ashore' and the way seemed open for the invaders to push rapidly forward. The American commander, however – with what posterity at least has deemed misguided caution – decided to dig in. The Germans were quick to rally and the force that should have been triumphantly advancing towards Rome instead found itself besieged. Jeffery spent about two months in the bridgehead, under almost incessant mortar fire, disliking it intensely, and all the more so for his suspicion that he should never have been there in the first place. It was an immense relief when, still with no explanation, he was pulled out, sent to a transit camp in Naples and told he would be on the next ship to the United Kingdom.

Jeffery arrived in Scotland the Friday before D-Day – too late to rejoin his battalion even if that had been the intention of the authorities. Instead he was kept in a transit camp in Glasgow for ten days or so and then sent home on leave. Lympstone was in a restricted area; he had to get a special pass to visit it and the journey by train took nineteen hours. And when he got there it was very different to what he had remembered. His father had rejoined the Navy and was with a motor torpedo boat based in Dartmouth. The boys he had known at school were away fighting, several of them were dead. Most of the girls had got married: 'The ones I'd had crushes on were all gone. I suppose they'd been in great demand.'

After nearly a month at home he felt curiously rootless. In so far as he had any loyalties outside the family they were to his regiment, but the Army showed no signs of allowing him to rejoin it. First he was sent to Morpeth for training, then to Ramsgate. 'You got shunted here, there and everywhere; you belonged to no one. I didn't mind where I went, really.' If *he* didn't mind, certainly no one else did. While at Morpeth he volunteered for one or two postings but was brushed off: 'It was "Oh, no, you've done enough" and that sort of patter.' He became so bored and irritated that at one time he thought seriously of desertion. He went up to London with a friend who said that he would be able to fix him up with a job, then thought better of his impulse and went back to Morpeth.

After that he was posted to a transit camp at Leeds, where there was even less to do, only odd jobs from time to time: 'One was just lost, one of a crowd. People spent the whole war lost.' He also made a bit of money on the side by selling Army boots and blankets: 'It wasn't right, but one had to live.' He spent his ill-gotten gains on a spree to London, went absent-without-leave for four days, was court-martialled and did a stint in the military prison. It was unpleasant but he knew that he had deserved it and at least it made a change.

In Leeds a friend took him to his house, where his parents and sister were living. The sister was called Dorothy, nineteen years old, very pretty and eager to embark on an affair with her first real boyfriend. The two quickly decided they were in love and that they should get married. In wartime such things tended to be done in haste and hugger-mugger; Jeffery only let his mother know what was going on by a letter which arrived after the wedding: 'It was quite a shock,' he admits. When he was sent back to Ramsgate – to a holding unit, 'whatever that may have been' – Dorothy came too; there were no married quarters to be had but the marriage allowance was sufficient to pay for some sort of accommodation. Their daughter, Christine, was born nine months to the day after their marriage.

Then, suddenly, the military machine creaked back into life. The Orderly Room clerk at Ramsgate was from Jeffery's old battalion. Jeffery asked whether there was any chance that he could at last rejoin the regiment. 'Why not?' said the clerk, surprised at so modest a request. Almost before Jeffery knew what was happening he was on a draft to Singapore.

Though the war was by now over there was no question of a private being allowed to take his wife with him to South-East Asia. According to Jeffery, Dorothy was not too put out by his departure, but for a girl of twenty with a baby it must have been painful and alarming to be so abruptly abandoned. And that, effectively, was the end of their relationship. 'It's difficult to put your finger on when the marriage ended,' says Jeffery vaguely. 'Probably it was my fault more than anybody else's; not what I did do, but what I didn't do.' One of the things he didn't do was write letters to his wife; the paralysis which had bedevilled his relationship with his parents still afflicted him. Dorothy took their daughter back to Leeds and lived with her grandmother. She wrote to her husband, wrote again, then wrote again. Finally she seems to have despaired. Jeffery is unclear about the details but thinks she must have decided to end the marriage: 'Divorce was in the pipeline, if I remember rightly.' Even if he had wanted to, he had no time to do anything about it. Long before the process could be completed, when it was barely launched indeed, Dorothy developed tuberculosis. Within a few months she was dead. Jeffery knew that his wife's grandmother was a good woman who would look after their baby daughter. As he had taken for granted the inexplicable vagaries of military life, so he accepted this new bludgeoning of fate. He shrugged his shoulders and got on with life.

The 1st Battalion of the Devonshire Regiment was in Singapore when he joined it in October 1946, but within three months it moved to Hong Kong. By now he had again become a lance-corporal; the promotion which he had rejected previously now seemed acceptable, even desirable. He welcomed the responsibility, not to mention the extra money which he needed for his contributions to his daughter's maintenance: 'It was different to the time in Malta. I'd got a little wiser.' Hong Kong at first was bleakly cold; the food was terrible – 'we lived on rabbits from Australia'; the commandos who had occupied the barracks before them had ripped up the floors for firewood. Things got better in the spring when they moved to the New Territories where they patrolled the border with China and paid visits to various off-shore islands. The transfer of power in Hong Kong still seemed unimaginably far away, prosperity was returning, confidence growing; the only excitement came when the battalion was placed on stand-by to move to Shanghai so as to protect the British community in the growing civil disorder. In the event, it came to nothing. Instead they moved back to Singapore, a posting which seemed at first likely to be only a humdrum stage in their eventual return to Britain but became considerably more exciting when the Emergency broke out in 1948.

From the time that the British returned to Malaya in September 1945, it had seemed likely that the Chinese Communists would eventually seek to take power. The 'Malayan People's Liberation Army' never had more than four or five thousand guerrillas operating in the jungle at one time, but they enjoyed the tacit support of some half a million Chinese scattered around the countryside, many of whom were poised to join in the battle if at any moment their services were required. They operated in small gangs, acting independently and at the whim of the local commander; a policy which may have limited their effectiveness overall but also made them extraordinarily difficult to forestall or track down. Jeffery found himself involved in long and arduous jungle patrols, perpetually seeking an elusive enemy who was rumoured to be here, suspected of being there, but rarely turned out to be where the British troops expected. Luckily the Chinese were less successful when it came to engaging British troops in action; when they laid ambushes the results were rarely to their satisfaction and the terror which they inspired in the local peasants and white rubber planters did not extend to the men of the Devonshire Regiment. Jeffery came under fire several times and remembers the burial of a man from another company, but the dangers from disease or snakebite were quite as menacing as anything arising from enemy action.

By the spring of 1949, the strength of the British forces was building up, Iban trackers from Borneo were proving extraordinarily adept in leading the pursuit of the Chinese guerrillas, intelligence was improving. For the first time Jeffery felt that eventual victory was certain. He had no burning wish to see the job through himself, however, and was pleased when he returned to the United Kingdom for discharge in May.

It had been open for him to leave the Army at the end of the war. For a time he had considered the possibility but he had known that he would have to wait several months, perhaps a year, for his demobilisation and it had seemed easier to stay in and serve out his ten years. Now he felt that he had had enough. He would retire, he would get a secure and well-paid job, he would take responsibility for his daughter, he would settle down. These admirable resolutions lasted about a month, then reality prevailed. 'I was like a fish out of water. I didn't have a clue about civvy street.' He had no trade qualifications and no useful contacts. After some searching around he got a job stoking in a gasworks and detested it: 'I was shut in all day. It was hard work and I'd been out of doors most of my life. It was awful. Gradually I realised how big a fool I had been.' He went to visit his daughter in Leeds. Christine was a pretty child with curly auburn hair and he played with the idea of taking her away from her great-grandmother to live with him in Folkestone. Then he realised that he could never give her the stability that she needed – 'her granny was her mainstay'. It hurt him each time he had to leave her behind so his visits became less frequent and in the end he gave up going altogether. He never wrote to her and did not see her again for twenty years. Without a job that he found tolerable or a home to which he could bring his daughter, the attractions of Army life began to seem irresistible.

Meanwhile he had found another woman. Pearl was four or five years younger than him, physically not unlike his first wife but a tougher character, less quiet and introverted. She came from a military family – her father had been thirty years in the Buffs – and encouraged him to re-enlist, even though she knew that the Devons were still abroad and that he would be likely to disappear for a year or more. She was in no great hurry to marry, but by the time Jeffery took the plunge and rejoined the Army they were engaged.

The Devons were happy to welcome back their prodigal son and within a month he was on the way to rejoin them in Malaya. He was back in the battalion by January 1950, finding it 150 or so miles north of where they had been the previous year. The patrolling followed the same lines but the atmosphere was very different. By now General Templer was in command and the situation had been transformed; the Army was better organised, they had good maps and air-support, equipment suitable for the jungle had replaced the leather boots and leaky groundsheets to which Jeffery had grown accustomed. Above all, new techniques had been devised to win the confidence of the local inhabitants and to ensure that once the Communists had been driven from a particular area, they did not quickly return. By the time the Devons left Malaya at the end of the year, the war was effectively won. Part of the battalion went to Hong Kong; Jeffery, by now a full corporal, with 120 other men returned to England.

For the sake of his marital prospects it was just as well he did so. Pearl had written to him regularly but had had only a handful of letters in return and was reproachful if not indignant. She did not bear him too lasting a grudge, however – 'after a while everything was forgiven,' says Jeffery gratefully – and almost before he had touched ground he found himself securely married. He was due twenty-eight days' leave and he took his new wife to Devon. She settled there among his relations and his first son was born just before he set out on his travels again.

In October 1951, the battalion was transferred to Cyrenaica in North Africa. He remembered what had happened to his first wife when he left her behind and resolved that this time he would keep regularly in touch. He did not invariably live up to this admirable intention, but he managed a great deal better than in the past: 'Now and again I did write, not very often though, but when I did write I always wrote a long, a good letter.'

The regime of King Farouk in neighbouring Egypt was in trouble and the British government wanted to have additional troops nearby in case it was necessary at short notice to protect British lives and property. The Devons were sent first to Tripoli, then, after a month, to Derna, nearer the Egyptian frontier. It was an 'excellent training area', wrote the regimental historian, by which he meant that there was a great deal of sand and precious little else: 'There was nothing there, it was miserable,' remembers Jeffery feelingly. It was a frustrating period: several times it seemed as if British troops would be called upon to intervene in Cairo, each time the crisis passed and the Devons remained stranded in their gloomy desert staging-post. Once, when Farouk was eventually driven from power, they actually boarded a landing craft to go to Alexandria; then the risks of intervention seemed too great, the politicians thought better of it – having marched his men up the hill the grand old Duke of York marched them down again.

But the Devons were not doomed to perpetual inaction. Now another part of the Empire demanded their attention. During 1952 the Mau Mau revolt had been gathering force in Kenya. The largest of the Kenyan tribes, the Kikuyu, under their charismatic leader, Jomo Kenyatta, had legitimate grievances over land and the intrusion of Christian missionaries into their religious practices, but nothing could excuse the savagery with which the terrorist Mau Mau pursued their campaign. As so often in such operations, it was the innocent local civilians who bore the brunt of the violence; in March 1953 alone eighty-three Kikuyu, two-thirds of them women and children, were massacred by the Mau Mau for being insufficiently enthusiastic in the cause of liberty. The following month 39 Infantry Brigade, including the 1st Battalion of the Devonshire Regiment, flew out to reinforce the inadequate imperial garrison.

Before going into action the Devons were given six weeks in the White Highlands of Kenya to acclimatise. They were made much of by the settlers and Jeffery was impressed by the concern some of these felt for the welfare of their native workers. But on the whole he thought them a decadent bunch who did not deserve the luxurious style of life which they enjoyed: 'The white settlers were gods and the blacks were just blacks. I never bothered about them, one way or another.' He would not have been surprised if he had been told that within ten years Kenya would be independent; nothing he saw of the inhabitants made him think it likely that the Africans would make a conspicuous success of running their own country but he could see no reason why they should not be allowed to try. That did not alter the fact that there was a job to be done and a particularly vicious bunch of terrorists to be put down. The battalion was deployed in the area of the Aberdare Forest and

Jeffery, now promoted to platoon sergeant, soon found himself doing much the same work as he had undertaken in Malaya.

The task was in many ways easier. The Mau Mau, though brave and resourceful, were worse armed and less adroit than their Chinese counterparts. The terrain was easier, more like Richmond Park in its appearance than the dense forests of South-East Asia. There was also less difficulty in distinguishing friend from foe; the Army cut a strip a mile deep around the forest and assumed that anybody within must be an enemy. Once the strip was in place the farmlands outside the forest were usually secure, but there were still bloody incidents from time to time; Jeffery remembers coming across one farm where half a dozen Kikuyu labourers had had their hamstrings cut and been slit down the back with pangas, a couple of women had been beaten up and raped, the cows were left with their bellies slashed and their entrails leaking over the ground around them.

The British strategy was to confine the Mau Mau to the forest, to intercept the porters who were bringing them supplies, and eventually to starve them out. Forays into the forest itself were limited in scope and usually failed to end in any serious engagement with the enemy; Jeffery was only in action twice and his platoon suffered no casualties during its eighteen months in Kenya.

For the first few months he was with a machine-gun platoon; then he was transferred to a rifle company, with a major, a captain as second-in-command, three platoon subalterns, a company sergeant-major and three sergeants, of whom he was one. Jeffery liked and got on well with them all, except for the Company Sergeant-Major, of whom he had already fallen foul while still in Britain and who now tried to have him transferred as being unsuitable for the job. Fortunately the Sergeant-Major was disliked by everyone and his complaints did Jeffery little harm. 'In our estimation he was an idiot,' says Jeffery bluntly, who considers that he had no common sense and was woefully deficient in the skills of man-management. But then, after the Kenyan campaign was over, the Sergeant-Major was given a commission and transferred to another unit: 'So he can't have been that stupid, can he?'

Pearl came out for four months during the period her husband was in Kenya and lived in a bungalow near Nairobi. By now there were three children: a son, a daughter, and a second son born just before the trip to Kenya. Jeffery was glad to know that they were there but did not see much of them; he only managed to get to Nairobi three times during their visit and the longest he spent with them was a day and two nights.

When she got back to England Pearl was disconcerted to find the Devonshire Regiment pilloried in the press as murderers. The Commanding Officer had rashly offered a prize of £5 to the first patrol to kill a Mau Mau terrorist. The story was leaked to a Labour Member of Parliament by a disgruntled national service officer and the *Daily Herald* proclaimed that the Devons were being paid bounty money for killing terrorists and that innocent Africans were being slaughtered as a result. 'Is Your Son A Murderer?' was their headline. A court of enquiry was set up and the Colonel exonerated but there was much resentment among the troops who felt, with some reason, that they were being unfairly traduced.

At the end of 1954 the battalion, which had been operating in largely independent companies over the previous twelve months, assembled at Thika for its return to the United Kingdom. Jeffery went back a few weeks before the rest and was far from gratified to find that he was being detached from the Regiment to serve with a territorial unit at Plymouth. He was a Permanent Staff Instructor, still with the rank of sergeant and probably selected for the job because of his experience with machine- and anti-tank guns. The prospect was dismal: 'Nobody chooses the Territorial Army,' he explains. 'You were a dogsbody, at everyone's beck and call.' He worked every weekday from 8 a.m. to 10 p.m. and then often found himself on duty at weekends, firing on the ranges on

Dartmoor or taking his unit on exercises. There was no mess life and as well as all his other work he was responsible for the accountancy and much of the driving. There was at least decent married accommodation for his family, but this was small consolation given the limited amount of time he was able to spend there.

Jeffery didn't argue when he was told his fate — partly because he didn't know how awful it was going to be, more because he had imbibed the military doctrine that a soldier goes where he is sent — but he did all he could to escape from it. His technique was to be so bloody-minded that the Company Commander would long to see him transferred elsewhere, without behaving so outrageously that a bad report would be filed which might be damaging to his future career. Whether he managed to bring off this delicate tightrope walk he never knew but at least he was allowed to return to his regimental depot after only eighteen months. He longed for another posting overseas and applied to be attached to the Malayan Federation Army, a job which would have entailed not only a return to a country he much liked but also a handsome increase in pay. It seemed the job was his, he was due to leave on his thirty-fifth birthday in April 1957, then with only a week to go he was told that the posting was cancelled. Typically he was given no reason for this change of heart. Instead he was offered a job with the Territorial Army in Hong Kong. His experience in Plymouth made him chary of any territorial posting, but Hong Kong, he was assured, would be different. He agreed to go and embarked on some of the most enjoyable years of his life.

His task was to be instructor in the Support Company, responsible for the unit's machine-guns and mortars. Most of the men were British expatriates, many of them former officers and some holding important jobs in banks and business houses. There were also a few conspicuously affluent Chinese with British passports. The atmosphere was relaxed but enthusiastic; the headquarters was in Happy Valley near the racecourse — to visit the

Sergeants' Mess Jeffery had to make an expedition into the town but there was a bar on the premises in Happy Valley which stayed open from 7.30 a.m. to the time that the last celebrant left, often long after midnight. Married accommodation was luxurious, there were good schools for the children, limitless opportunities for swimming and yachting. They had two servants and were regularly invited to the houses of the territorials: 'Hong Kong was like one big holiday for me.'

Among the Chinese territorials was a multi-millionaire contractor who held the rank of lance-corporal. He had a beautiful Chinese wife but liked occasionally to escape from her in the evenings or at weekends. Jeffery would oblige by sending him a letter ordering him to parade for training. As a *quid pro quo* Jeffery was given an all-expenses-paid trip to Tokyo. The only trouble was that his benefactor – like the other Chinese who showered him with invitations – assumed that his wife would stay contentedly at home. Pearl was prepared as an exception to miss out on the week in Japan but she became somewhat disgruntled if too often excluded from such treats. Jeffery stuck up for her rights and eventually persuaded his Chinese friends that English women had these odd ideas which needed to be pandered to for the sake of domestic harmony.

The Hong Kong territorials would have been happy to extend his appointment and he equally happy to stay, but the War Office ruled that such plums must be equitably distributed and that he had enjoyed the privilege long enough. He then considered joining the Trucial Scouts in Oman, but once again his plan was vetoed, he was told that he had already been away for too undesirably long a period and must now rejoin the regiment. So after a happy three years in the Far East and a leisurely journey home he returned to Britain and was given two months' leave.

He found the pattern of his domestic life curiously changed. His own parents and younger siblings had emigrated to Australia, his links with Devonshire had largely parted, they spent most of their leave with his wife's mother in Folkestone. He got on well enough with his mother-in-law – 'she was all right to a great extent' – but two months were more than enough. With relief he returned to the Devonshire Regiment, which was now in Cyprus.

While he had been in Hong Kong the Devons had amalgamated with the Dorsets. Though the two regiments knew each other well and had often served alongside each other, neither was keen to lose its identity. The merger was inevitably uneasy and a feeling of 'us and them' persisted strongly for a while. The worst was over by the time Jeffery rejoined the battalion, but the atmosphere was still uncomfortable. Nor did he much enjoy life in Cyprus. By the beginning of 1961 the troubles with EOKA were almost over. The battalion was free to concentrate on the normal preoccupations of peacetime soldiering – almost the first time Jeffery had been so engaged since before the war in Malta. Parade square drills, room inspections, endless fussing about polish on boots and brasses, gave him little satisfaction. 'Soldiers like trouble,' he admits frankly. 'It does away with bullshit.' There had been plenty of trouble in Malta, Sicily and Italy, Malaya and Kenya. There had also been much danger and discomfort, which he would happily have done without. But there had been a redeeming simplicity. Life in wartime might offer fewer amenities – hot showers, regular meals – but it also meant informality, independence, excitement. For Jeffery at least the price was worth paying.

This brush with the realities of peacetime soldiering made Jeffery think again about a world outside the Army. When the battalion returned to England he was within a few months of his retirement. If he could have been guaranteed ten, or even five more years of service he would probably have applied to re-enlist, but the best he could hope for was a twelve months' extension, with the possibility of further extensions year by year if it suited the convenience of the Army. He was forty-one, young enough to make a life outside. He decided that he must go. The Adjutant knew that he planned to settle in Colchester so arranged for him to be posted to the Military Correction Training Centre in that town. It meant 'learning to be a screw', and Jeffery hated it – he was still enough of a rebel himself to feel as much sympathy for the gaoled as for the gaoler – but he appreciated the Adjutant's good intentions and in his last few months as a soldier began to look around for a future job.

He was discharged on 11 January 1963. 'It was like leaving an orphanage at the age of sixteen after living in it all one's life,' he now says. He had no idea how to set about the business of administering his life. If his unit had been in England he might have got some help, but the battalion was by now in Germany. He had no home, and a lump-sum payment from the Army of £600 was the total of his resources. Worse still, his marriage had foundered: 'Don't ask me why. There were no other women, there were no other men.' His father-in-law had died a few years before, without warning and giving Pearl no chance to reach his deathbed. She had been greatly depressed and gradually withdrew more and more into herself. By the time Jeffery was discharged she had settled with her mother in Folkestone and showed no sign of wishing to resume married life. Then he heard that she was ill; next, that she was in hospital. What the trouble was he never understood – it was in some way 'mental'. In any case, she was lost to him for ever. Jeffery found himself with no job, no home, no wife, precious little money, and three children of twelve or under.

He had already concluded that the best chance of work was to be found in London. His first job was as a cashier in a branch of Barclay's Bank in the City. Quickly he found that it was intolerable not to be his own boss and to be 'shut up all day, caught for the rest of your life'. He appealed to an old acquaintance from Army days who had become a successful entrepreneur and, among other enterprises, owned a chain of newsagents. He offered Jeffery a job driving. That served as a stopgap, but Pearl's illness meant that Jeffery had to find accommodation for the children as well as himself. His friend suggested that he might take over the running of a newspaper shop in Kennington, which had rooms above it where the family could live. Jeffery accepted gratefully and soon discovered that he enjoyed retailing and was good at it; he worked hard, knew how to keep his stock under control and excelled at getting on with his customers. When it became clear that his employer was in trouble economically and that the shop was likely to be sold over his head, he had no trouble in moving to an off-licence in Brixton. A large number of his customers were 'coloured' but this caused him no concern: 'I didn't mind, I'd lived with them so much in the Army. I got on all right with them.' His good relationship with all his neighbours, he believes, explains the fact that his was the only shop on the street not to be burgled at least once and in some cases several times. It may have helped, too, that he had friends in the local police who used to drop in after closing time, sit on the barrels and boxes and have a drink.

The flats above the shop in Kennington and in Brixton were big enough for his three children. It was sometimes difficult to combine running a business with looking after a family but the children were old enough to fend largely for themselves and the elder ones helped out with the younger. At first they missed their mother but soon they settled down and, in an undemonstrative but affectionate way, were a united family. In due course the two boys joined the Army. Jeffery tried to talk them out of it; not because he thought it was a mistake but so as to be sure that this was really what they wanted and that they were not following blindly in his footsteps. The children kept in touch with their grandmother in Folkestone. Jeffery, in principle, was more than ready to do the same but he had little time for travelling and, as usual, found that the effort of sustaining a correspondence was beyond him. When his own parents came over from Australia they all fitted into the house at Brixton; it was a squash but the children didn't mind doubling up or sleeping on the floor for a few weeks. Soon only his daughter, Vivienne, was left at home; she was an intelligent and hardworking girl who excelled at school and eventually went on to the University of York.

Jeffery never ceased to miss the comradeship of Army life, the feeling that he belonged. In civilian life, he found, he had a great many acquaintances and some whom he would call friends but 'no real muckers you could depend on; who, if you needed help, were there at the drop of a hat'. But he hardly ever went to regimental reunions or kept in touch with his former Army friends, partly because money was always short, partly from inertia: 'I'm a bad one, as I said, for writing letters.' Once the boys had left home and he no longer needed so much accommodation, he looked around for a job that would given him rather more time to himself than the off-licence. The National Children's Bureau in Islington was looking for a man whose official designation would be 'security officer' but who would in fact turn his hand to anything that was needed. A pleasant flat went with the job. Jeffery liked the sound of it, they liked the look of him, he joined and stayed there for fourteen years. He worked pretty hard for the first few years, then, 'took it easy, though it wouldn't be true to say I didn't do *any* work'. The Bureau was satisfied, at all events, and would happily have kept him on after retirement age if he had wanted to continue.

Vivienne had developed a strong social conscience while in Hong Kong. At university she joined the Communist party, then she worked for a Russian newspaper published in English. She married a husband who was equally left-wing and equally dedicated. 'I'll be OK when the revolution comes. You'll look after me,' Jeffery used to tell them. He was himself decidedly right-wing in so far as he thought of politics at all and father and daughter used to argue incessantly if inconclusively about the issues of the day. They never quarrelled, though, and he felt no resentment at her views: 'You can't spend your life defending freedom of speech and then deny it to someone.'

One day the telephone rang in his flat in Islington. A voice asked whether he was Arthur Jeffery. 'Yes.' 'Do you have a daughter?' Without knowing why, for he had not seen her for twenty years while Vivienne was much in his thoughts, he replied 'Christine'. 'Would you like to meet her?' 'Of course.' Two days later Christine made the journey from Leeds to London. He had written to her a few times when she was very young but had soon stopped doing so and had not gone on contributing to her maintenance after his remarriage; she might well have been reproachful but instead accepted that it had probably been better for everyone concerned that there should have been a clean break. She had read in a newspaper how a journalist had successfully reunited a long-separated father and daughter and on an impulse had written to ask whether he could perform the same miracle for her. The journalist obliged. Christine and her father never lost touch again.

After he retired from the Children's Bureau Christine suggested that he should move to Leeds. 'I'm not going to live with you,' said Jeffery suspiciously. 'I wouldn't live with any of my children.' Christine offered to find him a flat, and did so, on the outskirts of Leeds, half a mile or so from where she was living. He stayed for six years, walking a lot, reading, listening to music, watching television, visiting Christine. He was glad to have settled down; he had seen enough of the world in the course of his life and had no wish to travel more. It was a pleasant life, never boring if sometimes a little lonely.

Then he began to get ill. One evening he felt an acute pain in his stomach, was taken to hospital, more or less restored to health and then discharged after a couple of days with nobody seeming to have any clear idea as to what had gone wrong. Six months later, on a torrentially rainy night, the same thing happened. He decided to take himself to hospital and waited for twenty minutes at a bus stop, soaked through and in increasing pain. Nobody offered him a lift, and when he eventually caught a bus he soon realised that he could not complete the journey. He got off and telephoned his daughter, who insisted on sending for an ambulance. At the hospital gall-stones and pancreatitis were diagnosed; he was starved for three days and then had an operation. Soon he was home again, but his confidence was shaken. He was uncertain how long he could manage alone, yet was determined not to be a burden on his children.

In the past he had occasionally wondered if he might end up in the Royal Hospital, but had imagined it as a bleak Peabody Buildings estate in which he could not bear to live. 'If I'd taken the trouble to get on to a No. 19 bus while I was in Islington I'd have applied to come in right away after retirement,' he now thinks. Belatedly, he did so and went to London for the trial visit. 'When I walked in through those gates I didn't have to go any further. That was me, right away.' When he told Christine what he planned to do she at first demurred; she would look after him whatever happened. 'Suppose I get ill again just as you're about to go on holiday,' he said. 'You'll have to stay and cope with me, won't you?' 'Of course.' 'Then your husband will think, if it wasn't for your bloody old man we'd be in Turkey or America.' She accepted his decision and when she visited him in the Hospital a few months later, she knew at once that she would never have to worry again. The lack of privacy, which she had feared might prove intolerable for her father, caused him no concern at all – 'You were used to sharing a barrack room with thirty other people', and, anyway, if one wanted to be alone one only had to shut the door of one's berth. The company, the comfort, the knowledge that whatever goes wrong there will be somebody to cope, all make him feel as secure and as much at home as he has ever been. But he is still no good at writing letters.

JAMES FERGUS

Sergeant Fergus, 1943

James Fergus

MUSSELBURGH is a dour fishing port a little to the east of Edinburgh. Today it is almost swamped by the city but eighty years ago there was open country between it and the neighbouring hamlet of Joppa and again between Joppa and the fringes of the capital at Portobello. The inhabitants are on the whole as rugged as their environment; life has never been easy in Musselburgh and to survive successfully required assiduity and strength of character. Jim Fergus was born there on 22 August 1922.

At that time his parents still lived with his father's mother, a formidable old lady who kept her premises spick and span and expected that everybody else would do the same. By the time that Jim remembered anything, however, the family had moved to their own house in Joppa. It was one of a pair of semi-detached cottages owned by the council, who let them for a low rent to their employees. Jim's father, David, had served in the Gloucestershire Regiment during the First World War and was now a postman; the cottage was reasonably warm, dry and comfortable by the standards of the age, but shared an outside toilet with its neighbour. The family was poor but happy and united; when their father came home from work in the evening Jim and his younger brother, Andrew, would go to the bottom of the lane to meet him.

He would load them into his red Post Office barrow and wheel them back to the house, a cherished ritual which he insisted on performing even when he began to feel ill and was in considerable pain.

The pains grew worse. For over a week he was afflicted by some sort of stoppage in his bowels, was unable to use the lavatory, suffered more and more. If he had gone to see a doctor the problem could possibly have been quickly cleared up but he dared not risk losing a day's pay and struggled on, hoping all would come right in the end. Finally the pain became unendurable and late one night he collapsed in agony. His alarmed wife sent for help and Jim remembers watching him carried out on a stretcher on his way to hospital. It was the last time he saw his father. Next morning the news came that David Fergus was dead.

The family had been poor enough before, now they were almost entirely without resources. The cottage at Joppa was quickly reclaimed by the council but Susan Fergus managed to find a tiny flat in Portobello, on the fringes of Edinburgh. To feed and clothe her children she went out to work; by day cleaning the houses of two relatively prosperous old ladies who lived nearby, in the evenings scrubbing the floors of the local high school. She would come back exhausted, her hands covered with calluses and with 'spales' – chips of wood – lodged under her nails; but always her own house was warm, and nourishing if not lavish meals were provided. When the boys grew old enough they did their best to lend a hand; they would go to the school in the evening to help their mother move the desks. But the real responsibilities and the burdens were hers, and hers alone. Poverty was the norm in that part of Scotland in the 1920s; perhaps there were few who found it harder than the Ferguses to make both ends meet but they were far from unique and scarcely any of their neighbours were conspicuously richer.

Jim first went to school at the age of five, when his father was still alive. Every morning he would walk the two miles or so from

Joppa to the Tower Bank School in Portobello. The classes were large, up to forty boys and girls; of these a surprisingly high proportion seemed to be cousins of one sort or another, most of them on his father's side and many of them children of men who worked in the nearby coalmines. They had the same teacher for every subject except woodwork but, as was the case in most Scottish schools at the time, were given a sound grounding in the nuts and bolts of education. Outside school they would amuse themselves by playing marbles, sometimes in the gutter, the whole way back to Joppa, or by visiting the beach at Portobello. This was a favourite summer resort for holiday makers from Glasgow, there were slot-machines, ice-cream parlours, hoop-la stalls. Jim was rarely able to spend anything on such diversions but sometimes his mother would manage to scrape together a little pocket money. Once he won a set of crockery at bingo and bore it home in triumph – 'the cups must have been half an inch thick', the set was so heavy that he could hardly get it as far as the house.

He stayed contentedly at the Tower Bank School until he was eight or nine, but then things took a turn for the worse. His mother had been born a Roman Catholic, had become a Baptist to keep her husband company, but now was pressed by her relations to revert to her childhood faith. With some doubts she agreed, and sent her sons to a Catholic school. Jim found the discipline too strict after the relaxed atmosphere to which he was accustomed, he missed his friends, worst of all he fell seriously foul of his form mistress who decided that he was an idler and a troublemaker. 'She was just a bully, I think, and she was built like a tank as well,' Fergus remembers; no doubt she was from time to time provoked, but the severity with which she lashed his bare arm with a leather strap was out of all proportion to his mischief-making. By the end of each week his arm was nearly raw from the shoulder down. He bore his sufferings stoically but one day when he got home he found the pain too great to endure in silence and began to cry. His mother asked him what was the matter. He refused to say but his brother told Mrs Fergus to look at Jim's arm. She was horrified by what she saw. She was something of a disciplinarian herself and would sometimes slap her sons' behinds, but though she kept a brown stick in the cupboard it was only for show, she never used a cane or leather strap. Next day she stormed into the school, denounced the teacher and removed her sons. The behaviour was uncharacteristic; by nature she tended to be gentle, even docile; but when she felt that her children were being victimised she would rise in fury. One of her rules was never to strike a child on the head for fear of doing lasting harm. Once a relation of hers thought that Jim had done something naughty (in fact it turned out to be her own son who was guilty) and cuffed his ears. 'Be careful,' said Mrs Fergus, 'and never do that again. I smack my kids, but never across the head.'

Her disenchantment with the school was only part of her increasing alienation from the Roman Catholic church. When she had reverted herself she had told her sons that there was no need for them to follow suit. They had decided that they would do the same as her, but soon doubted the wisdom of conversion. They found the local Catholic priest 'a bit of an old devil'. If the boys didn't touch their hats to him when they passed him outside his church he would come round to the house to protest; he was most put out if for any reason they missed a service; his demands for money were insistent and importunate. Within two years the Ferguses had had enough. The boys' withdrawal from the Catholic school was soon followed by the family's return to the Baptist church. The Baptists welcomed back these prodigals with enthusiasm; the Ferguses were appreciative but they were never consistent churchgoers and their attendance was soon limited to the minimum compatible with respectability.

With his experience of Catholic education behind him, Jim moved on to the High School in Portobello, where he rejoined his friends and cousins from Tower Bank. He was reasonably good at his lessons but took little pleasure in them; arithmetic at least would be useful in later life but history and literature seemed to him irrelevant and so much wasted time. He quite enjoyed football but found cricket too slow to be tolerable. Running was his speciality and he carried away the prizes for almost all the sprints. When he reached the age of fourteen in August 1936, he accepted without regret that his schooling was over; he knew that he owed it to his mother to go out and earn some money but, even if the opportunity to continue his studies had existed, he would have wanted to get on with what he felt must be the more serious business of life.

For a while he worked as delivery boy to a baker but this, he knew, would lead to nothing. The majority of his friends followed their fathers into the mines but Jim wanted to see more of the world and was repelled by the idea of working underground. He wanted to 'do something worthwhile. I suppose I was more serious-minded than most youngsters. I wanted to do something that would ensure me a bit of money later on in life.' If he joined the armed services he would at least be sure of a pension. He considered the Navy, but before he could look deeply into the possibility, found himself outside a recruiting office for the Black Watch. With a Scottish regiment, he felt, he would be among people who shared the same accent and some at least of the same experiences. At the age of fifteen he enlisted. It would be another two years before he would qualify as a full soldier and he would have to wait until he was eighteen before he would begin to earn towards the coveted pension, but a beginning had been made.

The Black Watch was founded in 1739 and, though deemed a Highland regiment, recruited in Perth, Angus and Fife; Fergus, from East Lothian, was a little outside even that catchment area, but numbers were below strength and the regiment was happy to pick up youngsters from further afield. 'The Jock,' wrote Wavell in his foreword to the regimental history, 'today comes from the city as often as from the hill or the fields. But he still inherits the spirit and traditions of his Highland forebears – the clan feeling, the toughness, the fierceness in assault, the independence of character, the boundless self-confidence . . .' In none of these was Fergus lacking, though the clan feeling was something that would grow from practice rather than come ready-made. From the first moment that he wore uniform he was made to feel that he was joining a rare elite and that to be a member of it carried responsibilities as well as privileges. The regimental history was thrust upon him, and though he was temperamentally as unready to devote much time to the history of the Black Watch as to that of any other feature of British history, he would have been unusually unimpressionable if he had not emerged with some pride in and reverence for the institution he had joined.

His mother questioned him closely about his intentions but made little attempt to dissuade him. 'I don't think she wanted me to go,' he remembers. Since the death of her husband her life had been emotionally starved, mother and son had grown very close. At least she would not be financially the worse off for his absence; out of the exiguous 14 shillings a week which he would earn as a boy soldier, 2/6d would automatically be deducted to send to his mother; Fergus voluntarily raised the amount to 3/6d. He knew how much the money was needed; only three years later did he discover that his mother had been putting it scrupulously to one side. On his eighteenth birthday she returned him the full amount.

Any recruit to the Black Watch belonged from the start to one of its battalions. Fergus found himself allocated to the 1st, which happened to be in India at the time. It was, however, due to return in two years and, rather than send him east for a short period, it was decided that he should spend this time with the 2nd Battalion. To the outsider the difference between one battalion and another might appear trivial and it anyway seems that it would have been sensible to have assigned the new recruit permanently to the battalion with which he was destined to pass his first two years. This was not how the Black Watch worked, however. The 1st

Battalion was short in numbers, so to the 1st Battalion Fergus must be assigned.

Within the overall structure of the regiment each battalion commanded fierce allegiance, so that at once Fergus found himself confused in his loyalties. He knew that he was working alongside other boys from whom he would soon be separated, was commanded by officers and non-commissioned officers who were not his own. For somebody naturally disposed to be combative and rebellious, the circumstance was disturbing. On top of this, the work was physically far harder than anything he had experienced before; the discipline was rigorous; the slightest deviation from the standards of smartness that the sergeant felt appropriate was severely punished. Fergus reacted badly and earned himself a reputation as a ne'er-do-well: 'I was a very bad boy. I was always in trouble.'

The climax came when the battalion moved south to Colchester to take part in the annual tattoo. The boy soldiers were left behind in the charge of a senior private who resented the fact that he had been singled out for this boring task and took it out on his youthful charges. Any boy soldier in the Black Watch was expected to study a range of musical instruments so as to equip him for a possible place in the regimental band. Their temporary master made them practise at what seemed to them unreasonable hours; they amused themselves by playing popular tunes instead of the regulation military or religious music, were caught red-handed and told that they would be put on a charge. Fergus and a friend decided that enough was enough, they left the barracks for a walk 'and just kept walking'. They did not intend to desert, merely to assert themselves and make a protest by taking a few days off.

They spent their time doing odd jobs and sleeping rough, then ended up at the home of Fergus's companion. His friend's father had himself served in the Black Watch; he was horrified at the boys' escapade and packed them off back to the barracks. The Colonel, already dissatisfied with Fergus, decided that this time he had gone too far and that he should be discharged. Fergus's mother might not have been gratified by his choice of career but she had no intention of letting it end in such ignominy. She rushed to the barracks and pleaded that her fatherless son should be given another chance. The Colonel relented and Fergus, greatly relieved, vowed to turn over a new leaf. This was the end of his rebellious career, he says: 'I changed before I became a soldier.' In fact his Army life was to be marked by periodic outbursts of turbulence, but the worst was certainly over.

The 2nd Battalion was sent off to Palestine and Fergus was despatched to Dover to await the return of the 1st Battalion, now only a few months away. Most of the time was devoted to training for the band. He had the chance to be a piper, a drummer or a bandsman on some other instrument. He chose the third but proved a restless exponent of the art, moving from instrument to instrument, showing some ability at each but a reluctance to settle down and master any one of them. When the 1st Battalion finally returned from India he was on the fringes of the band but not fully part of it. Then he was promised that, if he would take over the E-flat bass from a soldier who was on the point of retirement, and really work at it, he could have a place in the band when it went on a trip to New York in September 1939. His long-term ambition was to put music behind him and to become a foot-soldier, but this chance was too good to miss. He accepted the offer with delight, earned his place, and was within a few days of embarkation when the growing German threat to Poland and the near certainty of war led to the cancellation of the visit. When war broke out on 3 September Fergus was seventeen years and twelve days old.

The loss of the jaunt to New York was a disappointment, but far more distressing was the fact that he and the other boy soldiers were left behind when the 1st Battalion was sent to France. He would anyway not have been allowed into the front line until he was eighteen but at least in France he would have been on the way to his objective. Instead he went back to the depot at Perth and continued his work as a bandsman. When he was seventeen and a half, though still not eligible for France, he was at least allowed to become a full soldier and to start his primary training. The emphasis was on drill and small arms; the young soldier who did well at these was deemed to have potential as a non-commissioned officer and might hope for early promotion. Fergus shone and was duly recommended for promotion; but those responsible in this case did not believe in unduly encouraging youthful enthusiasm and ruled that he must wait till he had become eighteen.

As soon as that landmark was reached he applied to join the 1st Battalion in France. Once more he was frustrated. The Regimental Sergeant-Major thought highly of his abilities and wanted to retain him as an instructor. Fergus knew there was little point in protest; theoretically the War Office or the officers of the regiment might control his future but in fact the RSM was close to all-powerful – 'He was the man who had everybody in his sights and guided their lives.' As a result, after a short further period at the regimental depot, he found himself posted as lance-corporal to the 70th Battalion at Kinross. He did not realise at the time that every year away from the 1st Battalion, and indeed every promotion, made it less likely that he would ever be allowed to rejoin his proper unit. Like constituency parties selecting a new Member of Parliament, the battalions jealously guarded their independence and preferred to manage their own promotions; they looked with some doubt on people who had obtained their experience elsewhere and whom the depot tried to thrust on them. As it happened the RSM's obduracy may have saved Fergus's life or, at least, his liberty. The Highland Brigade was cut off and hideously mauled south-west of Dieppe after the German breakthrough in May 1940; only thirty survivors of the 1st Battalion fought their way through to St Valéry and evacuation by the Royal Navy.

The 70th Battalion was a unit devoted to the training of young soldiers on the fringes of maturity, including a number of seventeen-year-olds destined to become officers. The other instructors consisted for the most part of elderly survivors from the First World War, one of whom had no fingers on his right hand, none of whom was fully able to undertake an energetic training schedule. Fergus would have impressed in any company, here he shone with an almost indecent radiance. Within a few weeks he had been promoted to the rank of corporal and given what was in effect a staff sergeant's job in charge of a squad of forty or so potential officers. He was not particularly impressed by the calibre of those who were one day destined to command him – 'They didn't show much common sense,' he considers – though he concedes that in time most of them turned into good officers. He felt that he was as well qualified as any of them and would have been perfectly capable of being an officer himself. But though at one point it was suggested to him that he might apply for a commission, he felt no urge to do so. For one thing he did not think he could afford it; the pay would have been better but the mess bills and other expenses would have more than outweighed this advantage: 'It took you a long time to make any money, you had to be a captain or a major first.' For another, he felt that he would have been made to feel uncomfortable and out of place in the Officers' Mess. He sensed that there would always be a distinction between those who had taken a commission on joining the Army and those who had risen from the ranks. Rankers were made to feel inferior; less so, certainly in the closely knit Black Watch than in the Brigade of Guards, but 'the stigma was always there'.

Fergus had a reputation among the officer cadets for being something of a martinet but fair and a man to be respected. With one exception he got on well with all of them. The odd man out was the son of one of Fergus's company commanders, a 'bit of a tearaway' and quick to resent junior non-commissioned officers who ordered him around too assertively. Once Fergus put him on a charge for throwing bread in the mess hall, and ensured that he was confined to barracks. The incident rankled in the young man's mind. Normally when an officer was commissioned he was not sent back to the unit where he had done his training in the ranks, but for some reason in this case the new Second-Lieutenant found himself back in Kinross in command of a platoon. He was gratified to discover that Fergus was still there, now his subordinate. On the first morning he sent for him. Fergus was at the time teaching a squad of recruits, and sent back a message that he would come as soon as he was free. Half an hour later he turned up. By this time the newly arrived platoon commander was seething with indignation. 'You haven't changed much, Fergus!' he exclaimed. 'Don't know what you mean, sir,' was the reply, then, as an afterthought, 'You haven't changed much either!' Fortunately the RSM had a healthy respect for Fergus's abilities and little for those of the new officer; he made sure that the Commanding Officer knew the background to the incident and no harm came to Fergus's career.

In fact newly commissioned officers were sent to Kinross more to learn themselves than to instruct others. Once a tyro platoon commander was scheduled to give a lesson. As was the usual practice, he assumed that the non-commissioned officer concerned would do the bulk of the work. Fergus that day was in a mood to be difficult. He lined up the men and then rapped out: 'All present and correct, sir! Your lesson, sir!' The Second-Lieutenant was 'flummoxed', Fergus remembers with satisfaction. 'They weren't up to field training.'

Fergus was himself somewhat flummoxed when he was sent on a six weeks' course with the Guards at Caterham, to bring his drill and weaponry up to a standard which he thought he had already achieved. He soon found that he had not. It was a gruelling and in some ways salutary experience, but though he respected their discipline and technical expertise, he was in no way disposed to accept the superiority of his temporary instructors. He has never been a lover of the Guards, he admits: 'I'm afraid I find the standard of intelligence in non-commissioned and warrant officers is not as high as in the Black Watch.'

In January 1943, he found himself back in the regimental depot and in March was promoted to lance-sergeant. By now he knew that his chances of getting back to the 1st Battalion were slight but he was resolved that he would not sit out the whole war training other soldiers to fight the Germans or Japanese. He appealed to his company commander, who told him that his best chance was to apply direct to the War Office for a posting outside the regiment. He would have to wait a few more months to become a substantive rather than a lance-sergeant but then the Regimental Sergeant-Major would no longer be able to frustrate him. Fergus followed this advice, to the considerable annoyance of the RSM who had intended to keep him with the regiment in Scotland as an instructor. There were not many places, though, to which a War Office posting could be secured. The area most usually applied for was West Africa, and it was there that Fergus asked to go.

Between his decision to apply for a War Office posting and his eventual departure, the course of Fergus's life was changed. Before his return to the depot at Perth early in 1943 he had had little time for girls. Money had been short, the demands of the Army on his time insatiable, there always seemed to be something else to do. With a sergeant's pay and the pressure of work temporarily eased, he had time to look around. He was twenty-one; this was still unreasonably young for marriage in the eyes of the Army but the uncertainties of war had lent urgency to courtship and even the most traditional of commanding officers had to admit that standards might be relaxed. Fergus almost immediately found what he was looking for. Annie was a pretty and lively girl, working in a canteen just outside the barrack gates; she knew her own mind and quickly made it obvious that Fergus suited her quite as well as she suited him.

For him it was almost as if he wanted to marry her family as well

as her. Her father had been a company sergeant-major in the Black
Watch who had retired and was now working as an insurance
agent. They were comfortably off and their house was always full
of friends and relations, relaxed, cheerful, having a good time.
After the straitened austerity of his own home it seemed a new
world to Fergus. Annie's parents were 'two of the finest people I've
known in my life,' he feels. 'There were never any arguments, no
disharmony at all.' They made Fergus welcome from the start.
Annie's father must have thought his future son-in-law on the
young side for taking on the responsible role of a husband but he
did not even suggest a delay: 'You've thought about it, and if you've
decided you're doing the right thing, that's OK by me.' His
Company Commander proved equally acquiescent; Fergus was in
most ways conspicuously mature for his age and not likely to rush
into any relationship he might later regret. The couple married a
year or so after they met, in the spring of 1944. They took up
residence in the home of Annie's parents; it was uncomfortably
crowded but the young couple could not have been made more
welcome.

Almost immediately Fergus was posted to Sierra Leone to join
the 1st Battalion of the West African Frontier Force. He knew
that this unit would shortly be on its way to active service in some
part of the world, but had no idea where this might be or when he
would see Annie again. 'I missed her,' he confesses. 'I didn't enjoy
the first time I went abroad because I'd just got married.' But it
never occurred to him to try to cancel or even postpone his posting,
nor did his new wife, a Regular soldier's daughter, doubt that he
must go where he was sent. In wartime, of course, family ties had
to take second place; but even in peacetime Fergus would have
taken it for granted that the demands of the service were pre-
eminent. Two institutions commanded loyalty in Fergus's life, the
Army and the family, and of these the Army was both the more
demanding and the more inflexible.

The West African Frontier Force was recruited from the

inhabitants of the British colonies of Nigeria, the Gold Coast and Sierra Leone. It was run by British officers and senior non-commissioned officers. A few of the sergeants and more junior NCOs were black Africans but their wages were far lower than those of their white counterparts, they were not trusted with similar responsibilities and were never billeted within three hundred yards of the British lines. There was no question of the African sergeants using the facilities of the British Sergeants' Mess. 'To be honest, they were treated more as slaves,' says Fergus. 'They were very, very backward.' He did not feel that this was unfair; his view was that the African NCOs had no leadership qualities, actual or potential, and that it would have been unfair to them, as well as to the men, if they had been encouraged to take on duties beyond their powers.

In May, 1945, the 1st Battalion of the Frontier Force took ship for India. Fergus accompanied them as far as Bombay but was then detached for special duties. He said goodbye to his African colleagues without regret and was unsurprised to hear that, when they went into action in Burma, 'they didn't make a very good show of themselves'. According to a British acquaintance from the battalion whom he later met, the African troops fled when they were fired on by the Japanese and left the battalions to the right and left of them in the lurch: 'As soon as they got ambushed the buggers ran away and left us,' reported Fergus's friend.

Fergus himself was despatched to a site on the east coast of India, north of Madras, and told to lay out a camp for a battalion getting ready to invade Malaya. In the event the war ended so quickly that nothing was ever built but Fergus completed all the preparations before he was sent on a course to the Small Arms School at Saugor. Possibly the authorities were at a loss to know what else to do with him – certainly the course was elementary by his standards. After three days the major in command admitted that there was nothing they could teach him; instead he asked

Fergus to take on certain lecturing duties and offered the prospect that he might join the School as a full-time instructor.

This would have suited Fergus well, but things then turned sour. One night in the Sergeants' Mess an African sergeant-major walked in, accompanied by another sergeant. Fergus at once challenged him and told him he had no right to be in a building reserved for Europeans. 'Once these people went to India they got spoiled,' he complains. 'British troops treated them as equals, which, of course, they weren't. They got above themselves.' The Africans left under protest and next day the Sergeant-Major complained to the School Commander. Fergus was summoned. Boldly, he told the Major that he did not understand the relationship between the British and Africans: 'He thought that these people were on an equal basis with us, which was wrong.' He sees no reason today to revise his position. If the Sergeant-Major had been Indian rather than African he would have felt less sure of his ground, but then, he does not think that such a situation would have arisen. In 1945, he believes, no Indian non-commissioned officer would have contemplated intruding into a British Sergeants' Mess.

Fergus paid the price for his attitude when he was expelled from the Small Arms School and found himself in a transit camp. At once he volunteered for service in Burma. The 2nd Battalion of the Black Watch was there and he hoped that he might eventually link up with them, but initially he knew that he would have to rejoin the West Africans. Before he could do so, however, the atom bomb precipitated the Japanese surrender. Fergus had not relished the thought of a jungle campaign but he was still disappointed that he had been deprived of seeing action. He had served throughout the war as a member of one of Britain's finest fighting regiments yet had not heard a shot fired in anger. He could legitimately maintain that this was none of his doing, but the reflection was still not one that gave him any satisfaction.

He returned to the United Kingdom in February 1946, travelling back neither with the Black Watch nor with the West African Frontier Force but as an individual. Any lingering hopes that he might at last serve with the 1st Battalion were quickly quashed; it was back to the regimental depot in Perth. This had now become an Infantry Training Centre, for the Argylls as well as the Black Watch, and Fergus found himself a platoon sergeant, training mainly national service recruits in drill and small arms. It was a job that he could have done in his sleep, and though he performed it competently and conscientiously he could not help feeling bored. It was some consolation that his wife joined him and they set up in married quarters; it was the first time they had enjoyed life on their own and they wasted no time in starting a family. His daughter, Frances, was born in December 1946.

By the autumn of 1947 he had had enough. He took the same escape route as he had followed four years before and volunteered for service in West Africa. This time he went to Lagos. He found the Nigerians, particularly the Ibos, more advanced than the Sierra Leonians but was struck by the harshness of the discipline that they meted out to each other – 'very cruel, they were'. There were tentative moves afoot to assimilate black and white troops at all but the highest level but Fergus was not in Nigeria for long enough to have to come to terms with this trend. Even before his wife and child were able to join him he had contracted serious bronchitis and spent several weeks in hospital. The doctors decided that the climate was responsible and sent him back to Britain; he quickly recovered and the condition never recurred.

In July 1948, Fergus found himself once more back at the depot. He was still only twenty-six but it was already clear that the job he coveted above all others – that of Regimental Sergeant-Major of the Black Watch – was likely to evade him. He had no wish to leave the service, though – 'the Army was still my life' – and there seemed no option but to carry on, hoping something would turn up. Most of the next six years were spent as a sergeant in the

Highland Brigade Training Centre at Fort George, Inverness. He
was in charge of a platoon of recruits who were being prepared for
Korea and would happily have accompanied them there, but the
Company Commander had his eye on him as a future sergeant-
major. After a short stint at the depot, now as a colour-sergeant, he
was soon back for a second term at Fort George.

It was in some ways an unsatisfactory period. Fort George was
the depot of the Seaforth Highlanders. The Company Sergeant-
Major, who was himself a Seaforth, fell ill, was sent away sick and
was 'Y-listed' – which according to the usual rules should have
meant that he was posted away permanently from the battalion.
Fergus put up the crown on his sleeve which marked him as a
sergeant-major and rejoiced at what he imagined would be a
permanent appointment. His predecessor had powerful friends,
however; he reappeared at Fort George and took up his old duties.
Fergus reverted to his sergeant's stripes. This would have been bad
enough if it had happened only once but three times Fergus found
himself temporarily glorified and then demoted. He would have
preferred not to put up his crown, only to lose it again, but was
told that while he exercised the duties of sergeant-major he must
be dressed accordingly.

Worse was to follow. While Fergus was acting company
sergeant-major he was ordered to take a batch of ninety men to
Portsmouth to put them on a ship for Korea. The day before he
was due to go, it appeared in the Adjutant's Orders that he was to
revert to the rank of sergeant. Furiously he went home, took off his
crown and once more put back his stripes. Next day he presented
himself at the Adjutant's office and was asked why he was
inappropriately dressed. Fergus lost control of himself; 'I was very
cheeky,' he admits. 'You signed the order, *sir*,' he said, emphasising
the 'sir' so as to make it sound an insult rather than an honorific,
'So *you* should know why I've got three stripes on my arm. As far
as I'm concerned you can keep your bloody badge!' 'Well, that's the
finish of it,' said the Adjutant. 'You were being posted away from

here as acting sergeant-major.' 'Then why did you sign an order saying that I was to revert to sergeant? If you'd told me yesterday that I was going away as an acting warrant officer, and to take no notice of the order, then I wouldn't have done so. But I'm a soldier. If you sign an order, I obey the order. If you can't read your own orders, you shouldn't be doing the job you're in!'

No doubt the Adjutant would have given a very different account of the misunderstanding which led up to this explosion. Whatever the rights or wrongs, Fergus's behaviour had been, to put it mildly, injudicious. 'I didn't do myself any good,' he admits, 'but I don't regret it. I can't abide fools, I'm afraid.' He was never again made acting company sergeant-major.

In 1954 it was once more back to the depot. There were new problems. Fergus was now a substantive colour-sergeant. There was no vacancy for such an individual at Perth, the only way he could be given a new job was if he displaced the acting Colour-Sergeant, a man called Smith. This he was most reluctant to do: 'I was responsible for Mr Smith getting his first tape,' he told the company commander. 'I wouldn't want any harm to come to him.' The Company Commander appreciated his generosity and promised to try to find him a good berth outside the regiment. He succeeded, and a few weeks later Fergus was offered a job as sergeant-major with the Royal Electrical and Mechanical Engineers at Malvern. It was a temporary assignment and for the first year or so Fergus felt himself a visitor, but the work and the company were congenial, he was appreciated and sought after, so early in 1956 he took the plunge and left the Black Watch to join the REME.

The REME had its origins in the nineteenth century but it did not split off from the Ordnance Corps and achieve full independence until 1941. By 1950, by which time it had responsibility for all repairs and maintenance carried out in or near the front line, it was nearly ten thousand strong. It was a young corps, and decidedly unglamorous by the standards of the infantry or cavalry regiments, but the job it did was none the less essential and professionally satisfying. Fergus could not help feeling that it was a come-down to leave the Black Watch for such an employer, he cherished his Scottish roots and wore the kilt when any suitable opportunities offered, but the prospects for promotion were obviously far greater in his new arm, and he never doubted that he had made the right decision.

'I couldn't do a thing wrong with the REME, just couldn't do a thing wrong,' he recalls. He did, indeed, enjoy great success in his new career, but at one moment it came close to shipwreck. In 1956 he was transferred to Bordon and appointed Regimental Quarter-master-Sergeant in the Army Emergency Reserve. His Quarter-master was a lieutenant and, says Fergus, 'a very disagreeable chap', notorious for showing little consideration for the men under his command. On one occasion a squad had finished a hard day's work and was awaiting dismissal so that its members could catch a bus to go home. For no good reason that anyone could see, the Quartermaster kept them hanging about outside. Fergus stalked into the office and 'had a bit of an argument with him, quite a severe argument actually'. He was so offensive to the indignant officer that he could well have faced court martial for insubordina-tion. The fact that nothing of the sort transpired seems to him proof that the Quartermaster recognised he was in the wrong. As with Fergus's other imbroglios, it is at least possible that the other party involved would have seen things differently: 'I've always been outspoken, if I had anything to say I said it. It never did me any harm, anyway.'

His period with the Colours ran out in 1960, but he had no wish to end his military life before he had to and he applied to go on the Long Service List. He was offered an extension of three years with the probability of a further two to follow, and accepted gratefully. Usually renewal would have involved coming down in rank but the

REME were so anxious to keep him that they found him a slot at his existing level in the Army Apprentice College at Carlisle. It proved to be 'the cushiest job I ever did'. He was responsible for clothing for the whole unit as well as for everything within the buildings and the buildings themselves. It was no sinecure, but equally it involved little in the way of worry or sudden crisis. The Quartermaster was a major, an ex-ranker, who liked and trusted his Sergeant-Major and let him get on with the job in his own way. 'I wanted to stay on,' says Fergus. 'I'd have been a fool if I didn't with the job I had!'

He would have been happy to serve out the rest of his time at Carlisle but a more demanding task was offered him. In 1966 he was told he was to go as Regimental Quartermaster-Sergeant to SHAPE – the Supreme Headquarters of the Allied Powers in Europe. It was an important and difficult assignment and the Adjutant made much of the honour that was being done him by the offer. Then two days later came disappointment. Important and difficult though it might be, the evaluation team had ruled that in future the job should be done by a mere staff sergeant. The offer to Fergus was withdrawn. By way of consolation the Adjutant offered him two possibilities: either with the REME in Germany or as Regimental Quartermaster-Sergeant of the Middle East Command in Aden. Unlike the job in Germany the posting in Aden would allow him to retain his full rank. He accepted it without hesitation.

Meanwhile his children had been growing up. As a father Fergus had shown himself strict, exaggeratedly so in the view of his son and daughter, though they had no doubt that it was with the best intentions. His insistence that they should mind their manners and keep the house scrupulously tidy was sometimes burdensome to them, so too was his determination that they should study hard and pass their exams with credit. His son, who had been born in 1950 while they were in Scotland, bore the brunt of his father's attentions on the academic front; his daughter, whose education seemed decidedly less important, found that Fergus became oppressively over-protective when she showed signs of wanting to lead an independent life. When she began to go out with boys he always expected to be told who was involved, where they were going and when she would be home – however early a time she proposed he would always insist on something earlier still. Whether his wife shared his attitude his children never knew; certainly she never intervened forcefully on their behalf. Fergus showed no wish to bully his wife, who was well able to look after herself, but there was no room for doubt as to who was in overall charge of the household. His insistence that everything should be done exactly according to his wishes often sorely tried his family and when they moved on from an army quarter he became almost obsessive in his resolve that everything should be left in apple-pie order and that the next occupants should find nothing about which they could possibly complain.

By the time the Ferguses left for Aden their daughter was twenty years old and had just married. Their sixteen-year-old son was at boarding school and would join them in Aden only for such holidays as the Army would authorise and pay for. The Ferguses therefore set off by themselves. It did not seem likely to be a tranquil posting. A state of emergency had been in existence for three years while the various factions struggled to be best placed when the British finally departed. Most active of these was the National Liberation Front, who wanted the British not merely to give the colony independence but also to quit the military base which they had originally intended to retain. The Front's aim was a Marxist state linked with the Yemen and Egypt, and it had free recourse to terrorism to achieve its end. In 1965 a bomb had been thrown at a party of seventy-three British children preparing to fly home; five of them were injured. In 1966, the year of Fergus's arrival, there were 480 terrorist incidents causing 573 casualties, of whom five dead and 218 wounded were British servicemen. Amid this bloody mayhem Fergus's task was to pack up and prepare for evacuation.

It was a task for which his tidy-mindedness and passion for detail admirably equipped him. The REME had enjoyed a considerable presence in Aden for many years, with four major workshops including facilities for the support of light aircraft and helicopters, and there was an inordinate amount of material to be disposed of. Delays in announcing the date of independence meant that the schedules were constantly being revised; decisions as to which pieces of equipment should be returned to the United Kingdom, which sent to the Gulf, which re-allocated locally, were made on one day and remade the next. It was an unpleasant and messy job. 'No praise is too high for the outstanding work of our men – and this includes their NCOs and officers,' recorded the regimental history. 'They often worked prodigious hours, under conditions of extreme heat, discomfort and not infrequently danger.'

Fergus, in fact, rather enjoyed his time in Aden. The work was hard, indeed, but it was the sort of occupation he relished and at which he knew he excelled. He accepted that the danger from terrorists was omnipresent but had no direct responsibility for combating it and was never personally involved; the nearest he came to action was when gunmen shot at somebody in a car a little way ahead of him in a line of traffic. He did not hesitate to bring his son out for holidays: 'If you avoided the places where trouble was likely to happen you were all right, except for odd occurrences.' When he went out in a car with his wife and son he would look out to the front, his wife would keep an eye on the non-driver's side, his son would stand guard to the rear. The danger was real but it was also something of a game that would give his son something to boast about when he went back to school.

The situation in which the British Army found itself in Aden was in many ways distasteful. Fergus, probably more than most soldiers, felt that he had joined the Army to protect the interests of

King and Country. The Black Watch, one of the most traditional of regiments, had fortified this conviction. It had been his perceived duty to defend the Empire. Now he found himself involved in its disintegration, with the added chagrin of knowing that the friends of Britain, once their patrons and protectors had gone, would almost certainly end up on the losing side. But though this might be disagreeable to contemplate he did not waste much energy in lamenting it. He was sensible enough to realise that Aden had been of value above all as a staging-post on the way to India. With India independent since 1947 and Britain's Asian empire following after it, Aden had become little more than an expensive and insalubrious encumbrance. If the Empire could have regained its glory he would have been delighted; failing that, the sooner we were shot of Aden the better it would be.

By August 1967, evacuation was far advanced. The bulk of the stores had been disposed of; now only three hundred or so packing cases remained. It had originally been intended that Fergus should stay until the final pull-out on 1 January 1968 but he had little left to do, he was bored, and when his wife left on the last plane taking female personnel back to Britain he gave notice of his intentions and flew back as well. For some reason that he could never understand the Army thought it necessary to send out a replacement of the same rank to see out the final phase of the evacuation.

This time there could be no further renewal. He was discharged in August 1967. The parting caused him less pain than he would have expected a few years before. The Army was changing, and he did not like what was going on. Standards were being allowed to slip. 'It's my own feeling that the Army was a much happier place when we had very strict discipline. When the discipline went, the attraction for me went as well. It didn't seem to me to be as smart as it used to be.'

Besides, though he left the womb, the umbilical cord was not completely severed. He might be no longer *in* the Army but he was still very near to it, even perhaps *of* it. He became a Barracks Inventory Accountant, his job being to settle soldiers in their quarters and to move them out, to account for all the stores and furnishings, to write off items of no further value and to ensure that losses were paid for and damages made good at the culprit's cost. His responsibility ended at the barrack gate, but in the hinterland within a few miles of the Army town of Tidworth he was responsible for all military accommodation. He wore civilian clothes, indeed was a civilian, but he reported to majors and to colonels; he was no longer a soldier but was still a cog in the great machine of Army life.

It was not a role in which a man as inflexibly meticulous as Fergus could expect to make many friends. The worst friction arose at the moment military tenants handed over their quarters at the end of periods of occupation – which had sometimes lasted several years. Invariably they thought that they had looked after the property well. Fergus rarely agreed. There was some leeway overwhat constituted fair wear and tear, he admits, 'but not much if you did the job conscientiously'. People were always cheating, denying the existence of items that appeared on the inventory, claiming that scratches on furniture had been there when they arrived, indignant that recompense should be sought for mattresses spoiled by children wetting their beds – 'there were some very dirty people'. The problems grew worse when soldiers were allowed to import their own furniture when they took over official quarters. They would return from a posting in Germany with large cupboards or tables, dispense with the War Office allocation, then find that their German pieces did not fit happily in their new home and try to reverse the decision. The result was confusion, wasted effort and, since Fergus was not particularly sympathetic to such vacillation, a certain amount of ill-will and frustration.

As a general rule he was responsible for the accommodation for other ranks while officers were left to one of his colleagues, but from time to time he found himself looking after the officers' quarters as well. His reputation as a martinet went before him. When it came to losing or 'liberating' pieces of domestic equipment or leaving their houses in a mess, Fergus found that officers were every bit as bad if not worse than the men. He refused to make any concessions: 'If you are going to charge an other rank £90 or £100, you can't let an officer off.' If his victim complained to the quartermaster or commanding officer that he was being hardly used Fergus would not yield an inch: 'Well, that was what I found. You should know me by this time. Do I make any unfair charges? If you want to come in and inspect it yourself, please do so.' They never did, and they knew that he did not make unfair charges, but his attitude still inspired resentment. He is convinced that it was the hostility caused by his firmness which led to his never being appointed Assistant Barracks Officer, a promotion that would have earned him an extra £500 a year. The atmosphere improved during the last few years before his retirement when he was transferred to do the same job at the helicopter station at Middle Wallop, a few miles away. Perhaps he had mellowed with time; perhaps his idiosyncrasies were well known and discounted in advance; in any case all went smoothly: 'I got on very well with everyone there, including the officers. They all knew what to expect and I got on fine with them.'

During these years the Ferguses lived in a bungalow which they had bought at Porton. His wife worked at the nearby Microbiological Research Establishment as a research assistant, and Fergus would drop her off on his way to work. The children were off their hands: their daughter living in Colchester; their son, who had at first followed Fergus into the Army, also married and now settled in civilian life. With their joint salaries and Fergus's Army pension, they were comfortably off and they could face the prospect of retirement with equanimity. They had originally intended to make their final home in Perth where Annie's mother was still living but by the time the need to make a decision arose all their near relations were dead or had moved away. Left to himself Fergus would probably still have gone back to Scotland but his wife was nervous about the climate and anyway wanted to be near their daughter. Fergus gave way without too much reluctance. In December 1986, they bought a bungalow at Colchester and settled in contentedly. Fergus played golf three times a week and gardened vigorously. He never lost his habit of speaking his mind freely when provoked but he was perhaps provoked less easily, he got on well with his neighbours and had a pleasantly undemanding social life.

Then in the early 1990s his wife had a heart attack. Annie had suffered from rheumatic fever when a child but had recovered well; she never found it easy to support the cold, however, and from time to time had difficulty breathing. Her first heart attack was not serious and she soon seemed more or less restored, but over the next years her angina grew progressively worse. She was still able to walk around and enjoy life until the end but in 1995 a stroke proved fatal.

As so often, the survivor of a marriage only discovers how dependent he or she has grown on their partner after the other one has died. Fergus was still active; played golf regularly, saw his daughter's family every Sunday, kept up the garden; but he was lonely and felt that he was keeping himself busy so as to avoid being bored, not because he really wanted to do the things he did. He had often jokingly said to his wife, 'If anything happens to you I'm off to Chelsea!' and every time he got the annual statement of his pension a pamphlet from the Royal Hospital reminded him that he was eligible for a place. The possibility that he might become a Pensioner was therefore often in his mind but at first he rejected it; he did not like the idea of depending on others and resolved to die where he was.

To this day he is uncertain what made him change his mind; it was not decrepitude, though he recognised that the garden might become too much for him in a few years. When he told his children that he was thinking of applying to the Royal Hospital they did what they could to dissuade him – they needed him amongst them, there would always be a place for him in their homes – but they privately accepted that if it worked out it would be the best solution. Whether it *would* work was another question: they knew how hard their father found it to accommodate himself to the demands of others and feared that he might find so close-knit a community uncongenial and claustrophobic. He had the same doubts himself but eventually took the plunge. He sold the bungalow, thereby making retreat more difficult, and entered the Royal Hospital in October 1998.

He is still not entirely convinced that he has made the right decision. 'We do have our independence,' he feels, 'and it's a good life really; I just find it hard to get used to communal feeding and communal facilities – ablutions and things. I don't think that I like that very much. There's got to be a drawback to everything, I suppose.' If he did go, it would not be his relationship with the other Pensioners that drove him out. The astringency and impulsiveness that marked his military career seems to have abated and he finds no difficulty in getting on with those around him. But he still maintains that it would not take an awful lot to make him leave the Hospital. What deters him most is the thought that he would have to resume all those burdens that he shuffled off when he came to Chelsea: the council tax; the water, gas and electricity bills; pension arrangements; negotiations with the Inland Revenue. There is a marvellous simplicity, almost irresponsibility, about life in the Royal Hospital; it would take a considerable effort of will to renounce it. Nobody has ever doubted the strength of Fergus's will but every month that passes makes it less likely that he will think the price of independence is one that is worth paying.

ALWYN HOLMES

Sergeant Holmes (front, right) with members of his
platoon at Celle in Germany, *c* 1955

Alwyn Holmes

I F his parents had been more meticulous about their spelling, Alwyn Ronald Holmes believes he would have been christened Aylwyn. This is the Old English word for 'elf'. Why they should have expected their eldest child to be elfin in appearance or in character is uncertain. Since he was invariably addressed as 'Ron', it anyway mattered little.

It does not seem likely that this flight of fancy emanated from the paternal side of the family. Grandfather Holmes was a sour and curmudgeonly old miser – 'a tight-fisted old sod' is Ron's concise summary. In his grandchildren's memory he was dressed invariably in a starched wing collar and was never seen without hat and cane; when he came to the house the children had to tiptoe around and speak only in subdued whispers. He owned and ran a sweetshop-cum-tobacconist, but when Ron as a five-year-old asked if he could have a penny bar of chocolate, he made his grandson pay for it. He also owned a string of houses, which he rented out. Ron once asked his mother why their family had never been given the chance to live in one of them. 'Oh, he would have if I'd gone to bed with him,' was the unpromising reply.

There was little love lost between Nellie Holmes and her

husband, Henry, let alone her father-in-law. Harry Holmes – to his own mind at any rate – had had one great stroke of luck, when an ingot of white-hot steel had snaked across the floor of the Sheffield foundry where he worked and run over his foot. It did little more than superficial damage but the foundry had clearly been guilty of negligence and its owners were anxious to hush the matter up. They offered their employee either compensation of £1,000 or the guarantee of a job for life. Mr Holmes at first proposed to take the cash – worth over £25,000 at current values – but the union representative urged him to look to the future and accept the lifetime job. He took the advice and never regretted it. Short of theft or some grossly disorderly conduct he was now secure; he was not a lazy man and did his job well enough to escape censure, but felt no need to make any special effort. In fact, he *did* make a special effort, in that he got little pleasure from being at home and regularly worked on Saturdays for high overtime rates. His family benefited little from his industry; only when he died did his widow discover that a substantial part of his pay-packet had been held back, to be spent, it seems, on drink and other women.

So far as Harry's children were concerned, it seemed to Ron that 'he just didn't want to know'. As well as Ron, who was born on 2 January 1925, there were two daughters and, much later, a second son; their father more or less ignored his sons and the younger daughter but showed some affection for the elder. When his favourite married an American soldier and left for the United States, he got seriously drunk on Christmas Day, ranted and swore, and finally said to his younger daughter, Elizabeth: 'It should have been you who went over the water!' Ron, in the view of the victim at any rate, he seems actively to have disliked; partly, perhaps, because he experienced the jealousy of a man who feels that he has been displaced in his wife's affections. He resented any sign that his son might shine in a field where he felt himself well-established. He was a competent spin bowler but never coached Ron or encouraged him to play cricket; when Ron showed some aptitude for snooker, his father jeered at his efforts and advised him to give up. On the rare occasion that he was invited to go on a fishing expedition, Ron was not allowed to touch the rod and was cuffed painfully across the ears if he made any noise that might disturb the fish.

Mr and Mrs Holmes had so little in common that it is hard to understand how they had managed to produce four children. In another age or social group the marriage would probably have broken up; as it was they struggled on with little satisfaction to either party. All the blame did not lie with Harry Holmes. Nellie had originally wanted to marry someone else, had lost him when he went abroad, and always felt that her husband was a second best. Her father ran a bookstall in Sheffield market and collected debts for a doctor; occupations which she felt established her socially at a higher level than her husband had any right to claim for himself. She never ceased to rub in her superiority and by so doing incited her husband to behave with exaggerated uncouthness if not downright brutality. The result, from the point of view of the children, was an atmosphere of continued turbulence and sour resentment. Ron never saw his father actually strike his wife but Harry Holmes would often come home drunk, abuse and threaten her, and teeter on the edge of violence. Once his behaviour was so outrageous that the six-year-old Ron attacked him with his tiny fists and cried: 'When I'm big enough, I'll give you a good hiding!' 'Just make sure that when you're big enough you're good enough as well,' his father retorted. Ron stored up his memory of this exchange for future reference.

The real difference between the couple, their daughter believes, was not so much social as religious: 'He had the pub, she had the Church.' Nellie was a verger at the local church and managed to invest three out of her four children with strong religious convictions. She herself, though fervent, was eclectic in her beliefs: she was an Anglican, but felt equally at home in a Methodist chapel and ended up as a Mormon, when her younger son, to whom she was particularly devoted, converted to the Latter-Day-Saints out of sympathy with his girlfriend: 'She couldn't even let him do that on his own,' remarks Ron, with a touch of bitterness.

This black vision of life in the Holmes family is that of Ron; the daughters had rosier memories of their childhood. Much of the time, particularly when Harry Holmes was absent, the house was a happy one. 'It wasn't all that bad,' even Ron admits. 'Mother was all right with the kids.' In spite of Harry's self-indulgence there was enough money to keep the house warm, the children adequately clothed and fed. There were always books around and Ron was encouraged to read; he remembers in particular the *Speed Book for Boys*, featuring the 'catch-as-catch-can car', a Maserati endowed with miscellaneous gadgets that would have graced the models that thirty years later Q was to prepare so lovingly for James Bond. But books were treated with respect if not reverence; there would be a sharp rebuke for any child who left one lying open face downwards or with the corner of a page turned back.

The family led a nomadic life. Ron was born in a semi-detached house in a modern terrace, then moved to council flats in the centre of Sheffield. This proved disastrous: the building was high-rise and Ron, who disliked heights, hardly dared go within a few feet of the window. Nellie Holmes insisted they must come down to earth and so they moved to a series of terraced houses in different parts of Sheffield. Ron believes that the constant shifts were made necessary by his father's reluctance to pay the rent: he always disliked parting with his money, 'tight as a duck's arse'. If so the inhibition must finally have been overcome; they settled in a house in Hillsborough, in North Sheffield, and stayed there for the next twenty years.

Ron was not a particularly healthy child; he had all the traditional childish ailments in their most virulent form and was cosseted by his mother as something of an invalid. He went to council schools in Sheffield at the age of five and stayed till he was fourteen; for two years at the Walkley infant school, then to the main school across the road. He was bright but naturally left-handed and his teachers, as was the practice at the time, dragooned him into writing with his right hand. In spite of this, he might still have prospered with encouragement. This, however, was not forthcoming; the hard-pressed teachers had neither the time nor the inclination to pay much attention to individuals: 'They never bothered; they were just there to teach the boys how to count 2 + 2 and to spell "cat".' For the last two years of his education, his parents' migrations took him to a new school at Hillsborough. Shortly before he left he was required to sit an examination – exactly with what end he was not told, but he understood vaguely that it was related to possible further education at some sort of technical school. After the papers had been marked, the headmaster sent for him and told him that he was just below the required standard, what had tipped the balance against him had been his atrocious handwriting. 'Doesn't your father teach you?' he asked. 'He's got a beautiful hand.' He urged Ron to appeal for help to his parents, but when he did so his father had other, more pressing things to do while his mother had no time to do more than put him in the front room with a writing pad and tell him to get on with it. Ron was unconcerned; he had had enough of school and was more than ready to start life outside. His father, he thinks, in spite of his general indifference to his children's doings, would have been pleased if he had gone on to some form of further education. Both the girls did so, and he enjoyed boasting to his friends about 'my daughters at the grammar school'.

By the time Ron left school it was obvious that war was imminent. The idea of being a Regular soldier had never occurred to him: he did not feel himself to be a pacifist but found the idea of fighting and killing vaguely repugnant. He was an active and successful Boy Scout, however, so much so that he had risen to be an Assistant Scout Master by the time he was fifteen – this accelerated promotion no doubt owing something to the fact that by that time most of the senior Scouts had joined the services and were at war. He found his Scouting responsibilities challenging and exciting, of far greater interest than his daily work. This at first was as an errand boy making deliveries for a grocery chain. His employers issued him with no protective clothing, and after he had got soaked through three times in a single day his mother put her foot down and insisted that he should transfer to something less uncomfortable. He began to work as a baker's boy, and so great was the shortage of adult workers that as soon as he reached the legal age – seventeen, in wartime – he was allowed to drive a delivery van. Nobody ever gave him any formal tuition: he watched what the other drivers were doing, asked questions, and picked it up as he went along. He used a provisional licence and did not bother to apply for a full one until 1947, by which time he had driven many thousands of miles, often in the most difficult conditions.

By this time France had fallen and the Home Guard had taken over responsibility for much of Britain's defences against invasion. Ron joined the Home Guard as soon as he was allowed to, on his sixteenth birthday. The heroic days of Dad's Army, with octogenarians dressed in corduroy trousers and carrying out their drill with pikes, were already over but there were still colourful characters around. The Commanding Officer was Colonel Bassett, of the Liquorice Allsorts family, and his firm's vans, with the addition of a minimal amount of camouflage, provided the unit's transport. The Company Sergeant-Major was the local fishmonger; like most of the veterans he had had First World War experience and could drop a grenade into a motor-car tyre on the ground at twenty-five yards with impressive consistency. The weapons they trained with were lethal enough if not always entirely efficient: phosphorus bombs with a layer of water and rubber on the outside that, on exploding, would splatter the target with white-hot fragments that could not be scraped off; the Blacker bombard – renowned for killing the man who fired it almost as often as the intended victims; a flame thrower that emitted an impressive jet of fire but could only be used once every two and a half hours. Night patrols were particularly hazardous. Once, in the countryside, Ron spotted a German sniper up a telegraph pole. He raised his rifle and requested permission to shoot the intruder. His Corporal told him to hold on until he could see the target more clearly, by which time the sniper had been transmogrified into an electrical transformer with a projecting arm: 'What the hell a sniper was doing in the middle of a field of cows, we didn't think!'

The reality of war came home to them with the blitz on Sheffield. The city suffered two nights of devastating attack – the 'Thursday' and the 'Sunday' – in December 1940, and many minor raids. The Holmeses had an Anderson shelter in their garden, but as it was only half covered with earth at the time of the first raid, it would not have provided much protection against a near miss. At every lull in the attack, the family would rush out and shovel earth over the exposed parts of the roof. Fortunately for them, the German attack concentrated on the centre of the city and the nearest bomb fell several hundred yards away. Harry Holmes was fire-watching on the roof of the steelworks on the 'Sunday'. He looked out to see a parachute mine dangling from a tree a few yards away. He flung himself towards the stairs and was halfway down when the bomb exploded. The blast picked him up and deposited him, surprised but unhurt, on a pile of ingots on the foundry floor.

Ron's last two years in Sheffield were intensely active; on top of a full-time job he had the Scouts on Monday and Wednesday nights, the Cubs on Friday, Home Guard training on Tuesday and Thursday, guard duty on Saturday. He was far too tired to indulge in any social life. The Army, he felt, could hardly be more strenuous and would at least take him away from the poisoned atmosphere at home. He was liable to be called up any time after his eighteenth birthday and in fact was left in civilian life for three months more, but he viewed the prospect of military service with equanimity if not enthusiasm. His mother did not share his attitude; after he had left to join the Army his sister remembers that Nellie sat in the dining room and cried. 'He's only a boy,' she wailed, and then, remembering his childish illnesses, 'It seems hard that after all that he should have to go to war.' Even Harry Holmes was impressed enough by the occasion to accompany his son to the railway station. After Ron went away the back door was left permanently unlocked in case he returned unexpectedly – a practice which says as much about the law-abiding nature of the times as it does about Mrs Holmes's affection for her son.

When Ron Holmes had registered for military service at the age of seventeen he had asked to join as a driver/mechanic in the Royal Army Ordnance Corps. Recruits who could already drive were relative rarities and the needs of the Royal Army Service Corps were felt by the authorities to be more urgent. Holmes did his primary training in the grounds of Bradford University, harried from dawn to dusk by Sergeant Job: 'I haven't got the patience of my famous counterpart,' the Sergeant announced grimly. Holmes had been told that the Home Guard was viewed with some disfavour by the Regular Army and that he would do well to keep quiet about his service, but in fact he found that his early training served him well. Job used to enjoy catching out the former Home Guards by occasionally giving them orders that he knew they would never have encountered previously, but he recognised that they had already acquired much of the basic knowledge and made no effort to make them feel inadequate.

Within a few months Holmes was posted to Yeovil where he was put in charge of a three-ton lorry. The build-up for D-Day was already on and he spent every hour of daylight and many of darkness carrying ammunition and other material to dumps all over the West Country. Then, in September 1943, he was attached to the airborne forces. Parachuting, he was told, was entirely voluntary; he would initially be assigned to the glider-borne element of the Airborne Division. When Holmes discovered that passengers on gliders carried no parachutes he was outraged: 'Blow this for a lark. I want to be able to get out and walk!' He volunteered for parachuting; a skill which earned the practitioner much prestige and an extra 2 shillings a day. He was asked if he wanted to make an allotment to his parents and declined to do so. But if he did, the Sergeant explained, his mother would be able to claim a larger dependant's allowance if her husband died. Holmes then agreed to allot 5 shillings a week to his mother, and each week Mrs Holmes sent him a postal order for the same amount.

The move to parachuting might seem an odd choice for a man whose fear of heights had forced his parents to leave their high-rise flat, but to Holmes it was perfectly logical: 'Don't forget, in a parachute you're psychologically enclosed. You've got straps all round you.' It took him six months to arrange his transfer and even then there were doubts about his suitability because he wore glasses. The Regimental Sergeant-Major took him off to the rifle range, watched his performance approvingly and said: 'That's OK, you're in.'

To qualify as a paratrooper the volunteer had to complete a course of ten jumps, which Holmes did at Ridgway, near Manchester. The first two were from a balloon, theoretically easier than from an aeroplane but in fact more frightening because there was no slipstream to open the parachute and the parachutist had to fall more than two hundred feet before the speed of his fall did the same job. The second jump was the worst, 'by then you knew what was coming'. After that the jumps from a Whitley seemed relatively easy. As it happened, the first person killed in a practice jump at Ridgway was another RASC driver, but though one man dislocated his shoulder and Holmes himself sprained his ankle in a night jump, there were no serious accidents while he was training.

As a driver Holmes's main function was to be on the ground, preparing landing sites and receiving material as it was dropped. He did not take part in the D-Day drops, indeed he never jumped in action, but he was in France two days after the initial landings and stayed with the Sixth Airborne Division until it reached the Seine. He was always near the front line but like many, even perhaps most soldiers, did not see much in the way of fighting: 'I did fire a few times but I don't know if I hit anyone.' His worst moment came when a sergeant-major grabbed him and a fellow driver and said: 'You two! There's a dead Kraut up there. Go and plant him.' They gingerly approached the body. 'There's definitely a different smell about a German corpse and a British one, it must be the diet. We found this bloke – cor, the stench – and buried him in his trench.' Then they heard 'the hell of a clatter', looked up and saw a German Tiger tank almost on top of them. They dived into the nearest trench just as a battery of 75 mm-howitzers opened up on the tank above their heads. The individual shells were too small to do any damage but the impact of five shells simultaneously was enough to cripple the tank and push it off the road. The German crew 'jumped out and scarpered'.

Holmes would have been pleased if he had been involved more directly in the action but his habit was to do what he was told and not to think too much about the why and wherefore. An American Red Cross worker once asked him why he was fighting. 'Because I've got no flaming option,' he replied. 'We have a job to do, so we just go on and do it.' He would have been ashamed to seem cowardly but had no aspirations to be a hero. Once he saw an elderly man from the Salvation Army dishing out tea from a mobile canteen just behind the front line. A German mortar opened fire and the paratroopers dived for the ditch. 'Get down, you silly old fool!' shouted one of them. The Salvationist calmly went on pouring tea. 'If the Lord wants me, he'll take me,' was his comment. Holmes wondered at the faith and admired the courage, but knew that, if the situation were to recur, he would always be found in the ditch.

After a few months the Sixth Airborne Division was withdrawn from France to train for the crossing of the Rhine. Holmes was based at Minstead, in the New Forest. With their red berets, extra pay and reputation for daring, the airborne troops lorded it over the rest of the Army and were much resented as a consequence. There were frequent punch-ups in the local pubs, so much so that the nearby town of Lyndhurst was divided into sectors and the paratroopers confined to a particular area. When he was not drinking or fighting Holmes spent his time mastering the new techniques of preparing and marking out dropping sites. He did some more jumps too. The rule was that everybody had to report after their twelfth jump so as to ensure that the thirteenth took place over friendly soil. The paratroopers were particularly addicted to such superstitions; when numbering off on getting into planes the men would call out: 'ten, eleven, twelve, twelve A, fourteen . . .' Holmes made his thirteenth jump over Salisbury Plain.

Crowned as he was by the glamorous aura of a paratrooper, it was particularly pleasant for Holmes to return home and exhibit himself proudly around his former haunts. On one occasion his return caused consternation. In 1944 a telegram was associated with bad news, and when a telegraph boy was seen advancing towards the front door, Mrs Holmes feared the worst. Then her son appeared from nowhere, seized the telegram and said that he would deliver it himself. In fact it contained the news that he was coming home on leave. 'Never do that again,' said his mother. 'Just come.' Though his sister, Elizabeth, believes that her father was secretly proud of his warrior son, the two men got on no better. One night Harry Holmes got drunk and abused his wife. His son remembered the incident of fifteen or so years before. He grabbed hold of his father's coat and thrust him against the wall. 'Now I'm big enough, and good enough, so shut it!' he threatened. Things were no better when they went out together. In a pub Harry Holmes left his son to pay for the drinks. 'Come on, Harry, put your hand in your pocket,' said a friend. 'Don't let your kid do all the paying. He's only a private soldier.' 'It's about time he started paying me back for some of what he's cost me!' Harry retorted. For his son this was too much. He threw himself against his father and had to be held back. 'He's not worth it,' advised one of the lookers-on.

As Harry Holmes's friend had pointed out, Ron Holmes at this time was still a private soldier, or 'Driver', and had no thought of being anything else. His concern was to get the war over and then begin a real life in the civilian world. Even if he had been interested in promotion, his prospects would anyway have been set back by an accident incurred when training with a Canadian paratroop battalion on Salisbury Plain. He slipped on an assault course, landed awkwardly, and tore a ligament in his left ankle. He spent several weeks in plaster and was then despatched to a rehabilitation centre at Richmond. The centre was so overcrowded that Holmes and a few others were sent on to Glasgow. Shortly after he left a V2 hit the corner of the square where he would have been during the daily muster parade. 'How lucky can you get?' Holmes muses.

He rejoined the Airborne Division shortly after the Rhine crossing, by which time the Germans were in headlong retreat. Their advance took them through the forests of Lower Saxony, near the little town of Belsen. It was April 1945. They stopped in a quiet glade to have a meal, then saw skeletal figures in striped uniforms tottering through the trees towards them. Horrified, they began to offer these apparitions food. At that moment an officer ran up, shouting: 'Don't feed them! Don't feed them! They're starving. If you give them solid food it'll kill them!' If Holmes's course had been slightly different he might have found himself in the camp itself. There 35,000 bodies lay unburied; the sights were so horrific that it is said they turned white the hair of some of those who saw them.

The Sixth Airborne Division ended up at Vismar on the Baltic coast, where they met the advancing Russians. There was little contact between the Allied armies but Holmes was amused when he was asked why he was driving a Russian jeep and was armed with a Russian machine-gun. When he replied that one was American and the other British, the Russian was incredulous. He had used such equipment for years but had never been given any reason to suspect that it had not been designed and manufactured in the Soviet Union.

The paratroopers were involved in rehabilitating former prisoners-of-war and displaced persons; the latter were horrifying in their abject misery, they were 'so diseased it wasn't true'. The German civilians were almost equally impoverished, sullen and resentful of the British troops but far more concerned about the proximity of the Russians. When all the prisoners-of-war had been sent home and the paratroopers began to pack up for their return to Britain, the Germans became seriously alarmed. 'If you're going, who's coming?' they asked. 'The Russkies,' was the reply. A panic-stricken exodus towards the Western zones at once began. 'They were on the road before we were,' Holmes remembers. 'Once they heard the Russians were coming they moved out in droves. We had to push them out of the way.'

The sight of the survivors from Belsen and the desolation around him made Holmes reflect how lucky he was to be a soldier and on the winning side. He did not feel much pity for the defeated Germans, but he realised that for many of them their worst troubles were just beginning. For him, at least, the war was over, though sometimes the violence still seemed very close. Once Holmes was fishing with a friend in a boat in Vismar harbour. He looked up and saw a Focke-Wulf 109 diving straight at him with a Spitfire in pursuit. He thought his end had come, only to find out later that the Royal Air Force were experimenting so as to establish the strengths and weaknesses of the two aircraft. The Focke-Wulf proved to be far more manoeuvrable: 'It flew rings round the Spitfire.'

The Airborne Division drove from Vismar to Ostend and Britain, where they enjoyed some leave. Then it was time to train for jungle warfare; the war with Japan was still on and there seemed no reason to believe that it would end without much more fierce fighting. Holmes's 716 Paratroop Company of the RASC, held by its members at least to be the elite contingent of the Corps, had already sent a platoon in advance to the Far East. Then came the atom bomb, and the operations in which they would have been involved became unnecessary. Holmes was glad not to go but did not feel that he had been spared a terrifying ordeal. The spectre of the all-conquering Japanese army had finally vanished and the Sixth Airborne Division felt they need be afraid of nobody. 'They're not so big as you; they're not so tough as you,' the British troops had been told, and they believed it. 'We were so full of confidence.'

The war was over, but since he had not joined up until 1943 Holmes knew that it would be a year or more before he would be demobilised. The general election came and went without his paying much attention. When he had been offered a proxy vote he told his mother he wanted her to vote Labour on his behalf 'because I'd got nothing to conserve'; but in July 1945 he was still only twenty and so too young to vote. He saw no reason to believe that the Labour victory would make much difference to his life and resigned himself philosophically to serving out the rest of his military career wherever the Army might choose to send him.

This turned out to be Palestine. In theory the Airborne Division was supposed to be part of a mobile reserve available for the whole of Southern Europe, the Middle East and Africa, but inevitably they found themselves drawn into the mounting conflict between Jew and Arab. It was the twilight of the British mandate and men like Holmes found themselves uneasily trying to act as policemen in a conflict which they did not feel was their concern. They were disliked and distrusted by both camps, but at the end of 1945 the Jews, who felt that they had been betrayed by the British failure to set up an independent homeland for them and who bitterly resented the limits put on Jewish immigration, were the more obviously hostile. They called the airborne troops 'poppies' – red tops, black hearts – 'just because we wouldn't be messed about. We reminded them in no uncertain terms that we'd just fought a bloody war to free them and now they were shooting us in the back.' This somewhat *simpliste* interpretation of events summed up the paratroopers' point of view. They were unequivocally pro-Arab and anti-Jew. A much quoted parody of Kipling's poem, 'Tommy', ran:

> Then they sent me out to Palestine to fight the bloody Yid,
> Who kills at night, without a fight, which Jerry never did.

The official rule was that, if a convoy came under fire, it was to accelerate away as fast as possible. General 'Boy' Browning, the Paratroop commander, was having none of this. He put armoured vehicles at the front and rear of every convoy and ordered them to return fire if anyone was rash enough to engage them. 'You probably won't hit the terrorists,' he said, 'but you'll frighten the life out of them.' The result certainly seemed to be that the airborne convoys were treated with respect. Holmes himself only came under fire a few times, but it was an unpleasant period of constant tension and threats from an ill-defined and usually invisible enemy. He managed to fit in some sightseeing during local leave in Egypt and Jordan but was not particularly impressed by what he saw: the Pyramids were disappointingly small, the Sphinx at that time was largely covered by sand. What struck him most about Petra were the perfectly squared edges of the building blocks.

He returned to England to be demobilised in June 1947. He felt no regrets at leaving the Army, only excitement and slight apprehension about the future. He was sent to York, went into the depot as a soldier, emerged as a civilian. Almost at once he met a childhood friend, Jean Hazlewood, took up with her, and was married early the following year.

Then everything began to go wrong. Holmes got on with his mother-in-law and would have been happy to spend the first few months of his married life in her house but unfortunately she had recently remarried and worked with her new husband as a caretaker which meant that there was no room for her daughter and son-in-law. The young couple could not afford their own home and so were forced back on Ron Holmes's parents. They were taken in but hardly made welcome. Nellie Holmes treated his wife as a servant: 'When visitors came she would say, "Go and make some tea." "Do this and do that." We soon got fed up with it.' Holmes blames the difficulties of his early married life largely on his parents. 'They always held us back. We could never get in front.'

Things would no doubt have been different if he had been able to settle in a secure job with prospects. He initially found employment with the Post Office, working on repairs to telephone wires. His old fear of heights returned to plague him; he did not mind swinging around at the top of a telegraph pole or working on roofs but getting from the ladder to the roof made him acutely anxious. He found the Post Office systems old-fashioned and inefficient and the equipment antiquated. Worst of all, the pay was bad and prospects for promotion limited. After eighteen months he gave up the job; 'I couldn't work up any enthusiasm.' He tried two jobs in the steel industry and disliked them both. By the beginning of 1950 the chances of escaping from his parents' home and establishing his wife in a house of their own seemed as remote as ever.

The Army, which had been so unappealing a few years before, now became more attractive by the day: 'If I'd known then what I know now, I'd never have come out,' he reflects. Jean, even more anxious than he was to escape from her mother-in-law, urged him to re-enlist. In February 1950, he took the plunge. To his relief he was welcomed back with enthusiasm: the Army had a plethora of raw recruits doing their national service and relatively few veterans to train them. Within a few weeks of applying he found himself back with the Army Service Corps at Aldershot for primary training, posted to a platoon which contained young recruits for the Regular Army or doing national service as well as a handful of re-enlisted men. The Sergeant called out the older men, to find out how much they knew. Holmes excelled. The Sergeant, impressed, asked him what he had been in. 'RASC, Sergeant.' 'What Company?' '716 Company,' replied Holmes proudly. 'Ah, I thought so.' The Sergeant-Major sent for him. A boy soldier with the rank of corporal was sitting at the desk in the outer office and treated him with some disdain. Holmes was about to explode in indignation when the Sergeant-Major emerged and sent the Corporal off to fetch tea and biscuits. 'By the way, boy Corporal,' he remarked, 'Driver Holmes was swinging on a parachute when you were still swinging on the school gate.' Holmes would have got immediate promotion to lance-corporal in the Boys' Company as soon as he had finished his training but he would not have been allowed to live out and when his wife turned up and demanded married quarters the job fell through.

Instead he found himself sent to York, driving staff cars for the headquarters of Northern Command. He was given one of the best cars, a pre-war Wolsley 18 with walnut veneer and leather seats. The work was agreeable enough but not really what he had expected when he rejoined the Army; he might as well have been working for a taxi service. He was relieved when early in 1951 he was sent to Bielefeld in Germany. The 11th Armoured Division was being re-formed and Holmes was assigned to the support unit, 107 Company of the RASC. Almost immediately he was given his belated promotion to lance-corporal. The accolade was gratefully received. In the wartime Army, when he had had no intention of staying on, promotion would have seemed unimportant, even unwelcome. Now he accepted that the Army was to be his life and he was anxious to get ahead as quickly as possible.

But he found that marriage and a military career were not always easy to reconcile. His sister believes that he married without proper consideration and that both he and Jean were too young for each other. Certainly things would have gone better with rather more wisdom and patience on both sides. As a young lance-corporal Holmes was sent on many courses to gain new qualifications. Jean felt lonely and neglected. 'It wasn't easy, I know, being alone so much,' Holmes now admits, but at the time he was preoccupied by his career. Resentful, Jean had an affair with a former Welsh Guardsman who was now a sergeant in the military prison. 'She told me about it and I misread the signals,' says Holmes. Her admission, he now believes, was a cry for attention; she was hoping for a display of jealousy, a reaffirmation of their marriage. Instead, her husband sulked: 'If she prefers him then she can have him.'

Things got worse. Holmes was posted to Berlin. 'I'm not going to Berlin. I'm going home,' decided Jean. In fact she remained for some time in the married quarters at Bielefeld. Holmes, now a corporal, sent her the marriage allowance each week by postal order. She had been told that, if she was receiving nothing from her husband, she would get a larger allowance from the Army, so she kept quiet about the weekly payments. In due course his Major sent for Holmes and accused him of leaving his wife destitute in Bielefeld while he lived a life of luxury in Berlin. Indignantly Holmes retorted that he had sent his wife her allowance every week, and was able to prove that he had posted the money orders by registered mail. The Major was sympathetic but Holmes was still told that he must pay back the difference between the allowance his wife had improperly claimed and that to which she was entitled. Even more annoying, when he got back to Bielefeld he found that she had left their quarters in a state of squalid disorder: 'I was ashamed. There wasn't a clean piece of linen in the house, or clean crockery. The place was filthy.'

Today, he believes that his wife was given bad advice. 'It can't affect Ron if you claim the extra money or leave the billet in chaos,' she was told. 'He isn't responsible.' At the time he was not disposed to make allowances. The marriage was doomed. Jean made one effort to talk to him from England but, embittered, he told her to get lost and put down the telephone. Soon the divorce papers came through. Now he feels it was 'a damned silly divorce which neither of us wanted'; at the time it seemed inevitable. It was more than thirty years before they spoke to each other again.

Even before he had finished paying off Jean's ill-gotten allowances he was remarried. His new wife was called Olive, a Huddersfield girl who was serving as a cook-corporal in the Women's Royal Army Corps. She had been married twice already, had two children, and was forty-one years old to Holmes's twenty-eight. 'You remind me of a film star,' was her opening gambit. 'I know – Pluto.' 'No, but I can't remember who.' Holmes knew well; only a few weeks before, when he was lighting a cigar in the canteen, another soldier had looked up and said: 'Jesus Christ! Groucho Marx his bloody self!' The resemblance was remarkable. It does not seem to have deterred Olive. Within ten minutes of their meeting Holmes asked her if she was married. 'No'. 'Will you marry me?' She gave no immediate reply but that night drank him under the table. 'And that was how it went. She was one hell of a party-goer.' When Holmes recovered from his hangover and renewed his proposal, she accepted with little hesitation. Ten weeks later they married.

The marriage proved a happy one. Holmes's mother was horrified by the difference in age and advised her son to think again but his sister Elizabeth liked Olive at once and in time became very fond of her. Olive made it clear that she wanted no more children, which came as a relief to her new husband, since he had failed to have any by his first wife. 'It wasn't for want of trying,' he says; he thinks that possibly he was sterile as the result of mumps when he was young. Now he told himself that he was lucky to be spared the heartache and worry that children could bring. Probably he believed it at the time but 'it was a defence mechanism. I did miss having kids. Although I had stepchildren it's not the same.'

He became sergeant shortly after his remarriage; a promotion which caused some problems of protocol. Once he looked into the kitchen where Olive was working, to see if he could scrounge a cup of tea. He sat on a table. 'Get off that bloody table!' his wife commanded. 'Are *you* telling *me*?' 'Tables are made for rissoles, not arse-holes. Get off!' 'Corporals don't tell *me* what to do!' That episode was soon forgotten, but there was more embarrassment when Olive wanted to go into the Sergeants' Mess and was admitted only as the wife of Sergeant Holmes. After a few months the time came for her to renew her term of service. She was told that, if she did so, she would be posted away. A sergeant and a corporal could be married to each other on the same station only on the most temporary basis. With mingled irritation and relief she retired from the Army; she was not sorry to escape the rigours of the cookhouse but the corporal's pay and ration allowance had come in very useful.

Unlike his first wife, Olive was happy to accompany Ron Holmes when he was posted to Berlin. The city was just beginning to recover from the devastation of the war and the Women's Royal Voluntary Service used to conduct tours around the points of interest. Civilians were not allowed to take buses into the Russian zone and non-commissioned officers from the British Army used to volunteer to drive the visitors in their stead. Holmes was impressed by the amount of rebuilding that the East Germans had already done, then one day in Karl Marx Strasse he was obliged to divert into a side street. To his surprise he found that the buildings only went up to the first floor, after that there was no more than a façade hiding a void behind. His wife made some friends among the Germans but though he had scores of German drivers under his command he never really got to know them. He found them pleasant enough: 'There were a few arrogant ones among them but most of them were all right.'

His next station in Germany, Celle, provided some of the happiest days of his military life. The officer commanding 110 Company, Major Capel Smith, believed that transport was meant to be used, not left to rust in a car park. There was plenty of driver training, and junior NCOs were encouraged to use their initiative and take responsibilities beyond their rank. Holmes's platoon won his complete confidence and he fought for its rights. Once he was made responsible for operating an experimental batch of trucks. The Company Transport Sergeant proposed to draft in some of the more experienced drivers from other platoons to help out. Holmes protested strongly: 'I've got the best platoon I've ever had. I don't want to change one of them.' To the platoon he put it less fervently – 'I told him I'd keep the heap I'd got' – but they knew what he meant and appreciated it.

There was a tradition that men were confined to barracks on Friday night so as to prepare for the billet inspection on the Saturday. Holmes believed that he was dealing with grown men and trained soldiers and that they did not have to be instructed when and how to clean a sink. He told them that they were welcome to go out if they wanted to, 'but any clangers tomorrow morning and you'll know about it'. When the men presented themselves at the entrance to the camp the Corporal acting as guard commander refused to let them out. Holmes rounded up his young and inexperienced 2nd-Lieutenant, Gavin Edwards, and told him that he needed his support. 'This is part of your training, sir. Listen and back me up.' He then marched into the guardroom, stood to attention, saluted the startled Corporal and began: 'Now, Mr Edwards, sir . . .' 'I'm not Mr Edwards!' 'Exactly! Nobody but Mr Edwards can countermand my orders. When I say they can go out, they can go out.'

The billets the next day were spick and span. The platoon never let him down. 'I was loyal to them and they were loyal to me. We had a lovely working relationship.' He was particularly touched when they prepared him a lavish and carefully inscribed Christmas card and to this day keeps it with him in his berth at the Royal Hospital. 'I'm so proud of it. I get very emotional these days, you know.'

In the autumn of 1956 the company was moved to Cyprus to take part in the build-up for the Suez operation. The Prime Minister had sent the message: 'We cannot afford the great British propensity for first engaging in a war and then preparing for it,' and the RASC was busily employed moving stores and ammunition from A to B and sometimes back again. They were so pleased to be doing what they were supposed to do, instead of indulging in yet more interminable training, that morale was high. They rarely discussed either the ethics or the expediency of the invasion: 'Regular soldiers get into the habit; the Army says go and do that, so you go and do it.' When the campaign spluttered out in ignominy they were as one in laying the blame on the Americans: 'They dropped us in it as usual,' says Holmes. 'You can imagine British soldiers have a low opinion of the Americans.'

For the first three months of their short stay in Cyprus 110 Company kept its lorries painted the standard green as opposed to the sand-colour suitable for Egypt adopted by the other vehicles. Major Capel Smith, who probably expected that the operation would be aborted before the RASC played a part in it, opposed any suggestion that his unit should conform with the rest. Eventually he was forced to give way. The sand-coloured spray was still wet on the last vehicle when the company was ordered back to Celle. From being the only green-painted unit in Cyprus, 110 Company found itself the only sand-coloured unit in Germany.

Though they never came within five hundred miles of Egypt, life in Cyprus was not entirely peaceful. It was the height of the EOKA campaign and the Greek Cypriots were determined to achieve independence without accepting any restrictions designed to protect the Turkish minority. The British Governor, Field Marshal Harding, tried to do a deal with the Cypriot leader, Archbishop Makarios, but met with a blunt refusal to compromise on the main issue. Makarios was exiled to an island in the Indian Ocean – a sure indication to those who studied the history of British decolonisation that it would not be long before he was installed as first President of an independent Cyprus. In the meantime, however, EOKA terrorists (or freedom-fighters, depending on one's point of view) planted a bomb under Harding's bed and staged many attacks on British servicemen.

Whenever RASC trucks drove in convoy, Holmes, holding a loaded bren-gun, would stand in the last vehicle looking out for potential terrorists. Once he almost caused a serious incident. The convoy was passing a group of road menders when he saw an arm go back in what seemed to him the classic posture for throwing a grenade. He swung round with his bren-gun cocked, but before he could fire a priest who happened to be present threw himself forward with his arms outstretched. Holmes lowered his gun and a relieved Greek labourer dropped the stone which he had been about to throw into the ditch. Another time Holmes was prowling about the camp at dusk with a revolver when a figure suddenly appeared between two vehicles in a place where no figure should have been. Holmes raised his revolver. 'Don't shoot, don't shoot!' said the Officer Commanding. 'That was a bloody silly trick to play, sir!' 'I'm sorry, I didn't think.' 'Famous last words,' said Sergeant Holmes sourly.

Shortly after their return to Celle the company was broken up. Holmes found himself with the Territorial Army at Folkestone, attached to the permanent staff. As a place to live he and his wife found it most congenial but the work was depressing. He was instructor to the Transport Platoon and the Administration Officer had foolishly advertised for recruits with the slogan: 'Learn to drive and be paid for doing it.' Volunteers poured in, but they wanted to do exactly what the advertisement suggested and nothing more: 'They didn't want to know about inspections and things like that.' One Saturday they got out the vehicles and Holmes announced that a 1000-mile service was due and must be carried out. The platoon began to melt away. Holmes asked one of the deserters why he was leaving. 'Oh, we're here to drive, not to do grease-monkey work.'

He was relieved to return to the Regulars at Bulford, though the Army was being run down and men seemed to disappear every day. It was now 1961 and he had been a sergeant for the best part of ten years. His promotion after he rejoined the Army had been unusually rapid and he had always taken it for granted that his career would continue to prosper. It did not seem out of the question that he should become that most refulgent of beings, a regimental sergeant-major, or perhaps even be commissioned as an officer. But at Bulford things went wrong. Holmes ascribes his troubles to an incident with the major in command of his company. The Major was 'a bit of the old-fashioned kind' and disapproved of the steps the Army was taking to make life more attractive for the other ranks. When an order came round saying that the polishing of brasses on equipment was to cease except in the case of those on belt and gaiters, the Major chose to ignore it. 'Get those brasses polished,' he ordered during an inspection. Holmes produced a board with the order from the War Office. 'Don't want to know!' said the Major, knocking it from his hand. 'Get those brasses polished!' 'It wasn't so much what he said as the way he said it,' explains Holmes. 'No, sir, I won't,' he replied.

That was the end of it for the moment; the Major knew that he was in the wrong and did not pursue the matter. But Holmes had made a formidable enemy. Words were dropped into the right ears, promotion prospects were blighted. Holmes went on a course for appointment as Company Quartermaster-Sergeant and passed with flying colours, but found himself categorised as 'obstinate, cantankerous and unco-operative'. 'I fell foul of the system,' he says. How far this one incident was in fact responsible for his setback is impossible to say. Holmes did not suffer fools gladly, least of all fools with commissions, and this Major was not the only officer who had found him obstinate and unco-operative. He had made life difficult for himself, but he knew that he had been denied promotion for which he was well qualified and he had the right to feel a sense of grievance.

More foreign service followed. In November 1962, he went to Malaya to assist in the moving of the RASC depot from Taiping to Penang. It was the time of the confrontation with Indonesia, whose government was infiltrating troops into Borneo, Sabah and Sarawak in the hope of destabilising and eventually dismembering the newly independent Malaysia. Once his work at the depot was over Holmes was despatched to Terendak Camp in Malacca to take charge of the Motor Transport section of 16 Field Ambulance of the Royal Army Medical Corps. He found the unit in chaos, with four non-existent Ford ambulances theoretically on the strength and a store filled with spare parts for their support. Holmes got the former struck off the inventory and disposed of the latter, then began to put in order the air-portable Land-Rovers with stretcher units which were their main resource.

Most of the fighting took place in Borneo but he tells of one bloody clash. The Indonesians sent over a raiding party which went to ground in a mangrove swamp on the coast of Malacca. The British Brigadier in command in the area turned out 28 Commonwealth Brigade, to which Holmes's unit was attached, surrounded the swamp and ordered the Indonesians, by loud-hailer, to come out. When this achieved nothing he began to shell the area. A few men came out and gave themselves up. After a pause shelling was resumed. Another party came out. After interrogation of the prisoners the Brigadier established that a lieutenant, a sergeant and about twelve privates were still in the swamp. He sent in the Gurkhas, stressing that if possible he wanted the Indonesian officer brought out alive. The Gurkhas set off expectantly, brandishing their kukris. After a short time they emerged, escorting the officer. 'Where are the men?' asked the Brigadier. 'What men, sahib?' asked the leading Gurkha. 'Oh, all right,' said the Brigadier. Dates and places are hard to verify, but Holmes's recollection is a vivid one.

By the time he left Malacca, he had only three years of his service to run. If he had applied to go on the Long Service list he could probably have secured a few more years in the Army, but only at the price of staying in the United Kingdom and coming down a rank to corporal. He and his wife decided that it was better to make a clean break while he was still young enough to make a life outside. In the meantime he went back to Bielefeld where he found himself working in the same office as he had occupied when a corporal fifteen years before. His job was to transport Honest John missiles for the Royal Artillery; the nuclear war heads which made these weapons so controversial a part of the armoury of the Army of the Rhine were mercifully not attached, but would have been delivered rapidly in case of emergency.

For the last twelve months of a man's service the Army had the civilised practice of employing him as near as possible to the place where he proposed to retire. Holmes had discussed this endlessly with his wife and they had decided that they would settle in Folkestone. The best the Army could do for him was Redhill, more than fifty miles away, but at least the work was congenial. He was attached to the Territorial Army again, this time to an ambulance squadron, but the atmosphere was as different as could be imagined from the unenthusiastic grumpiness he had experienced at Folkestone. Everyone was eager to learn and to help; 'You only had to say you wanted a thing for it to be done.' It was a happy end to what had been on the whole a happy, if slightly disappointing, military career.

The Holmeses installed themselves in a flat in Folkestone. Olive got a job in a firm called Portex at Hythe, which made surgical plastics, while Ron worked in a local garage. It was run by a young and ambitious man whose eagerness to expand was greater than either his judgement or his financial resources. Holmes thought the concern badly run and did not hesitate to say so. 'What do you miss most about the Army, Ron?' his employer asked him once. 'Organisation,' replied Holmes drily. The sales manager had the habit of eavesdropping on what was going on in the garage by keeping the intercom switched on. Holmes retaliated by singing bawdy barrack-room songs into the microphone. His employer got word of what was happening and asked for an explanation. Holmes replied that he didn't like being spied on: 'It's a good job for you this isn't a union shop,' he concluded. The eavesdropping stopped but Holmes gained a reputation for being a troublemaker. It was unsurprising that, when the firm ran into financial difficulties and staff had to be laid off, he was the first to be made redundant.

The timing could hardly have been more propitious. Holmes was given his notice on the Monday after Christmas. The following day he got a letter from Portex, offering him a job. Without saying a word to him, his wife had put forward his name as a possible employee. He accepted without hesitation and never regretted it, Portex were excellent employers and he stayed with them until he retired nearly twenty years later. He worked on a machine for injection moulding and within a few months went on to night shift, 'because it paid the heck of a lot more, almost twice as much'. The work was monotonous and undemanding, and grew more so as the machines became more sophisticated. By the end they could more or less look after themselves, and the operators' duties were confined to pressing the occasional button and making sure that nothing was going wrong. Holmes was bored but 'having been a platoon sergeant for so long, it wasn't long before I wound up running six to eight machines'. His work became more responsible and better paid, soon he had made himself almost indispensable.

That was just as well, for after a few years this firm too found the going hard and began to make what economies it could. One of the first casualties was Olive, who was now more than sixty years old. For a time she got a job in the kitchen of a nearby boarding school but her health was deteriorating and she soon retired altogether. 'So she was just mooching about, and that's when she really got worse,' says Holmes. She seemed to lose all interest in life, indeed in living, though she suffered from no diagnosable disease. Holmes got increasingly exasperated by her lethargy and tried to make her snap back into activity. 'I'm sure I'm not long for this world,' she would say. 'Are you making promises?' he retorted. He recalled the remark with regret when she suddenly became genuinely ill and was removed to hospital.

Still it seemed that nobody could decide what was wrong. Holmes was at the hospital one day when she decided to go to the lavatory. He took advantage of the break to go into the garden for a cigarette. A nurse called him into her room: 'You can smoke in here, the doctors always do.' They had just got the results of the last test, an endoscopy, she told him. It had shown nothing wrong. All that was left was to try a barium enema; they were reluctant to do so because it was most unpleasant for the patient, but could see no alternative. Olive came back from the lavatory and went back to bed. He sat beside her and held her hand. Then, without warning or apparent stress, she stopped breathing. Holmes called the nurse who pushed him out of the way. Olive was beyond revival. The nurses had clearly seen that this was a possibility. 'Well, you could have warned me,' said Holmes reproachfully. They still did not know why she had died: 'She just gave up the will to live.'

A few weeks before Olive died Holmes had heard that his first wife, Jean, had also lost her husband. He let a little time pass, then, on an impulse, telephoned her. They were both lonely, time had dulled the bitterness which they each had once felt, the fond memories survived. They began to speak to each other regularly. 'We weren't having an affair,' Holmes stresses, but Jean said that only these conversations kept her sane: 'Our phone bills were horrendous.' She came to Folkestone to visit him and he went north to Sheffield. They used to lie in bed in their respective homes, playing sentimental music and talking affectionately. One day a record of Ken Dodd's was being broadcast; he was singing 'I'm the man whose wife one day you'll be'. 'Well, will you?' asked Holmes. 'Ask me again on December 18,' Jean replied – the day that they had first got married. He did, and it turned out that he wasn't, but only because Jean took a practical approach to the problem: 'You know very well that a bit of paper doesn't mean much. And, anyway, two single pensions are better than one couple's pension.'

For a time Jean came south and lived in the flat in Folkestone but she found that Olive's personality impregnated every room and that she could not settle. Besides, her daughter who was still in Sheffield had just had her first baby and Jean wanted to be near her. By this time Holmes was sixty-four, he felt no particular loyalty to Folkestone and so decided to retire and move up north to the city of his birth. For six years they lived contentedly together, but Jean was a chronic asthmatic and with old age her condition deteriorated drastically. She was the opposite of Olive; it was only too evident what was wrong with her and that she was seriously ill but she never complained, 'she used to play hell with me for trying to help her'. She died in 1993.

Old Mrs Holmes, now ninety-four, was still alive. She spent her last months in a hospital in Sheffield. Holmes visited her almost every day; the nurses were amazed at his constancy; so many people, they said, used to dump their elderly relatives there and then more or less forget them. Holmes had survived the death of both his wives with comparative equanimity but when his mother followed them he suddenly cracked. 'I'd been strong up to then,' he says, 'but when my mother died and we walked into the church they were playing "I'll be loving you, always", that did it. I just fell apart.' Jean's daughter, styled by courtesy his 'stepdaughter', more or less took him over. He used to meet the grandchildren from school and take them to his house and Lucy, the younger one, often spent Friday nights there as well. But from six in the evening until three in the afternoon he would usually be 'alone, twiddling my thumbs'. He was too short of money to take up anything in the way of a serious hobby, he had no garden, he knew few people in Sheffield and had neither the inclination nor the aptitude to strike out and make new friends. The grandchildren were growing up and becoming ever more independent, so even this resource would increasingly be denied him. He was bored, disconsolate, and increasingly apprehensive about the future.

Jean had once asked him what he would do if she died first and he became 'a lonely old man'. 'I won't be a lonely old man,' he replied. 'I'll go back where I belong, to the Army.' Now he *was* a lonely old man and the time had come to carry out his resolution. Whenever his pension was paid he was reminded of the possibility that he might join the Royal Hospital Chelsea; he told his stepdaughter that this was what he planned to do and found her regretful but reluctant to argue against a resolution that was so obviously in his best interests. She promised to bring the children to see him in London at regular intervals. In April 1997 he resolved the time had come and moved to Chelsea.

He has never doubted that he made the right decision. He prizes his privacy but finds that if he closes the door of his berth he is entirely alone – the lack of space causes him no distress. He plays old videos – *Singin' in the Rain* is the current favourite; tends the patch in the Hospital grounds which is assigned to him for his roses; reads a little, though not as much as he expected when he moved to Chelsea; chats with the other Pensioners in the club or dining hall. Compared with many of those around him he lacks the interests and the energy to make much of a life outside the Hospital routine, but he is content; more content, perhaps than he has ever been before.

EPILOGUE

Epilogue

ALL generalisations are suspect, and the more narrow the statistical base the greater the grounds for suspicion. Does one have any reason to believe that the nine Chelsea In-Pensioners whose stories comprise this book are representative of the institution as a whole? Or that the sort of man who becomes a Chelsea Pensioner is typical of the other ranks in the Regular Army? The only honest answer must be that one does not. But from the interviews I have had with these Pensioners and members of their families, from my conversations with other Pensioners and with veterans of the Regular Army who are not at Chelsea, from innumerable regimental histories and memoirs of military life, a pattern of a sort emerges: imprecise, certainly; impressionistic, perhaps to a fault; but not without some validity.

One thing that has struck me forcibly is the contrast between what soldiers thought they were going to do when they joined the Army and what they actually did do. The first of the nine Pensioners joined the Army in 1917, the last in 1940, and it is with the other ranks of that generation that this book deals. They enlisted at a time when the British Empire in geographical terms was at its zenith; Britain was still one of the greatest powers on earth, if no longer the greatest. To the politically or economically sophisticated it was obvious that the fabric was already crumbling, that the gigantic bluff which had allowed this tiny offshore European island to dominate so much of the world's surface had at last been called. But few of those who joined the ranks of the Regular British Army between 1917 and 1940 had any political or economic awareness, let alone sophistication. To them the Empire seemed free from all challenge, the vast tracts of pink that covered the map of the world on the wall of their schools would forever remain so. Empire Day was a bright light in the scholastic year, celebrated with much marching, flag-flying and singing of patriotic songs.

Traditionally, the principal function of the British Army had been to defend that Empire – the First World War with its involvement on the mainland of Europe had been an aberration which it was hoped would never be repeated. When young men enlisted in the 1920s or 1930s they took it for granted that this would be their function: almost certainly in India, probably at one time or another in other colonies or protectorates, they would be policing the Empire against dissension from within or protecting it against attack from without. They did indeed spend much of their military careers in imperial or quasi-imperial stations. The nine Pensioners whose stories are told in this book served in peacetime at one time or another in India and Ceylon; Malaya; Hong Kong; Malta and Cyprus; Palestine, Syria, Iraq, Aden and the states of the Persian Gulf; Libya and Egypt; Kenya, Nigeria, Sierra Leone and the Cameroons. Another nine would have yielded a list as long which would have overlapped in certain areas but would also have revealed further parts of the world where British interests were involved. But though imperial considerations took them to these outposts, after the Second World War they found that they were not there to defend the Empire but, hesitantly at first, then with increasing speed, to preside over its disintegration. Their careers in the Army were conducted to the accompaniment of a melancholy, long, withdrawing roar, as the imperial tide rolled back with the same inevitability as Matthew Arnold's sea of faith a century or so before.

To join an all-conquering team only to find that it slips inexorably down the table and is finally relegated to a lower division must be a depressing and disillusioning experience. Soldiers who served over these years were disheartened by what had happened. They did not blame their officers or even the remote and impersonal War Office. To a degree they felt 'the government' was to blame, no soldier has ever had much use for politicians. For the most part, however, they preferred to look further afield, to economic or demographic forces beyond the control of any earthly being, or to the Americans whose resolute opposition to the idea of Empire was, they felt, more directly responsible than any other factor for the decline in British power. But only the most thoughtful among them gave such matters prolonged consideration. Neither the depression nor the disillusionment were as profound as might have been expected; the vast majority of those in the ranks of the British Army gave little consideration to the downturn in their country's fortunes but just got on with the job in hand.

The truth was that, though they had joined the Army with the assumption that they would devote much of their energies to the defence of Empire, they had not done so with any burning desire to carry out this task. Certainly they were better disposed toward the imperialist ideal and more ready to envisage defending national interests by force than would be the case with most of their grandchildren today. Patriotism, a sentiment unfashionable in the new millennium if not politically incorrect, was far more prevalent in the 1920s and 1930s. Schoolchildren were taught to abhor the enemies of King and Country. Those Regular soldiers who are at the Royal Hospital today were in their youth quite as patriotic, more so indeed, than most of the civilians who were their contemporaries. They were as ready as any to defend the flag and maintain the greatness of their nation. But that was not primarily why they joined the Army. Their main preoccupation was to escape from almost intolerable conditions at home and to seek a better and less restricted life. The vast majority of recruits to the ranks of the British Army between the two World Wars came from a milieu that was poor or very poor. They wanted to put behind them homes that were cold, damp and overcrowded; food that was monotonous and inadequate; work that was unfulfilling and probably precarious. They were young and spirited, they craved a change and sought adventure, but it was security and decent living conditions that were their first consideration. That they would have the honour of fighting and perhaps dying for their country no doubt occurred to them, but as a motive for joining the Army it would have seemed romantic and irrelevant. To fight and perhaps die for one's country was just part of the job.

And if it turned out to be part of the job to assist in the demolition of the Empire rather than to shore it up, then this too would be accepted. To the outsider, one of the most remarkable features of the other ranks of the Regular Army – of most of the officers too, for that matter – was their readiness to accept whatever they were told to do without asking any questions, still less criticising the judgement of their superiors. 'Theirs not to make reply, theirs not to reason why': the British soldier would have ridden into the valley of death with the same unquestioning resignation in 1954 as in the Crimea a hundred years before. Albert Alexandre did not challenge an unreasonable posting, even though he knew that his sergeant-major would enthusiastically have supported his efforts if he had done so: 'Once they'd put me down for it, I wouldn't back out of it.' The arguments for instilling instinctive obedience into a soldier are, of course, compelling; if in battle an order to advance or retreat is followed by prolonged debate about the wisdom of the proposed line of action, casualties are likely to be heavy. By extension this automatic acquiescence applied at any level and in every contingency; if a battalion, having been trained for operations in the Arctic and equipped with snow boots and thermal underwear, had been despatched to combat terrorism in a tropical jungle, the colonel might privately have doubted the sanity of his superiors but he would not openly have questioned his orders, still less permitted any criticism of them from his officers or men.

It is easier to obey orders blindly if one has implicit faith in the person who is issuing them. On the whole relations between officers and men in the British Army were excellent; officers were respected and liked and it was believed that whatever instructions they might give were likely to be the right ones. Even when the men knew that their officer was inexperienced and suspected that he was a bloody fool as well, it was usually assumed that he had access to information or was in receipt of orders from above which justified an otherwise inexplicable decision. At the least, he was given the benefit of the doubt. The British other ranks liked a touch of divinity to hedge their officers. When Arthur Jeffery found himself briefly assigned to an American unit the informal relationship between officers and men caused him disquiet. In the British Army 'you always knew where you stood . . . there was no familiarity between us'; among the Americans familiarity was the norm and bred its proverbial concomitant: 'They were so friendly that they became contemptuous, you know.' Of course there were exceptions. Everyone has heard rumours of officers shot by their own men in the course of battle (though remarkably few such stories stand up to serious examination). Sam Small certainly felt a measure of contempt for his drunken major. But there was no habitual hostility – the feeling of 'them' and 'us' was unaccompanied by the tinge of bitterness which is often found in other walks of life.

So far as the higher strategy was concerned, or indeed anything which did not relate exclusively to the everyday minutiae of military life, the average British soldier was anyway inhibited from comment, still more from criticism, by the fact that he knew almost nothing about what was going on. Between the two World Wars the ignorance of the private soldier and many non-commissioned officers as well, was daunting in its completeness. The Army had done an excellent job of teaching even the most illiterate of its recruits to read, but it did not then take much trouble to ensure that the ability was put to good use. They read no newspapers, they rarely listened to the radio, no one made any attempt to brief them on the background to their activities. If an infantry private in a line regiment had been required to explain the Munich Crisis or to describe the events that had led up to the outbreak of war in 1939, he would have shown himself to be not merely inarticulate but almost entirely uninformed.

The same was true on the smallest scale. In battle the private would know the identity of the man to his left and his right. He would be aware more or less where his platoon was with relation to the other platoons of his company. It was possible that he would know that a battalion of the Lincolnshire Regiment was to one side or of the Coldstream Guards to the other. But how the battle was going, what the strategy might be, what the enemy was seeking to achieve, were subjects not merely beyond his ken but outside his sphere of interest.

Those greatest of all fictional battle scenes, Stendhal's Waterloo and Tolstoy's Borodino, portray vividly the thick fog of uncertainty in which even the most senior and experienced commanders conduct their operations. In the front line the fog became impenetrable; the most notable difference between general and private being that, while the general at least strove to establish what was going on and sometimes deluded himself that he had succeeded, the private had neither pretension nor desire to comprehend the wider picture and was preoccupied solely by his wish to stay alive and to kill as many as possible of the enemy.

In the eyes of the more circumscribed of commanders such ignorance was positively desirable. An informed soldier was potentially a questioning soldier, questions led to insubordination:

better bovine acquiescence than challenges to authority. By the outbreak of the Second World War such views were on the wane but their shadow at least must survive whenever men are required to risk their lives at another's command. 'Cannon fodder' is an ugly expression, implying an indifference to the lives of soldiers which was rarely encountered within the British Army. Nevertheless, the concept of the private soldier as a pawn which should be properly valued, employed with caution, might even one day reach the back line and become a queen, but is in the last resort expendable, is inseparable from any vision of warfare in any nation and in any century.

This blinkered vision of the average soldier meant that his loyalties were correspondingly limited. They were none the less intense for that; indeed perhaps the most essential element for a successful army is that its members should feel committed to the unit in which they serve. Once they were in the trenches, wrote Sir Michael Howard of the private soldiers in the First World War, they fought not for the mother country or any vague concept of glory or patriotism but 'basically because they had to, and from group loyalty to their mates'. 'In an infantry advance,' said Arthur Jeffery of the Second World War, 'you realise your mates are to the left and right of you.' It was to those mates, the members of his platoon, that the soldier owed his primary allegiance. Only after that came loyalty to the Battalion, then to the Regiment.

The Regiment as anything but an abstract concept, was almost beyond the comprehension of the average recruit; the Colonel, the Regimental Sergeant-Major, were God-like figures so remote as barely to exist as material entities. From the moment that a recruit joined, however, the tradition of the Regiment, its battle honours, its idiosyncrasies in dress or drill, were force-fed him so that willy-nilly he absorbed and took pride in them. The vision of the Regiment as an ideal was at the centre of the soldier's thinking. When James Fergus left the Black Watch to join the Royal Electrical and Mechanical Engineers he knew that in terms of his career he was taking a prudent step but he bitterly regretted the loss of something that was still precious to him; when Sam Small felt that the Northamptonshire Regiment had let him down his distress was the greater because the Regiment had meant so much to him and he had given so much of his life to it.

Still more diffuse yet none the less real was a soldier's loyalty to the British Army. He took pride in his profession. The postman, the railway worker, the farm labourer, may have enjoyed his work and respected his employer but he did not feel that he was a member of a race apart. The Regular soldier knew that he was different. Even after decades of civilian life he still felt a sense of solidarity with others of his species and a secret superiority to the generality of mankind. In the Army he had known where he fitted in, he was part of a close-knit and surprisingly homogeneous society, he belonged. In the Army, Archie Harrington stresses: 'Let me tell you, one is something.' In civilian life he had been 'Mr Harrington, an anonymous man'; once he had found his way to the Royal Hospital he 'was recognised as a man who'd given something'. Such recognition owed little to his rank or his accomplishments. Harrington had enjoyed outstanding success in his career but others of lesser achievement had still been 'something'. In the British Army there were no anonymous men.

To a remarkable degree, the Army deserved the loyalty that it commanded from its members. It provided those who joined it not merely with accommodation, food, clothing, a secure if ill-paid job, but also a self-contained environment, catering for every need, covering every eventuality. 'The Army was my family' is a phrase that I have heard repeatedly over the last years, and it did indeed supply the close-knit stability that is traditionally found within the home. The analogy with the family is one which the Army itself would have recognised and in which it would have taken pride. A song popular in the Second World War contained the lines:

> Kiss me goodnight, Sergeant-Major,
> Sergeant-Major be a mother to me.

This was, of course, written in mockery of one of the arch hobgoblins of British mythology: the sergeant-major, everyone knows, is an ogre, devoid of any trace of human weakness, a ruthless martinet demanding impossibly high standards of discipline and smartness. So indeed, up to a point, he had to be; a sergeant-major who lowered his guard and let his men take liberties over their appearance or behaviour would not have been doing his job. But the good non-commissioned officer also exercised a pastoral role, he knew the individuals under him, was aware of the pressures under which they laboured, made allowances for their weaknesses, intervened to protect them if forces from the outside world impinged damagingly on their cloistered lives. The Army was a family more stratified and rigidly disciplined than most of those which its members had known in their childhood. It rarely achieved the relaxed informality of the home which all but the least fortunate had enjoyed. But it was not without humanity, it respected the individual provided that the individual respected it, and it offered security and prospects for the future beyond anything which most soldiers could have found outside.

To any young man of ambition it provided a ladder up which he could climb to advancement beyond what he could have expected to find elsewhere in the Britain of the 1920s and 1930s. The field marshal's baton which the French *poilu* was traditionally believed to have within his knapsack was infinitely remote from the average British other rank, but for anyone who was prepared to work, who possessed energy and resourcefulness, who knew the rules and adhered to them, the sergeant's stripes and the sergeant-major's crown were eminently accessible. The Army felt that it had a responsibility to offer its members the education which they had often failed to secure in civilian life. Albert Alexandre joined the Army able to read and write only with difficulty and entirely at sea with even the most elementary arithmetic; by the time the Army had finished with him, he had passed his Second Grade, was reading books with pleasure and could grapple with the quite complex mathematics called for from the non-commissioned officers of the Royal Artillery. Not merely did recruits learn themselves, they were made to recognise the value of learning and most of them resolved to pass it on to their children. It is remarkable how many Chelsea Pensioners with children can boast that their sons – and often their daughters too – are earning more money, holding down more responsible jobs, availing themselves of more opportunities, than their parents ever had the chance to do.

Where the Army let them down in the years that followed the Second World War was in its failure to help them when the time came for them to leave the service. Most other ranks had twenty years or more of working life ahead of them when they became civilians. Their former employer presented them with a small cash gratuity and a still more exiguous pension, gave them its blessing and sent them on their way to fare as best they could. The former soldiers emerged like monks expelled from a monastery, blinking nervously in the light of the outside world, no longer sheltered under the umbrella of a vast organisation, having to grapple with all the problems of daily life with little or no knowledge of how the system worked. Many of them had been used to performing tasks of great responsibility, now they found that their skills were irrelevant, authority was denied them, they were given work that was menial and monotonous. Most of them coped, came to terms with the demands of civilian life, made a new career; but the process was painful and protracted and they could have been better prepared for what lay ahead. Small wonder that when the opportunity arose they sank back gratefully into the structured good order provided by the Royal Hospital.

And who are the Chelsea Pensioners? Do they, or other military veterans for that matter, differ to any noticeable extent from the generality of mankind? The Pensioners to whom I spoke varied widely in background, temperament and experience. They were as different from each other as any group of bank clerks or bus conductors. Yet, unlike the bank clerk or the bus conductor, they held in common certain rock-like standards and values. For better or worse, the Army had marked them as its own, stamped them with beliefs that were unquestioned and ineradicable. The sort of men who become Chelsea Pensioners are perhaps those who are predisposed to accept the beliefs of military life. It is impossible, though, to trace the development of these Pensioners without realising how very different they would have been if the Army had not shaped their lives.

All of them believe unquestioningly in the importance of discipline; self-discipline first, then discipline for others. Without firm discipline, they believe, society cannot work, the unrighteous will triumph, the weak will be trampled underfoot. They learnt themselves, sometimes painfully, that rules must be obeyed and natural instincts curbed; the fact that those rules are often inconvenient and sometimes irrational may be a reason for changing but never for disobeying them. Kipling wrote:

Now these are the laws of the Jungle, and many and mighty are they;
But the head and the hoof of the Law and the haunch and the hump is
  – Obey!

The Army is not a jungle, nor usually is civilian life, but the soldier is taught that they would quickly become so if the law were disobeyed. Soldiers, whether retired or not, rarely lose their conviction that standards of good order and discipline should apply as much in the family as in the regiment. Almost every child of a Pensioner to whom I have spoken has complained, albeit usually with affection, about their father's obsession with punctuality, cleanliness, good manners.

Soldiers are not hardened killers. Few of them enjoy talking about the bloodier aspect of their career, some close their minds to it altogether. If killing is necessary, if the nature of the job in hand demands it, then it must be done, but it is a means to an end, not the end itself. It is the job that matters. The belief that whatever the job may be, it must be carried through successfully and to the end is one of the most conspicuous characteristics of the former Regular soldier. It never dies. No Chelsea Pensioner is dragooned into taking on a duty in the Hospital unless he wishes to do so, but once he has said he will do it then it will be done. Sometimes an octogenarian will continue to man a gateway in the pouring rain even though he is feeling ill, suspects he may have a temperature and would instantly be sent to bed if he told the Duty Officer. It would not occur to him to do so. Manning a gate in Chelsea may seem pretty tame compared with holding a position in the front line in battle, but he will perform the task with equal fervour. To succumb to weakness is to risk letting down a colleague, and that is the ultimate offence. There may be many legitimate reasons why a civilian employer might wonder whether a former soldier would be the right choice for a certain job, but a fear that, if he were taken on, he would not apply himself wholeheartedly to his duties, is rarely justified.

Any great business must have its hierarchy: the chairman, the managing director, the members of the main board and so on down to the doormen and the cleaners. Only in the armed services, however, is hierarchy so enshrined at the heart of the organisation and so manifest in all its activities. The saluting, the insignia of rank, the separate messes, the different grades of married quarters: at every step the soldier is reminded who he is and how he fits in with everybody else. When he emerges into civilian life he has to adapt to a new, looser structure and does so with some discomfort. The hierarchical instinct, however, is not so easily expunged. When a new Pensioner settles at Chelsea he finds that his former rank carries no privileges; because he was once a sergeant-major he enjoys no more spacious a berth or superior a place in the dining hall than sergeants, corporals or privates. Nobody throws his rank about; if he tried to do so, he would receive short shrift from his fellow Pensioners. But everyone knows who he is and who everybody else is. The atmosphere is relaxed, informal, friendly, but the spirit of the Army permeates the great building and is cherished by its inmates.

Few people would number broadmindedness among the qualities most to be looked for in a Regular soldier. They have their fair share, perhaps more than their fair share of prejudice: racial, religious, social. But, paradoxically, narrowmindedness is accompanied by a striking tolerance. In the Army so many people of different habits and temperaments live cheek-by-jowl with each other that if a man did not tolerate the vagaries of human nature existence would become impossible. The soldier learns both to curb the more rebarbative of his own characteristics and to endure a measure of undesirable behaviour from his neighbour. He does not necessarily share the other man's point of view, he may not even understand it, but he will accept that it exists.

This tolerance, on the whole, extends into family life. One of the factors that most often propelled recruits into the British Army was a wish to escape from an unhappy home. Poverty was the norm, but it was intolerance and harsh discipline which proved the more unacceptable. Unhappy children, it is often said, make bad parents, but life in the Army seems somehow potent enough to break the pattern and turn potential tyrants into loving parents. Standards are not abandoned, or even lowered and this will sometimes lead to conflict. The old soldier demands that his children be well-mannered and properly turned out. But if they then declare themselves Communist or homosexual he may be surprised, hurt, even angry, but will not for that reason reject them. 'You can't spend your life defending freedom of speech and then deny it to someone,' says Arthur Jeffery. Soldiers are told many times in the course of their career that democracy, liberty, freedom of speech and thought, are the ideals for which they must be ready to fight.

Tolerance does not necessarily imply ease of communication.

The Army does not provide an environment where shows of feeling are held to be desirable. When Tom Parnell's wife died he could find no words to express his grief and had to ask a friend to break the news to his son. Archie Harrington's daughter is dismayed by the curtain of self-sufficiency that seems to cut her father off from the outside world. 'I sometimes say to myself, it's the Army that's done this. I think the Army is responsible for a great many fragmented families.'

But the soldier also found it easier to tolerate the views or behavioural oddities of his colleagues because they came from within the 'family' of the Army. If there is one feature more than any other which distinguishes the former soldier from those of other backgrounds, it is this sense of community. To belong wholeheartedly to some group or organisation is a heady drug, and once a taste for it has been acquired it is difficult to shed. The Regular soldier who puts his military service behind him and makes himself a new career in civilian life would love to recapture this sense of commitment. All too rarely does he find that his new employer either deserves or desires his allegiance. He is in a new world, with new rules, where the cash nexus reigns supreme and the worker relies upon his union to protect him against exploitation. The old soldier adjusts, he learns the new code, but he never wholly ceases to regret the lost simplicities and loyalties. In the Royal Hospital he at last recaptures the old commitment. When he emerges from its gates resplendent in scarlet coat he is determined to look his best; because such has been his lifetime practice, but still more because he feels that he is representing the Hospital and that this is an institution to which he is proud to belong and which he will never let down.

The Pensioners have done the state some service and few would begrudge them the comfort and security that the Royal Hospital has given them. Their true significance, however, rests not on what they have done but on the standards that they represent. Self-discipline, obedience, conscientiousness, loyalty: these are not the most fashionable of virtues – the Chelsea Pensioners are not the most fashionable of men – but they are virtues that have served the British Army well over many centuries and will be no less essential in any conflict in the future. They are virtues that are as important in society today as they have ever been. The Royal Hospital is not a museum of fossilised values nor yet another quaint reminder of Britain's imperial past. The old gentlemen in their fancy dress are a living reminder not of what put the Great into Great Britain but of the lessons that must be learnt and relearnt if a tolerable life is to be provided for every class and for every culture in this small, crowded but infinitely diverse land. It is for this above all that the Pensioners should be cherished.

Bibliographic Note

It would be pretentious and superfluous to try to list all the general studies which in one way or another have helped me in writing this book. I must mention, however, Field Marshal Lord Carver's *Britain's Army in the Twentieth Century*, London, 1999.

It may be of use if I mention certain more specialised regimental histories and studies of particular campaigns or operations which have been of value:

Brigadier G. N. Barclay, *History of the 16th/5th The Queen's Own Royal Lancers 1925–1961*, Aldershot, 1963

A. Stanley Blicq, *Norman Ten Hundred*, Guernsey, 1920

Victor Coysh, *A History of the Royal Guernsey Militia*, Guernsey, 1977

Brigadier G. F. Ellenberger, *History of The King's Own Yorkshire Light Infantry, Vol VI: 1939–1948*, Aldershot, 1953

Bernard Fergusson, *The Black Watch*, London, 1950

Brigadier Fernyhough, *History of the Royal Army Ordnance Corps 1920–1939*, London, 1967

Patrick Forbes, *The Grenadier Guards in the War of 1939–1945, Vol II: The Campaigns in North West Europe*, Aldershot, 1949

Major R. C. G. Foster, *History of The Queen's Royal Regiment, Vol VIII: 1924–1948* Aldershot, 1953

Major R. T. Gilchrist, *Malta Strikes Back*, Aldershot, 1946

Duncan Guthrie, *Jungle War*, London, 1946

Lt-Colonel Walter Hingston, *History of The Queen's Own Yorkshire Light Infantry Vol VI: 1919–1942*, London, 1960

Brigadier W. J. Jervois, *The History of the Northamptonshire Regiment 1939–1948*, Regimental History Committee, 1953

John Lodwick, *Raiders from the Sea*, London, 1990

Peter Mead, *Gunners at War*, London, 1982

General Sir Cameron Nicholson, *The History of the Royal Artillery 1919–1935*, RAI, 1978

Nigel Nicolson, *The Grenadier Guards in the War of 1939–1945, Vol II: The Mediterranean Campaigns*, Aldershot, 1949

Terence O'Brien, *The Moonlight War*, London, 1987

Major-General R. P. Pakenham-Walsh, *History of the Corps of Royal Engineers, Vol IX*, Chatham, 1958

Major-General R. P. Pakenham-Walsh, *History of the Corps of Royal Engineers, Vol X*, Chatham, 1958

John Parker, *SBS: The Inside Story of the Special Boat Service*, London, 1997

G. Peacock, *The Life of a Jungle Wallah*, Ilfracombe, 1958

Major-General L. T. H. Phelps, *A History of the Royal Army Ordnance Corps 1945–1982* (no date or place of publication specified)

J. A. Pitt-Rivers, *The Story of the Royal Dragoons 1938–1945*, London, 1956

Cyril Ray, *Algiers to Austria: a History of 78 Division in the Second World War*, London, 1952

Jeremy Taylor, *The Devons: a History of the Devonshire Regiment 1685–1945*, Bristol, 1951

Lt-Colonel A. W. Valentine, *We Landed in Sicily and Italy*, Aldershot, 1943

Lt-Colonel J. K. Windcott, *The Devonshire Regiment: August 1945–May 1958*, Aldershot, 1980

Anon, *The 10th Royal Hussars in the Second World War*, Aldershot, 1948

Anon, *Craftsmen of the Army: the Story of the Royal Electrical and Mechanical Engineers*, London, 1970

Index

Abyssinia, 67–8

Aden, 280–3, 324

Afrika Korps, 140, 198

Agira, 238–9

Ahwuz, 199–200

Alderney, 11–12, 14, 19–20

Aldershot, 90, 307

Alexander, General Sir Harold, later Field Marshal Viscount, 100–1, 142

Alexandre, Albert, 6, 9–45, 326, 331

Alexandre, Daphne, later Mrs Izod, 30, 35, 39

Alexandre, Dorothy, *née* Axcell, 25–42

Alexandre, Muriel 'Alex', later Mrs Jenkins, 27–30, 32, 35, 38–9, 42–44

Alexandria, 232, 235–6, 240, 248

Algiers, 96–7, 140

Alton, 49–51

Ambala, 26–7

America, United States of, 12, 39, 95, 176, 292, 312, 325

American Army, 199, 240–1, 327

A Month in the Country, 16

Amorgos, 172

Andaman Islands, 236

Anglesey, Isle of, 76

Anzio, 240–1

Archer-Shee, Colonel, 146

Argyll and Sutherland Highlanders, 276

Army Education Corps, 22, 193–4

Arnold, Matthew, 325

Atom Bomb, 33, 74, 174, 275, 304

Auchinleck, General Sir Claude, later Field-Marshal, 70, 135

Australian Army, 23

Austria, 143–4
Auxiliary Territorial Service, 32,
    102

Baghdad, 70, 72
Basra, 197
Bassett, Colonel, 296
Belgium, 164–7
Belsen, 302
Benghazi, 70, 211
Berlin, 308, 310
Bielefeld, 307–8, 316
Bihar, 31
Blackpool, 117, 168, 178
Black Watch, 6, 265–79, 283,
    329
Bolton, 125–8, 141
Bombay, 31, 63, 200, 274
Bomb Disposal, 209–10
Boy Scouts, 52, 295–7
Bristol, 209–10, 213–4, 217, 227
British army
    Demobilisation Policy, 18–19,
        34, 76, 181, 212, 254, 316,
        332
    Education in, 22–3, 57–8,
        192–4, 211, 229–30, 328,
        331–2
    'Family' Nature of, 20, 90–1,
        311, 330–1
    Inability to Communicate
        Information in, 14, 24, 67,
        143, 165, 234–5, 327–8
    Morale in, 15, 141, 165, 234,
        312, 325
    Music in, 227–9, 267–8

Organisational 'Black Holes'
    in, 31, 200, 240
Pay in, 14, 57, 91–2, 193, 195,
    230, 266
Postings Policy, 20, 22, 30,
    61–2, 115, 129, 201, 230,
    251, 266, 272, 280
Recruitment for, 12, 53, 61,
    89, 128, 162, 192, 228, 266
Role of, 20, 324–5
Structured Life in, 19, 35, 146,
    330, 334–5
Views on Matrimony, 24–5,
    58–9, 146, 272, 310
British Legion, 77, 184
Brothels, 24, 64, 132, 165–6,
    179, 231
Browning, General Sir Frederick,
    'Boy', 305
Buchan, John, 229
Burma, 30–2, 72–3, 201–9, 212,
    274–5

Cairo, 102, 247
Camberley, 29
Cambrai, Battle of, 14–15
Cameroons, The, 179–80, 324
Canadian Army, 23, 140, 302
Canadian Mounted Police, 148
Capel Smith, Major, 311
Carlisle, 34, 280
Carr, J L, 16
Caterham, 162–3, 169, 181, 271
Celle, 311–3
Ceylon, 201, 208, 324
Chamberlain, Neville, 94, 130,

194

Chanak, 23–4

Characteristics of
 regular soldier
(each sub-heading also covers its
 opposite – eg, for
 'Cowardice' see 'Courage'.)
 Acceptance of Orders, 22, 26,
  65, 98, 143, 165, 209, 240,
  251, 277, 312, 326–7, 336
 Adventurousness, 12, 31, 98,
  128, 173, 196, 326
 Ambition, 14, 57–9, 90–1, 169,
  195, 206, 235, 270, 302,
  307, 331
 Attitude towards Empire, 52,
  126, 226, 248, 282–3, 323–4
 Attitude towards Officers, 13,
  65–6, 99, 116, 134–5, 146,
  206, 212, 241, 270, 278,
  285, 315, 327
 Attitude towards Politics, 40,
  126–7, 150, 214, 256–7,
  304, 325
 Attitude towards Race, 64, 74,
  143–6, 180–1, 198, 248,
  274–6, 304–5, 335
 Attitude towards Religion, 32,
  52, 70, 138, 158, 188, 226,
  263–4
 Belligerency, 17, 24, 65, 94,
  143, 161, 165, 173, 235, 333
 Blinkered Vision, 21, 63, 234,
  327–8
 Camaraderie, 19, 35, 81–2,
  135, 145, 202, 238–9, 256,

311, 330, 336
Conscientiousness, 36, 284,
 334, 336
Courage, 15, 68, 97–8, 134,
 136, 173, 206, 239, 300
Discipline, 36, 98, 132, 169,
 180, 198, 239, 283, 333, 336
Honesty, 92–3, 113, 148, 242,
 285
Ignorance of Wider Issues,
 13–14, 67, 95–6, 143, 165,
 194–5, 234, 328–9
Impoverished Childhood, 9–11,
 49–51, 158–60, 189, 224,
 262–3, 326, 335
Inability to Express Emotions,
 80, 141, 149–50, 336
In Civilian Employment,
 36–8, 77–9, 117–9, 147–52,
 181–2, 213–7, 245–6, 254–7,
 284–5, 306, 317–9, 332
In Retirement, 41–2, 79–82,
 119–21, 152–4, 174–5,
 182–4, 217–20, 257–8,
 285–7, 319–20
Loyalty, 98, 120, 135, 202,
 238–9, 267, 311–2, 329–30,
 336
Patriotism, 12, 52, 126,
 189–90, 226, 282–3, 325
Prejudice, 58, 74, 274–6, 305,
 335
Pride in Regiment, 89, 120,
 135, 194, 266, 279, 307,
 329–30
Responsibility, 36, 59, 105,

113, 206, 215, 282, 317, 332

Sexuality, 24–5, 64, 69–70, 132, 166, 231, 272

Strictness as Parents, 39, 150, 214, 280–1, 333, 335

Tolerance, 39, 150–1, 248, 256–7, 335

Charles II, King, 3, 6

Chatham, 211–2, 214

Chaudhri, Lt Colonel, later General, 71–2

Chepstow, 192–5

China, 228, 244

Churchill, Winston, 135

Colchester, 44, 254, 267, 285–6

Cook, Major, 99, 101, 103

Corps of Commissionaires, 118

Coward, Noel, 73

Crete, 68

Cunningham, General Sir Alan, 67

Cyprus, 69–70, 173, 176–8, 180, 253, 312–3, 324

Dachau, 107

Daily Herald, 250

Daily Mail, 225

Daily Mirror, 234

Daily Telegraph, 210

Darlington, 187, 189

D-Day, 240–1, 299

Deal, 227–8

Derby, 196–7

Derna, 139, 247

Devizes, 29, 75–6, 147

Devonshire Regiment, 6, 85, 88,

228–54; merges with Dorsetshire Regiment, 253

Doncaster, 148, 152–4

Dorsetshire Regiment, 235, 237, 253

Dover, 268

Duke of Lancaster's Own Yeomanry, 6, 128

Dunkirk, 132, 166–8, 195, 232

Durban, 31, 169

Eden, Anthony, later Earl of Avon, 40

Eden, Sir Timothy, 190

Edinburgh, 261–2

Edwards, Gavin, 311

Egypt, 102–3, 132–3, 176, 198, 247, 281, 305, 312, 324

Eighth Army, 97, 99–100, 133–44

El Alamein, Battle of, 70, 133–9, 234

Elf Petroleum, 148–52

Elizabeth, Queen, 6, 44

Empire Day, 52, 126, 226

Entertainment National Service Association (ENSA), 73, 199

EOKA, 253, 312–3

Eos, 173

Eritrea, 67–9

Exeter, 89, 227–8

Falklands War, 5

Farouk, King, 247

Fergus, Anne, 272–3, 276, 281–3,

285–6
Fergus, David, 261–2
Fergus, Frances, later Mrs Bacon, 276, 280–1, 285–6
Fergus, James, 6, 261–87, 329
Fergus, Susan, 261–4
Ferozepur, 27
Focke Wulf 109 Fighter, 303
Folkestone, 196, 246, 253–6, 313–4, 316–9
Force 136, 201–8
Formby, George, 73
Fort George, Inverness, 277–8
Freyberg, Lieutenant General Sir Bernard, later Lord, 139

George V, King, 51
George VI, King, 27
German Army, 68, 96–7, 135–6, 238–9
Germany, British Forces in, 115–7, 144–6, 180, 302–3, 307–13, 316
Gibraltar, 34, 232
Gilchrist, Major R T, 234
Glasgow, 241, 263, 302
Gloster Gladiator Fighter, 232
Gloucestershire Regiment, 261
Gort Line, 165–7
Gothic Line, 103, 141
Graz, 144
Greece, 23, 68, 135
Grenadier Guards, 6, 162–70, 175–80
Guernsey, 10–13, 44
Guernsey Light Infantry, 6, 12–19

Gurkhas, 21, 113, 197, 315–6
Guthrie, Captain, 203–4
Gwyn, Nell, 3

Haile Selassie, Emperor, 80
Hampshire Regiment, 235, 237
Handley Page, 36–7
Harding, Field Marshal Sir John, later Lord, 313
Harington, Lieutenant General Sir Charles, 24
Harrington, Anne, 50–4, 59, 75
Harrington, Archibald, 6, 49–82, 336
Harrington, Frances, 58–66, 70–2, 77–80
Harrington, Vera, later Mrs Hayes, 66, 74–5, 336
Hart, Major ('Hartforce'), 97
Harvey, Colonel Roscoe, 134
Harwich, 114
Haslemere, 50–3
Hiroshima, 33, 74
Holmes, Alwyn, 6, 291–320
Holmes, Elizabeth, later Mrs Gill, 292–5, 301, 309
Holmes, Henry, 292–8, 301–2, 306
Holmes, Jean, née Hazlewood, 306–9, 318–20
Holmes, Nellie, 291–8, 306, 309, 319
Holmes, Olive, 309–10, 316–8
Home Guard, 296–8
Hong Kong, 244, 247, 256, 324
Hopton, Ernie, 137

Hore-Belisha, Leslie, later Lord, 195, 230
Howard, Sir Michael, 329
Hurricane Fighter, 232

Imperial Tobacco, 213–7
India, Significance to British Army, 20–1, 324; Alexandre in, 20–2, 25–33; Harrington in, 61–6, 72–4; Parnell in, 129–32; Pearson in, 200–2; 228, 230, 266, 268; Fergus in, 274–5; 283
Indian Army, 21, 30, 66–8, 70, 194, 200, 275
Indonesia, Confrontation with, 315–6
Iraq, 70–2, 324
Ireland, 20, 189
Ismailia, 102, 171
Italian Army, 68, 142–3, 237–8
Italy, 101–4, 141–4, 174, 239–41

Japan, 74, 174, 252
Japanese Army, 31, 202–6, 274, 304
Jeffery, Anne, 224–8, 231
Jeffery, Arthur, 6, 223–58, 327, 329, 335
Jeffery, Christine, later Mrs Pinkney, 243, 245–6, 257–8
Jeffery, Dorothy, 242–4
Jeffery, Ernest, 223–8, 242
Jeffery, Pearl, 246–7, 250, 252–4
Jeffery, Vivienne, 256–7
Jellicoe, George, Earl, 171–2

Jersey, 9–10
Job, Sergeant, 298
Joppa, 261–3
Junker Bomber, 232, 238

Kabrit, 171, 236
Karens, 201–5
Kent, Edward Duke of, 4–6
Kenya, 67, 200; Mau Mau Revolt in, 248–50; 324
Kenyatta, Jomo, 248
Keren, Battle of, 67–8
Khyber Pass, 27, 131
King's Royal Rifle Corps, 141
Kinross, 269–71
Kipling, Rudyard, 305, 333
Kohima, Battle of, 72
Korean War, 76, 115, 277

Lagos, 276
Lahore, 21
Lancashire Fusiliers, 99, 128
Larkhill, 58
Lassen, Anders, 171–3
Leeds, 242–3, 246, 257–8
Lemnos, 172
Lippizaner Horses, 144
Lübeck, 145–6
Lüneburg, 116–7
Lympstone, 225, 241–2

Madras, 274
Makarios, Archbishop, 313
Malacca, 315–6
Malaya, 30; Emergency in, 109–12, 244–7, 249; 274,

315, 324

Malta, 22–5, 176, 208, 230–6,
  244, 253, 324

Malvern, 278

Manchester Regiment, 140

Mansergh, Brigadier, later
  General, 69, 80

Mareth Line, 97, 139

Margaret Rose, Princess, 164

Mau Mau, 248–50

Messerschmitt Fighter, 168, 232

Miles, Frederick, 36

Military Police, 101, 102, 110–2,
  114, 136, 201

Monte Cassino, 101

Montgomery, General, later Field
  Marshal Viscount, 70–1,
  100, 135, 140

Morpeth, 242

Mountbatten, Lord Louis, later
  Earl Mountbatten of Burma,
  204

Munich Crisis, 130, 161, 328

Musselburgh, 261

Nairobi, 250

Naples, 240–1

Nasser, Gamal Abdel, 40

National Children's Bureau, 256

Newcastle, 60, 192

New York, 133, 268

Nigeria, 179, 274, 276, 324

Northampton, 89–90, 92–5, 109,
  118–9

Northamptonshire Regiment, 6,
  89–117, 120, 330

Northern Ireland, 5, 91–2

North Staffordshire Regiment, 13

North-West Frontier (India), 21,
  27, 63–6, 71, 130–1

Oman, 252

'Operation Character', 202–8

'Operation Torch', 96

Palestine, 129, 230, 268, 304–5,
  324

Paratrooper Training, 170–1, 202,
  298–301

Paris, 166

Parnell, Emily, 125–6, 141

Parnell, Harold, 126, 141

Parnell, Nigel, 147–53, 336

Parnell, Pearl Lee, née Robinson,
  145–52, 336

Parnell, Thomas, 6, 125–54, 336

Parnell, Thomas (Senior), 125–7

Passchendaele, Battle of, 5, 15–7,
  20, 28

Patton, General George, 107

Peacock, Colonel, 202–6

Pearson, Catherine, 187–91

Pearson, Eileen, née Roberts,
  210–20

Pearson, John, 187–91

Pearson, Leonard, 6, 187–220

Persia, 197–200

Perth, 265, 269, 272, 276–8, 285

Peshawar, 21, 27, 63, 130–1

Pieters, Colonel, 139–40

Pioneer Corps, 177

Pirbright, 180, 182

Platt, Major General, later
    General Sir William, 67
Plymouth, 19, 183–4, 208, 224,
    227, 250–1
Poles, Major, 202–3, 206
Poona, 33, 200–1
Portobello, 261–4
Poynton, 158, 181

Queen Mary, SS, 133
Queen's Royal Regiment, 6, 55

Rajputna Rifles, 207
Rangoon, 74, 204, 208
Rawalpindi, 21, 63
Remembrance Day, 81, 98
Risalpur, 130–2
Rome, 101–3, 141, 240–1
Rommel, Field Marshal Erwin,
    70, 97, 140
Royal Air Force, 33; in Eritrea,
    67; 204, 228
Royal Army Medical Corps
    (RAMC), 315
Royal Army Ordnance Corps
    (RAOC), 278, 298
Royal Army Service Corps
    (RASC), 6, 298–316
Royal Artillery, 6, 12, 19–35,
    54–77, 134, 316, 332
Royal Corps of Signals, 75
Royal Dragoons, 129
Royal Electrical and Mechanical
    Engineers (REME), 6, 119,
    278–83, 329
Royal Engineers, 6, 65, 165,
    192–213

Royal Horse Artillery, 56
Royal Hospital
    Chelsea
    Activities at, 43–4, 153, 320
    Admission to, 43, 81, 121,
        183–4, 219, 286–7
    Advantages of, 43, 82, 121,
        258, 287
    Death at, 45, 220
    Founder's Day Parade, 3–6,
        45, 140
    Organisation of, 4–5, 219–20,
        287, 334–5
    Privacy at, 43, 82, 258, 287,
        320
Royal Marines, 88, 160, 190,
    227–8
Royal Navy, 23, 85, 190, 208,
    213, 223, 225, 228, 231,
    242, 269
Royal West Kent Regiment,
    96–7
Russia (Union of Soviet Socialist
    Republics), 21, 145, 190,
    196
Russian Army, 145, 302–3

Salerno, 239
Salisbury Plain, 58, 147, 168, 302
Sandhurst, 71, 152, 194
Sardinia, 171
Sassoon, Siegfried, 13
Saugor, 274–5
Scott, Lieutenant, 238–9
Seaforth Highlanders, 277
78th Division, 95–103

Sharjah, 181

Sheffield, 149, 292–4, 297,
     319–20

Shell Petroleum, 147–8

Shoeburyness, 25–6

Shorncliffe, 62, 129, 195–6

Shrivenham, 92

Sicily, 101, 141, 230, 236–40

Sierra Leone, 273–4, 276, 324

Sim, Alistair, 138

Singapore, 74–5, 77; Prison in,
     110–2; 113–4, 117, 169,
     243–4

16/5th The Queen's Royal
     Lancers, 129–32

Sixth Airborne Division, 298–301

Slim, General, later Field
     Marshal Viscount, 32, 67,
     72–3

Slim, Lady, 32

Small, Ada, 86–7

Small, Blanche, née Rodhouse,
     94–5, 104–11, 114–20

Small, Fernley, 6, 85–121, 327,
     330

Small, Henry, 85–90

Small, Margaret, 112, 119

Small, Rita, later Mrs Derby,
     109, 111–2, 114, 119–21

Soldier Magazine, 148

South Africa, 31, 169

Southend, 25

Special Air Service, 98, 170

Special Boat Squadron, 6, 170–4

Spitfire Fighter, 232, 303

Stalag 7a, Moosburg, 105–7

Stuka Dive-bomber, 233, 238

Styal Prison, 182

Suez Canal, 33, 232

Suez Crisis (1956), 40, 173, 176,
     312

Suffolk Regiment, 231

Supreme Headquarters, Allied
     Powers in Europe
     (SHAPE), 280

Syria, 169–70, 324

Taranto, 101

Taylor, C F, 37–8

Teheran, 197–9

Templer, General Sir Gerald,
     later Field Marshal, 246

Tenth Royal Hussars, 6, 133–47

Territorial Army, Queen's Royal
     Regiment, 55; East Anglian
     Brigade, 61–2; Duke of
     Lancaster's Yeomanry, 128;
     Wiltshire Yeomanry, 147; at
     Plymouth, 250–1, at Hong
     Kong, 251–3 at Folkestone,
     313–4; at Redhill, 316

Thackeray, W M, 194

Thatcher, Margaret, later
     Baroness, 217

Tidworth, 147, 164, 179, 284

Times, The, 210

Toungoo, 204

Trieste, 143–4

Tripoli, 139–40, 247

Tunis, 96–9

Turkey, 23–4, 172

United Nations, 180

Vismar, 302–3

War Office, 131, 252, 272, 325
Waugh, Evelyn, 117
Wavell, Field Marshal Earl, 68,
 135, 265
West African Frontier Force,
 273–6
Windcott, Colonel, 234
Wokingham, 29–30, 36–8, 40
Women's Royal Army Corps,
 309

Woolwich, 56–7
Worcestershire Regiment, 16
Wren, Sir Christopher, 3
Wright, Adrienne, 174–9
Wright, Douglas, 6, 157–84
Wright, John Arthur, 157–62
Wuppertal, 115–6, 180

York, 150, 305, 307
Yugoslavia, 143–4, 172–3

Zambia, 148